# Archives and recordkeeping:
## theory into practice

# Archives and recordkeeping:
## theory into practice

Edited by
**Caroline Brown**

facet publishing

Published by Facet Publishing,
7 Ridgmount Street, London WC1E 7AE
www.facetpublishing.co.uk

Facet Publishing is wholly owned by CILIP: the Chartered Institute of Library and Information Professionals.



*British Library Cataloguing in Publication Data*
A catalogue record for this book is available from the British Library.

ISBN 978-1-85604-825-5

First published 2014

Text printed on FSC accredited material.

MIX
Paper from responsible sources
FSC® C013604

Typeset from editor's files by Flagholme Publishing Services in 10/14 pt Palatino and Frutiger.
Printed and made in Great Britain by CPI Group (UK) Ltd, Croydon, CR0 4YY.

# Contents

# Contributors

**Jeannette A. Bastian** is a Professor at the Graduate School of Library and Information Science, Simmons College, Boston, where she directs the Archives Management programme. She received her library degree from Shippensburg University, an MPhil from the University of the West Indies (Mona, Jamaica) in Caribbean literature, and a PhD from the University of Pittsburgh. Before moving into academia in 1999, she was Director of the Territorial Libraries and Archives of the United States Virgin Islands. Jeannette's research interests and writings are primarily in the areas of collective memory, post-colonialism and archives education. Her books include *West Indian Literature: an index to criticism, 1930–1975* (1981), *Owning Memory: how a Caribbean community lost its archives and found its history* (2003), and an edited volume, *Community Archives: the shaping of memory* (2009).

**Alan R. Bell** is the University of Dundee's Records Manager and Information Compliance Officer and Programme Leader and Honorary Lecturer for the records management programmes offered by the University's Centre for Archive and Information Studies (accredited by RIM (Records and Information Management) Professionals Australasia and the Archives and Records Association (UK & Ireland) (ARA)). He is the current Chair of the Scottish Higher Education Information Practitioners Group, was the previous Secretary of the Forum for Archives and Records Management Education and Research (FARMER) and is a corresponding member of the Section Bureau of the ICA Section for Archival Education (ICA/SAE). He speaks regularly on records and information management issues and has served previously on various professional committees, including ARA's

Education, Training and Development Committee, the Committee of ARA's Records Management Special Interest Group, the ARMA (Association of Records Managers and Administrators) International Higher Education Task Force and the Council of the Scottish Records Association.

**Caroline Brown** is the Programme Leader and Honorary Lecturer for the archives programmes at the Centre for Archive and Information Studies, University of Dundee, where she is also Deputy Archivist. She is a Chair of Archives and Records Association (UK & Ireland) Conference Committee, sits on its Professional Development Committee, having formerly served as the Chair of the Education, Training and Development Committee, and is a member of the Executive Committee for ARA Scotland. She sits on the Section Bureau of the International Council on Archives Section on Archival Education and is active in the Section on University and Research Institution Archives. She is an Arts and Humanities Research Council Peer Review College and Panel Member and has written and spoken on a range of archival and recordkeeping issues. Recent publications include an article on memory in *Archival Science* and two editions of *Archival Science* for which she was guest editor.

**Anne J. Gilliland** is Professor and Director of the Archival Studies specialization, Department of Information Studies, and Director of the Center for Information as Evidence, at the Graduate School of Education and Information Studies, University of California, Los Angeles. She also directs the Archival Education and Research Initiative that is led by a consortium of eight US universities. Her teaching and research interests relate to the design, evaluation and history of recordkeeping, cultural and community information systems; metadata creation, management and archaeology; community-based archiving and social justice concerns; and the use of digitized primary sources in K-12 education. Her most recent work is examining the role of records and recordkeeping in daily life in Croatia. Dr Gilliland is a Fellow of the Society of American Archivists.

**Rachel Hardiman** is a records manager and researcher, currently studying the semiotics of archives and records as an external PhD student at the University of Amsterdam. She has worked in a number of professional and academic roles since 2003, most recently as records management consultant to the Staff Council of the Organisation for the Prohibition of Chemical Weapons in the Hague. She has been responsible for strategic and operational records management services within the UK health and health regulation sector, and was a member of the research team for Northumbria University's three-year AC+erm (Accelerating positive change in electronic records management) project. Prior to entering the field of records and archives, she worked in publishing, financial services and the academic world, with roles including editor and researcher on specialist publications, business analyst in a financial software development company and temporary lecturer in Classics in Trinity College Dublin.

**Eric Ketelaar** is Professor Emeritus at the University of Amsterdam, where from 1997 to 2009 he was Professor of Archivistics in the Department of Mediastudies. As an honorary fellow of his former department he continues his research, which is concerned mainly with the social and cultural contexts of records creation and use. Educated as a lawyer and legal historian, he received his LLM and LLD (cum laude) degrees from Leiden University. He was Secretary of the Archives Council, Director of the Dutch State School of Archivists, Deputy General State Archivist and State Archivist in the province of Groningen. From 1989 to 1997 he was General State Archivist (National Archivist) of the Netherlands. From 1992 to 2002 he held the Chair of Archivistics in the Department of History of the University of Leiden. Eric was visiting professor at the University of Michigan (Ann Arbor), Gakushuin University (Tokyo), the University of Toronto (Canada) and Monash University (Melbourne), where he continues to be involved as a Senior Research Fellow. He is one of the four editors-in-chief of *Archival Science*. Eric served the International Council on Archives (ICA) for 20 years in various positions, before being appointed Honorary President of the ICA in 2000. He has served the Royal Society of Dutch Archivists as Vice President and President. He has been President of the Records Management Convention of The Netherlands, and Chairman of the DLM (Document Lifecyle Management) Forum on Information Governance across Europe. A full bibliography can be found on www.archivistics.nl.

**Jennifer Meehan** is the Associate Director of the Manuscript, Archives and Rare Book Library at Emory University. She directs the research services, arrangement and description, digital archives, university archives and rare book units at Emory. Before going to Emory, she was Head of Processing (2010–13) and Accessioning Archivist (2007–10) in the Manuscript Unit of the Beinecke Rare Book and Manuscript Library at Yale University. Previously, she held positions in the Archives of American Art at the Smithsonian Institution and the Digital Library and Archives at Virginia Polytechnic Institute and State University. She has written extensively on the theory and practice of archival arrangement and description and has taught professional workshops on archival processing.

**Caroline Williams** is an independent archival consultant, Senior Research Fellow at the University of Liverpool and Visiting Professor at Liverpool John Moores University. Her consultancy work has ranged from research into the applications of business intelligence systems in UK universities for JISC (the Joint Information Systems Committee) to the development of a professional competency framework for the Archives and Records Association (UK & Ireland). She was Head of Research and Collections Development at the UK National Archives from 2007 to 2009, developing a research and collections culture in support of its status as an Independent Research Organisation. Previously, as Director of the Liverpool University Centre for Archive Studies (1996–2007) she developed research, education and training for professional archivists and records managers and acted as a member of the International Council on Archives Section for Archival Education and Training. She is a member of the Arts and Humanities Research Council Peer Review College, President of the Archives and Records Association and co-editor of its journal. Areas of research include the history and diplomatic analysis of the record and the interface between theory and practice. A recent publication is *Managing Archives: foundations, principles and practice* (2006).

# Introduction

## Caroline Brown

> Thomas Carlyle … was once reproached by a businessman for being too interested in mere ideas. 'There was once a man called Rousseau', Carlyle replied, 'who wrote a book containing nothing but ideas. The second edition was bound in the skins of those who laughed at the first.'
>
> (Kenny, 2010, 573)[1]

The notion that archivists and recordkeepers may not be interested in ideas may seem absurd, but for many, faced with the day-to-day realities of managing the records, people and resources in their care, dealing with managers and stakeholders, and keeping in check the relentless tide of e-mails, there is little time for consideration of the big picture. Theory may seem impractical, irrelevant, costly or simply 'out there' and of no interest or consequence.

What is the point in knowing about theory if you are just starting out in your career, have no input into policy and spend your time re-housing photographs? If you are mid-career you may wonder why you should not just focus on expanding and enhancing those practical skills which have got you this far. As a manager you may be used to thinking strategically, but this might mean demonstrating the effective use of resources and aligning yourself with your organization's vision and aims: you see your role as thinking about concrete goals, rather than thinking conceptually.

In this book, however, we aim to demonstrate the value of thinking about theory and its relationship with the practical world. We want our readers to stop and think 'Why?' As archivists and records managers we're used to thinking about how and when, but spend less time reflecting on the why of what we do, at least on the why that doesn't involve short-term, reactive, resource-based goals. The authors in this book have all had the luxury of being able to consider the concepts and ideas behind the practicalities of archives and records management and to contemplate the purpose and goals of recordkeeping. Their chapters consider theories by exploring recordkeeping and other literature and aim to show their importance and how and why they impact on practice.

This introduction will examine, briefly (and we admit somewhat patchily), the debate about the role of archives and recordkeeping theory from the 1970s on. First, though, a word about definitions (the difficulties of which are considered by Caroline Williams in our first chapter); the title of the book deliberately contains both the words archives and recordkeeping. While the focus is primarily on the concepts and practice that relate to the management of archival material, we acknowledge and indeed wish to emphasize the overlap between the roles of archivists and records managers. Whether in terms of functions, responsibilities, purpose, legislation or education and training, the boundaries between the two, and the material for which they are responsible, are becoming more blurred. Our definitions are also blurred; recordkeeping is often used as a term that covers both the records and archives disciplines, but also has the connotation for some of focusing only on records as evidence of transactions. We do not use the expression in the latter sense, but in its broadest application, and reiterate that we hope this volume will be of use and interest to anyone involved in managing, preserving, or indeed using records and archives. We do not want to become like Carlyle's bookskins.

## 1 What is archival theory ...?

The 1970s and 1980s saw the beginnings of an expansion of interest in theoretical approaches to archive and records management. This can be seen, for example, in F. Gerald Ham's questionings of T. R. Schellenberg's essentially pragmatic approach to appraisal and Ham's call to build a 'representative record of human experience in our time' rather than focusing on informational and, specifically, historical value (Ham, 1975, 5).[2] While discussions on the nature and purpose of records and archives are not new (as is discussed by Jennifer Meehan in Chapter 3 – the so-called Dutch *Manual* (Muller, Feith and Fruin, 1898), despite its functional title, was an early examination of concepts such as the record group), clearly this 'new' focus on theory caused some raising of eyebrows regarding both the nature of archival theory and its purpose.

A series of articles in *American Archivist* and, later, in the Canadian journal, *Archivaria,* saw an increasingly tense exchange between authors seeking either to demonstrate that their profession had a theoretical basis or arguing that, if archival theory did exist, it was worthless and that archivists shouldn't waste their time discussing it. One of the early participants in the debate was Frank G. Burke, who took a distinctively positivist approach to the subject, berating the profession for the lack of theoretical approaches and urging archivists to address larger questions, thereby creating theoretical assumptions which could be tested in practice and, if valid, '[be] entered into the canon of archival thought and take their places as immutable laws of the profession' (Burke, 1981, 42). While Burke's belief in universal laws would not now be supported by many (nor was it in 1981), his insistence on the role of education in generating theoretical debate and his suggestions for 'larger questions' which included creating records, truth and interpretation, organizational structures and the role of archives in society, echo those of later writers.

Burke's approach, that theory consists of thoughts or ideas, tested in practice, then adopted as 'law', reflects a deductive approach to theory. While the debate he instigated was welcomed, his opinions, on the whole, were not. L. J. Cappon, taking a more inductive approach, saw Burke's views as confused and contradictory and argued that theory embodied archival principles which have 'emerged empirically, and from them specific rules have been shaped and modified for administering the records, the whole giving proof of a philosophy of archives for the advancement of knowledge' (Cappon, 1982, 21). Three years later the topic was revisited by Kimball, who agreed with Cappon that universal laws didn't exist, that theory was developed from empirical observation and that any identifiable general concepts would be a product of a particular point in history and particular circumstances, and therefore dependent on conditions (Kimball, 1985).

All this was too much for J. W. Roberts, who in 'Much Ado about Shelving' (and subsequent articles) delivered a forthright rejection of these notions of archival theory (1987, 1990, 1994). His argument was that archivists are involved either with the purely practical or, if they consider theory at all, with historiography. Principles such as provenance and original order are practical tools, and discussions about context and content are just archivists acting as historians. Writers attempting to theorize about 'mind-numbing' minutiae state the obvious in unduly complicated terms and discussions of levels of arrangement seek 'to conceptualize the mundane' (Roberts, 1987, 68). 'It is extreme intellectual silliness to boggle oneself with such preposterous phantoms as archival paradigms, [and] symbiotic links of medium and message' (Roberts, 1987, 73). The debate subsequently moved to *Archivaria*, where Terry Eastwood refuted Roberts' ideas, arguing for the existence, and importance, of archival theory (Eastwood, 1994). In a typically entertaining response Roberts claimed that Eastwood was mistaken in labelling him a theory denier: 'I consistently have maintained that archival theory does exist, and, moreover, that a considerable portion of it is abysmal claptrap', and finished his article urging the profession not to 'spend our time waiting for Godot to divulge the ultimate definition of respect des fonds' (Roberts, 1994, 132).

A further reluctance of archivists to engage with theory can perhaps be traced to Sir Hilary Jenkinson, Deputy Keeper of the Public Record Office in the United Kingdom and much-quoted writer on archival ideas. His insistence on impartiality and not compromising the integrity of archives (their 'moral defence', Jenkinson, 1965) can be viewed as a call for detachment from theory, as theory can represent a dangerous tendency towards interference in the archival process. Nesmith argued that 'Archiving has long been in the societal and intellectual shadows', partly blaming this on the emphasis on custody and neutrality (which had found eloquent voice through Jenkinson) (Nesmith, 2002).

Jenkinson, however, was a theorist. His emphasis on Truth and his definitions of archives and the responsibilities of archivists come close to being presented as the universal laws of which Burke was so fond. Jenkinson is criticized for this emphasis on Truth (the capitalization giving it an immutable status). As we have seen, most writers now would argue that however hard we think or conceptualize (deductive reasoning), or however often we observe or test or build rules (inductive reasoning), we are never going to emerge with something that will meet Jenkinson's concept of Truth.

Despite this, Jenkinson's insistence on the integrity of the archive is one of the concepts that has underpinned many of the theoretical debates from the 1990s to the present day, debates which moved beyond contemplation of the value of theory per se to a discussion of what the focus of this theory should be. Eastwood's championing of archival theory in *Archivaria* had been based, partly, on determining facts and characteristics, and this identifying of the characteristics and attributes of records and archives began to concern thinkers, theorists and research projects. Building on Jenkinsonian notions of integrity and authenticity, definitions were developed which focused on records as evidence and, frequently, as evidence of transactions (for example ISO 15489-1:2001 (International Organization for Standardization, 2001)). For many, however, providing an answer to what could be described as the key theoretical question, 'What are records and archives?' that was based restrictively on legal obligations and business activities was exclusive, and not viable as a theory at all.

It might be possible to argue that those who objected to this narrow focus on records as evidence of transactions were purely concerned with practicalities. It did not fit with their day-to-day work as manuscript librarians, community archivists or map curators. But can a theory that has no practical resonance for a large majority of the profession function as a theory at all, let alone one which claims to have a general application? Moreover, the critics were not rejecting theory per se, as Roberts had done, but just that particular approach. Mark Greene, for example, acknowledged that some authors had 'a subjective, relative, and essentially utilitarian approach to making appraisal decisions', but argued: 'It matters if the selection is done thoughtfully and with some explicit rationale, rather than ignorantly or completely without plan', and that, most importantly 'to think that by preserving "essential evidence" of transactions we will somehow be preserving a more "true" or more universally usable or meaningful sliver of a sliver of a window on our past is a fond delusion' (Greene, 2002, 53). Greene's search for a rationale can be viewed as a search for a kind of theoretical basis for his utilitarian approach.

In fact Greene's concern, throughout his writing, has been with the interplay between theory and practice, with an emphasis on theory that is useable and not exclusive; he is definitely not of the universal law school of thought. One of his objections to the defining of records and archives, and the consequent theory of 'recordness', was that it 'begins with the assertion that they have discovered the objective "nature" of records and of archives, and from it they have divined the immutable and incontrovertible "theory" of archives'. The view that archival theory is predicated on this 'nature' can be seen clearly in Luciana Duranti's writings on appraisal and archival theory in 1994: 'Examined in relation to the characteristics of archives, the idea of attributing value to archival documents is in clear conflict with each and all of them.' For Duranti, the nature of archives as evidence, their integrity and authenticity, means that no value can be attributed to them without compromising these characteristics. Duranti, in her article on 'The concept of appraisal and archival theory' at least, shows an aversion to an inductive approach to theory; for her, Schellenberg's definition of archives is flawed, not (interestingly, given the above) 'because he built into it the elements of value and use for research purposes', but 'because he arrived at it on purely pragmatic grounds' (Duranti, 1994, 334).

Greene is not the only author to demonstrate concern at this focus on the nature of records and archives, and at the definitions subsequently accorded to them. A search for definitions may imply the goal of a universal truth, or at least a narrowing of focus which leaves less room for the impact and importance of context. The context that is ignored is not just the context in which the records were created and used, but also the context of the wider world and the broader purpose of archives and records in society. Tom Nesmith has called for a re-concentration of theoretical discourse 'from a focus on what the classic archival texts say an archives, a record, or a public record is in "nature," to a study of how human perception, communication, and behavior shape the archives, records, and public records we actually locate and create as archivists and records creators' (Nesmith, 1999, 142).

Theoretical discourse increasingly allows for a 'fuzzy' rather than 'exact' approach (see Livelton, 1996 and the review by Nesmith, 1999 for other discussions of 'fuzziness'). Not only are definitions, truths or rigid approaches restrictive, but they are problematic. The postmodern discourse emphasizes subjectivity and interpretation rather than truth and fact. Definitions are difficult because of the limited and leading nature of language, because of different understandings and because everything is relative: 'all we can hope to find are interpretations answering to particular social or cultural needs. There can be legitimate parallel conceptions of the same phenomenon, and these are not fixed, but vary over time and across cultures, languages, and contexts of inquiry' (Yeo, 2007, 316).

Terry Cook suggests that we should no longer be talking about theory or paradigms but argues that 'perhaps these "paradigms" are better styled as *frameworks* for thinking about archives, or archival *mindsets*, ways of imagining archives and archiving. I want to explore the shared memories that we have as archivists, our identity, our sense of community' (Cook, 2013, 97). Just as postmodernism has liberated us from the truth, Cook's ways of imagining may liberate us from a ridged conception of theory. We can adopt a fluid mindset which acknowledges the importance of context and interrelationships. As more thinkers from outside the recordkeeping profession concern themselves with 'the archive', so recordkeepers should look to other disciplines to inform and broaden their thinking, they should look through other lenses to provide new perspectives on which to base their practical work. Verne Harris has written extensively on this, urging recordkeepers to go 'against the grain' to open up to and give out to other disciplines, arguing that 'the boundaries which define, distinguish and secure discourses are porous' (Harris, 2009, 135). We should not be waiting for Godot, we should be going out to meet him.

## 2 And why is it important?

So why, then, is theory important, particularly if we are viewing it not as an articulation of the truth or a universal law but as a fluid and changing approach or way of thinking? Arguing about and working towards an understanding of what archives and records are, what recordkeepers do and why they do it is one of the elements that contributes to our status as a profession. Having shared concepts and goals brings groups of people together and strengthens their sense of being part of a community (Yeo, 2007), but a theoretical underpinning is also something that society often sees as an essential characteristic of a profession. As Cox argued, one definition of a 'profession' requires evidence of

> Specialized knowledge or systematic theory. A profession has a body of knowledge that is the foundation of its work. Usually such knowledge is intellectual rather than based upon purely practical experience; such knowledge constitutes theory, and an understanding of this theory is a requisite for entry into the profession. The profession's specialized knowledge is developed through systematic research, primarily conducted at professional schools within a university.
>
> (Cox, 1986, 232)

Even Roberts acknowledged this connection: 'Moreover, the calls for developing a body of archival theory may derive less from an objective need for more archival theory than from an emotional need for greater professional acceptance' (Roberts, 1987, 67).

Professionalism does, to an extent, bring greater acceptance, and with this potentially broader influence and more resources. An ability to articulate is one of the most powerful advocacy tools, and articulation is possible only with clarity of thought. We need to be able to explain to our communities, our stakeholders and our funders why we keep archives and records and how we decide what to keep. We need to demonstrate that the methods we employ are based on careful consideration of these reasons, as well as upon available resources. We also need to satisfy ourselves that our approach to providing access to the material in our care is based on sound principles. If we can't do this, how do we expect our employers, depositors or users to understand what we do or to support us?

The theory and literature that we discuss in this book were developed for a reason. Recordkeeping theory is not just about increasing our understanding, or even about enhancing our professional status or approach to advocacy; it is primarily about making us better at what we do, which is why it should concern everyone involved in managing records and archives, and which is why theory is ultimately an ethical issue. Theory should have a direct impact on practice, and vice versa. An increasing number of research projects (for example the InterPARES project, which focuses on electronic records, www.interpares.org) have sought to develop a body of knowledge that has a direct practical relevance. Archivists and records managers are now frequently required to have degree-level qualifications which combine a theoretically based education with some elements of practical training. This rise of interest in (and understanding of the value of) the interplay between theory and practice can be seen in the number of publications which combine elements of both (for example McKemmish, 2005; Eastwood and MacNeil, 2010). Moreover, these have increasingly sought to include at least some elements that, as Harris would have it, go against the grain and take ideas from or seek to influence other disciplines. Perhaps the best example of these developments was the founding of the journal *Archival Science*, which aimed to be 'integrated, interdisciplinary, and intercultural' (Ketelaar, 2010, 345). Finally, standards such as ISO 15489: 2001 (International Organization for Standardization, 2001) and ISAD(G) (International Council on Archives, 2000) and codes of values and ethics all have an underpinning of theory and have, in turn, influenced the development of further theoretical approaches.

## 3 Why this book?

Any exploration of theoretical approaches in the literature brings to mind Harris' 'swirls': we find a shifting contemplation of theory, methodology and practice or 'imaginings' where boundaries are porous. Our swirls are further agitated by the inclusion of concepts from other disciplines, added to encourage clarity or to expand the horizons of our debate, but which may just serve to muddy our swirls because of their unfamiliarity or because we suspect, echoing Roberts, that they have been included to help us 'sit at the grown-ups' table' (Roberts, 1987, 74).

This book hopes to un-muddy some of those swirls. The authors describe some of the key recordkeeping theories (in the broadest sense of the term), examine some of the literature that has discussed these theories and consider some of the connections between these concepts and approaches and the practical world. It would be impossible to cover all aspects of recordkeeping in one volume, so it has been necessary to make a selection which, we hope, is reflective of the wider debates in the recordkeeping world. The first chapter seeks to provide a broad overview. Caroline Williams begins with what, for many, is the basis of any theory relating to archives and records management. She discusses the nature of records and archives and the role that they play in society. Underlying her analysis is an emphasis on the interplay between theory and practice and the evolving nature of this interplay and of the connections between recordkeepers, society and other disciplines.

The following chapters build on many of the topics introduced by Williams. In Chapter 2 Anne Gilliland looks at appraisal, the archival function which has, perhaps, attracted the most theoretical writing. Her aim is 'to provide practising archivists with a broad overview of what they need to know in terms of background, and what they need to reflect upon regarding appraisal in the constantly shifting sands of modern recordkeeping and information technology' (p. 33). She examines the concepts that have been developed and the methodologies they have influenced to avoid 'a selection process so random, so fragmented, so uncoordinated, and even … accidental' (Ham, 1975, 5). In Chapter 3 Jennifer Meehan focuses on another core archival function, arrangement and description. She uses an analysis of literature to consider how recordkeepers can balance theoretical and practical 'forces'; 'the needs of the records as both physical and intellectual objects; the needs of users; the demands of archival theory (the set of ideas about the nature of records); the practical limitations of archival methodology (the set of ideas about how to treat records based on their nature); and the even more practical limitations of available resources, systems and tools' (p. 64).

Elsewhere, Terry Cook has argued that archival theory has reflected 'broader societal phases'; theory does not evolve, but changes, being influenced by and dependent on the attitudes and concerns of the society in which it is formed (Cook, 1997). Late twentieth and early twenty-first century recordkeeping literature is a clear example of this, with discourse focusing on the role of records and archives in society and their influence on democracy, justice and culture, in particular. Writers such as Jimerson and Harris (Jimerson, 2009; Harris, 2007) have emphasized the power that recordkeepers hold and their consequent ethical responsibilities. Chapter 4 deals specifically with these concerns. Jeannette Bastian examines professionals' relationship with ethics both collectively and individually, through a discussion of the ethical perspective in general and the impact of these broader conceptual approaches on codes of ethics and real-life ethical dilemmas.

The relationship of archives and records to concepts such as power, justice, culture and memory is, as we have seen, often mentioned in literature, but frequently in a vague and undefined way. Eric Ketelaar's contribution takes two of these concepts, memory and identity, and seeks to articulate more clearly the connections between them and recordkeeping. As Ketelaar says, 'Many archivists claim that through the experience of archival documents identities are constructed and reconstructed.' In Chapter 5 he seeks to explore these claims, through a review of the literature and an analysis of how the policies and practices of archivists can use this knowledge to 'enhance the role of archives and archivists in the construction of individual and collective memories and identities' (p. 132). Ketelaar's discussion, naturally, references literature from outside the recordkeeping discipline.

One can only wonder why archival literature, seen in the context of his discourse, has been so reluctant to look elsewhere in its search for a theoretical underpinning of practice. In Chapter 6 Rachel Hardiman really takes us 'against the grain'. Drawing on the work of philosophers from the eighteenth century onwards, Hardiman demonstrates how an understanding of their work can enhance our conceptual approaches. Brien Brothman complained that '[T]he archival community has shown little interest in exploring possibilities for erecting any philosophical scaffolding for archival theory and practice ... [A]rchivists ... deem philosophy unhelpful in the face of practical problems' (Brothman, 1999, 69). This chapter represents a solid foundation for that scaffolding.

While each chapter stands alone, the book should be read as a whole so that the links between theoretical approaches are apparent. For example, an analysis of the nature of archives has an impact on approaches to appraisal and arrangement and description. Exploring the relationship between records and memory demonstrates the complexities behind decisions about what to keep and what not to keep and how to describe what is left. Running through the chapters (whether explicitly or implicitly) is an awareness of the importance of context, whether this be organizational, societal, conceptual or practical. Each author, while looking backwards, also looks to the present and future, describing current issues and reflecting on possible theoretical and practical developments in the future.

The final chapter looks back to the first, Caroline Williams' analysis of the concept of records and archives, but rather than focusing on extant literature it is firmly placed in the present and the future. Alan Bell reflects on 'the relevance of theoretical discourse in recordkeeping at a time when the role and purpose of the records professions is challenged continually by a rapidly evolving technical, informational and cultural landscape' (p. 228). He examines whether the rise of technological and cultural participatory cultures leaves recordkeepers both theoretically and practically irrelevant. Bell's chapter, with its emphasis on tensions and opportunities, is a timely reminder of the need for theory to be revisited and rearticulated in response to practical changes.

The different approaches taken by the authors and their different perspectives can only add value to this book. Theory is not static or agreed or the Truth but, rather, an arena in which debates can be had which lead us to new ways of thinking and different ways of understanding and, in turn, to a clearer articulation of our role and a greater understanding of practice. The chapters in this book are intended to encourage further exploration of the literature and theory and to encourage more practitioners to undertake research or to engage in conceptual debates. Mostly they are intended to give meaning to our everyday activities as recordkeepers and to add value to our actions as practitioners.

## Notes

1 I would like to thank Rachel Hardiman, author of Chapter 6 in this book, on philosophy, for drawing my attention to this quotation.

2 For further discussion of Schellenberg and Ham see Chapter 2, on appraisal, by Anne Gilliland.

## References and further reading

Brothman, B. (1999) Declining Derrida: integrity, tensegrity, and the preservation of archives from deconstruction, *Archivaria*, **48**, 64–88.

Burke, F. G. (1981) The Future of Archival Theory in the United States, *American Archivist*, **44** (1), 40–6.

Cappon, L. J. (1982) What, Then, Is There to Theorise about? *American Archivist*, **45** (1), 142–6.

Cook, T. (1997) What is Past is Prologue: a history of archival ideas since 1898, and the future paradigm shift, *Archivaria*, **43**, 17–63.

Cook, T. (2013) Evidence, Memory, Identity and Community: four shifting archival paradigms, *Archival Science*, **13** (2–3), 95–120.

Cox, R. (1986) Professionalism and Archivists in the United States, *American Archivist*, **49** (3), 229–47.

Duranti, L. (1994) The Concept of Appraisal and Archival Theory, *American Archivist*, **57** (2), 328–44.

Eastwood, T. (1994) What Is Archival Theory and Why Is It Important? *Archivaria*, **37**, 122–30.

Eastwood, T. and MacNeil, H. (2010) *Currents of Archival Thinking*, Libraries Unlimited.

Greene, M. A. (2002) The Power of Meaning: the archival mission in the postmodern age, *American Archivist*, **65** (1), 42–55.

Ham, F. G. (1975) The Archival Edge, *American Archivist*, **38** (1), 5–13.

Harris, V. (2007) *Archives and Justice: a South African perspective*, Society of American Archivists.

Harris, V. (2009) Against the Grain: psychologies and politics of secrecy, *Archival Science*, **9** (3–4), 133–42.

ICA (2000) *General International Standard Archival Description* (ISAD(G)) 2nd edn, International Council on Archives, www.ica.org/10207/standards/isadggeneralinternationalstandardarchivaldescriptionsecondedition.html.

ISO (2001) *ISO 15489-1: 2001 Information and Documentation: Records management. Part 1: General*, International Organization for Standardization.

Jenkinson, H. (1965) *A Manual of Archive Administration*, 2nd edn, Lund Humphries.

Jimerson, R. (2009) *Archives Power: memory, power and social justice*, American Library Association.

Kenny, A. (2010) *A New History of Western Philosophy*, Oxford University Press.

Ketelaar, E. (2010) Ten Years of Archival Science, *Archival Science*, **10** (4), 345–52.

Kimball, G. D. (1985) The Burke-Cappon Debate: some further criticisms and considerations for archival theory, *American Archivist*, **48** (4), 369–76.

Livelton, T. (1996) *Archival Theory, Records, and the Public*, Society of American Archivists and Scarecrow Press.

McKemmish, S. (2005) *Archives Recordkeeping in Society*, Charles Sturt University.

Muller, S., Feith, J. A. and Fruin, R. (1898) *Handleiding voor het Ordenen en Beschrijven van Archieven*, tr. 1940, *Manual for the Arrangement and Description of Archives*, H. Wilson Company.

Nesmith, T. (1999) Still Fuzzy but More Accurate: some thoughts on the 'ghosts' of archival theory, *Archivaria*, **47**, 136–50.

Nesmith, T. (2002) Seeing Archives: postmodernism and the changing intellectual place of archives, *American Archivist*, **65** (1), 24–41.

Neumayer, R. and Rauber, A. (2007) *Why Appraisal is not Utterly Useless and Why it is not the Way to Go Either*, Digital Preservation Europe, www.digitalpreservationeurope.eu/publications/appraisal_final.pdf.

Roberts, J. W. (1987) Much Ado about Shelving, *American Archivist*, **50** (1), 66–74.

Roberts, J. W. (1990) Archival Theory: myth or banality? *American Archivist*, **53** (1), 110–20.

Roberts, J. W. (1994) Practice Makes Perfect, theory makes theorists, *Archivaria*, **37**, 111–21.

Yeo, G. (2007) Concepts of Record (1): evidence, information and persistent representations, *American Archivist*, **70** (2), 315–43.

# CHAPTER 1

# Records and archives: concepts, roles and definitions

Caroline Williams

## 1 Introduction

Recordkeeping, as with other practice-based professions, involves substantial interplay between thinking and doing, between concept and practice. This chapter considers some of the underpinning concepts that support records and archives management, together with the degree to which they may – or may not be – directly applied in practice. It will look both at the roles of records and archives and at their influences upon individuals, organizations and society; and at interdisciplinary and intradisciplinary discussions about the nature and definitions of records and archives. As the literature that supports an understanding of these issues is examined it will become clear that thinking about such issues is not only forever evolving, but is engaging ever wider types of contributors and audiences.

It appears that perspectives on the multiple concepts and roles of records and archives and of their characteristics are proliferating, both within and beyond the recordkeeping profession. The ubiquitous nature and effects of technology; the consolidation of practices relating to governance, accountability and risk; the imperatives of freedom of information and data security; increasing adoption of 'the archive' by academic and creative disciplines; political and social imperatives for archives within cultural and heritage environments; philosophical debates – still largely influenced by postmodernism; and a shift from an 'expert' to a 'crowd-sourced' knowledge base ensure that lively discussions continue to contribute to an already solid base of understanding.

It is not the purpose of this chapter to explore all these influences in depth but, rather, to focus on the role of records and archives for individuals, organizations and society; their nature, definition and development; and the interaction of concept and practice. It will also demonstrate that concepts can have value even when they have no apparent direct practical application, not least in informing one's own professional knowledge base.

## 2 Records and archives: for individuals, organizations and society

Records have always had a range of meanings: they mean different things to different people. We 'look' at records in different ways, depending on what we want to find. This is not quite the same as saying that records have always had a range of uses (Craven, 2008, 16–17), but this also is true. When records are created it is generally for a specific purpose or function but, having been created, they develop the capacity to be used and perceived in a multitude of ways and to carry a multitude of meanings. In commenting on the roles of records McKemmish (2005, 15) argues that

> Records have multiple purposes in terms of their value to an individual, organization or society. They are vehicles of communication and interaction, facilitators of decision-making, enablers of continuity, consistency and effectiveness in human action, memory stores, repositories of experience, evidence of rights and obligations. On a darker note, they can also be instruments of repression and abuse of power.

Here we shall consider some of the similarities and differences between the records and archives that relate to, or are generated by, individuals and organizations, and their impact on society at large.

### 2.1 Individuals

Boundaries between the records of individuals, organizations and wider society are inevitably blurred, but some distinctive roles or purposes of records can be defined for each. The records we, our families, friends and acquaintances, as individuals, create and keep, or that are created about us, affect all our personal states – emotional, financial, legal, employment, identity, citizenship and so on. Personal narratives such as diaries, memoirs or autobiographies, correspondence and photographs reflect the details of a life lived, and their significance for personal meaning and memory may be profound. Fewer emotional connotations may be attached to the kinds of records required for conducting one's life effectively, but the consequences of failing to keep the evidence of financial, property, insurance and employment transactions efficiently, for example, could also be devastating. Personal vital documents (i.e. relating to life) such as passports, an example of those records of registration that connect individuals to the state, not only provide government with data from which to develop national policy and financial planning but directly impinge on people's access to citizenship and identity.

There have been accusations that recordkeepers (both records managers and archivists) have in the past paid less attention to personal records than to organizational ones. This was first highlighted by Australians Sue McKemmish (1996) and Adrian Cunningham (1996), who argued that there had been a failure to develop appropriate archival methodologies for managing personal papers partly because these were frequently deposited in and managed by libraries rather than archives. They suggested that it would be useful to employ the recordkeeping practices that were applied to the records of organizations to personal records as well, for example in relation to their arrangement and description. This essentially practical discussion evolved into a postmodern or poststructuralist debate between South African archivist Verne Harris (2001) and Upward and McKemmish (2001) not only about the nature of evidence left by individuals, but about the very personal effect that individual recordkeepers themselves have on the materials they manage. In Canada Catherine Hobbs (2001; 2010) has made the case for further developing understanding of personal records, emphasizing their differences when compared with the records of organizations, a theme which is taken up in some UK writing (Williams, 2008). While it might be desirable to apply the appraisal, arrangement, descriptive or other recordkeeping methodologies that work so well with organizational records to personal records, the often idiosyncratic, unstructured and unique content and context of the latter make these sometimes difficult to apply fully. The issue of personal recordkeeping is clearly linked to interests in genealogy and broader questions of identity, the latter a theme taken up in a range of conferences and publications (e.g. Kaplan, 2000).

## 2.2 Organizations

The successful operation of organizations (from governments to golf clubs) is equally dependent on the ability to create, keep and manage records and other kinds of information effectively. Imagine how a pharmaceutical company operates. Its ability to generate and access relevant information enables the ongoing operation, development and revision of its specific products and supports and informs future decision making. If these systems were not robust its exposure to risk would be greatly enhanced. Protection against legal or other challenges – made by auditors, clients or members of the public for example – is dependent on the creation of and ready access to those records that provide accurate evidence of its activity in specific instances. All organizations are accountable to their stakeholders, whether these are shareholders, citizens or employees. These bodies can provide evidence of accountability through records that show compliance with all necessary legal, fiscal, audit and other regulatory requirements. Accountability is linked to transparency: the more widely available the evidence of such compliance, the more transparent – and accountable – the organization.

The role of records and recordkeeping in organizations is supported in a variety of standards and literature. The key international standard, ISO 15489-1:2001 *Information and Documentation: Records management* (ISO, 2001), has been adopted in many Anglophone countries. Originally based on the Australian Records Management Standard, Part 1 of the standard comprises general information regarding records management requirements, including the characteristics of records; design and implementation of records systems; and records management processes and controls. Part 2 provides implementation guidelines, a methodology and an overview of the processes required for compliance with Part 1. Another international standard, ISO 14721:2003 *Space Data and Information Transfer Systems – Open Archival Information Systems – Reference Model* (ISO, 2003) is a core standard for managing digital data of all kinds and is being increasingly widely used by recordkeepers. There exists a range of textbooks on records management in the UK and elsewhere (for example, Shepherd and Yeo, 2003; McLeod and Hare, 2005; Bawden and Robinson, 2012; Bailey, 2008; Choksy, 2006). In addition, records managers need to be familiar with texts relating to allied information and data management disciplines and to the management of digital data, since many of the types of data and respective challenges and solutions overlap. In areas of governance such issues as data privacy, freedom of information, legal admissibility of information, information assurance and security and information risk are a key concern for recordkeepers and a central feature of their daily work.[1]

### 2.2.1 Use and reuse of records

The ongoing use and reuse of records and information either because they continue to have value as evidence or because they have developed a new purpose or use (such as freedom of information or archival information requests) may be a key concern both for the creating organization and for external parties. The management of organizations' archives either in-house or by national, local, business, university, charitable or other collecting archives ensures their continued accessibility to a wide range of audiences. As Shepherd and Yeo (2003, xii) note:

> Outside the organisation, the wider community also has expectations that records should be kept. When records are used for purposes of accountability they are not merely supporting organisational needs for compliance or self-defence, they also meet the requirements of society for transparency and the protection of rights. Other organisations and individuals may use records for historical, demographic, sociological, medical or scientific research. Records kept for cultural purposes also serve the values of society and its need for collective memory.

Organizations' archival records can be supported and maintained by any of a range of organizational models. Where an organization has no interest in the permanent preservation of its records/information/data as archives, recordkeeping supports solely current business needs. Some organizations have an integrated records and archives management set-up that provides a continuum of care for their own current and archival material. Other organizations outsource the management of their archives or hold them offsite – an arm's-length solution. Where the link between an organization and its archives has been broken, specific archival institutions take on the role of archival preservation, with a collecting remit embracing geographical, topical, biographical or other areas of interest (further discussed in Williams, 2006a, 35–49). Such institutions are also likely to receive the archives of their own parent body, and their role is to ensure the effective acquisition, description, promotion, access and dissemination of information about their holdings to a range of publics. There is a selection of literature available to those responsible for the management of archives; unlike in organizational recordkeeping, archival standards tend to be issued by professional rather than international or national standards organizations. The International Council on Archives (ICA) has produced four key descriptive standards (ICA, 2000; 2004; 2007; 2008), translated into some twelve languages; in addition a range of Anglophone textbooks (Williams, 2006a; Millar, 2010; Hunter, 2003; Bettington et al., 2008) are available.

## 2.3 Society

Beyond the individual and the organization, understanding the numerous roles of archives and records in 'society' is a complex matter touching on many areas of human life. Tom Nesmith (2010) comments:

> If you ask most Canadians what links the pursuit of Nazi criminals, climatology, Alzheimer's research, Aboriginal land claims, LSD medical experiments, chemical warfare experiments, unsolved murders from the American civil rights era, South Africa's Truth and Reconciliation Commission, the Stasi secret police, Japanese wartime compensation … few would answer *archives* …

Nesmith is focusing here on the role of archives in informing public policy, as do Johnson and Williams (2011). In addition to this and to the role of records and archives in helping people to understand past activity there are many other aspects of their interaction with society that have been readily seized upon by a number of writers within and beyond the recordkeeping profession. These aspects include the contribution of archives to issues of memory, accountability and social justice (Jimerson, 2009; Procter et al., 2005); societies' relationships with their records in a range of cultural, organizational and historical contexts (McKemmish et al., 2005); the connections between archives, justice and political power (Harris, 2002; 2005); the role of archives in memory and forgetting (Ketelaar, 2001; 2002; Schwarz and Cook, 2002; Blouin and Rosenberg, 2007); supporting democracy, human rights and recordkeeping in areas of conflict and truth and reconciliation (Peterson, 2005; Adami and Hunt, 2010); the effects of colonization on the colonized and their records (Bastian, 2003); and the growing involvement of local communities in generating and maintaining their own archives (Flinn, 2011). The literature noted here is a small example of writing largely by both professional and academic recordkeepers – a counter perhaps to those who continue to criticize the profession for its lack of engagement in wider intellectual issues. It also provides examples of how these writers' engagement in their particular areas of employment has impelled them to write about the wider effect of their experiences.

## 3 Interdisciplinary approaches to records and archives

Notions of 'the archive' have been seized or borrowed and developed by a wide range of disciplines as they experience an 'archival turn', and claim 'the archive' as a central hypothesis 'upon which to fashion their perspectives on human knowledge, memory and power'.[2] There are many descriptions of this, including Buchanan (2011) and Schwarz and Cook (2002). Considered to derive initially from Derridean and Foucaultian studies, the effect has been noted, for example, by McDonald (1996), Manoff (2004), Foster (2004), Spieker (2008), Mereweather (2006) and Magee and Waters (2011) in sociology, law, philosophy, political science, literary studies, anthropology, classics, cultural history and performance and visual art. Frequently highlighted are the writings of cultural historians such as Carolyn Steedman (2007), who has worked extensively in archives and record offices. She injects a note of reality into Derrida's well-known notion of 'archive fever' (Derrida, 1995), claiming that it bears little relation to the reality of archives and archival research. She argues that Derrida is anyway not just referring to archives and that his 'archive fever' is simply 'a metaphor capacious enough to encompass the whole of modern information technology, its storage, retrieval, and communication' (Steedman, 2007, 4). Steedman's own experience of archive fever occurs when she is visiting an archive or record office, and includes being faced with 'the great brown, slow-moving strandless river of Everything, and then there is its tiny flotsam that has ended up in the record office you are at work in' (Steedman, 2007, 18).

New terminologies are developing too, some of which may seem alien to recordkeepers. Manoff (2004, 11) notes that scholars from various disciplines have brought into the vocabulary such terms as the 'social archive', the 'raw archive', the 'imperial archive', the 'postcolonial archive', the 'popular archive', 'the ethnographic archive', the 'geographical archive', the 'liberal archive', 'archival reason', 'archival consciousness', 'archive cancer', and the 'poetics of the archive' as legitimate subjects of study. These may not be terms that we come across on a daily basis, but it is useful to be aware of them – and to be aware too that it is a two-way process, with recordkeepers also contributing to the discussion. Ketelaar (2001, 31) notes that recordkeepers too

> are exploring a multiplication of perspectives. They are learning (or relearning) from anthropologists, sociologists, philosophers, cultural and literary theorists: to look up from the record and through the record, looking beyond – and questioning – its boundaries, in new perspectives seeing with the archive (to use Tom Nesmith's magnificent expression), trying to read its tacit narratives of power and knowledge.

In practical terms, closer to home are those disciplines – sometimes referred to as 'fields of study' in acknowledgement of the fuzziness of disciplinary boundaries – that lie adjacent to our own and with which we do need to be familiar if we are to develop and broaden our own knowledge and skills. Bawden and Robinson's statements about information management emphasize the clear commonalities with records and archives management:

> Information management is a complicated subject, and can be understood in different ways. Sometimes it is understood as a wide and all-embracing concept, including records management, knowledge management, library management and so on, and sometimes with a much narrower focus.
>
> (Bawden and Robinson, 2012, 3)

And:

> We focus on the ideas that recorded information, instantiated in documents, can be understood as a resource … that information has a value … and that information management processes can be related to … communication chains and information lifecycles …
>
> (Bawden and Robinson, 2012, 252)

Information scientists define their discipline (alongside other definitions) as:

> the science and practice dealing with the effective collection, storage, retrieval and use of information. It is concerned with recordable information and knowledge, and the technologies and related services that facilitate their management and use.
>
> (Bawden and Robinson, 2012, 2)

To many, particularly to those at the 'records' end of the spectrum, it would make more sense for recordkeepers to align – and indeed integrate – directly with such a field of study. It is undoubtedly important to make links and to work alongside fellow information professionals whenever this can help to support and develop our services.

## 4 Defining records and archives

How are records and archives themselves actually defined? In general, as was inferred above, the term 'records' is applied to the output of individuals' and organizations' current operational processes and activities, while 'archives' is usually reserved for those records that are also available for use for additional purposes, including historical and other research. However, the fact that there is no clear distinction between the two (even if the role of the recordkeeper as either archivist or records manager is more clearly defined) will be discussed below. Associated terms, such as information and data will also be considered.

A definition is designed to explain the meaning of a word or phrase and thus to help us to understand concepts, their application and use. Definitions are essential for recordkeeping practitioners for purposes of communication with others, consistency of practice and decision making in the workplace. They help us to explain to interested parties what we do, to guide and instruct colleagues and to identify where our own professional boundaries lie in relation to those of others. If there is no consensus for example on the definition of a file or an evidence of title, then there can be no agreement about how to manage them either. However, the value of definitions – or, rather, the 'definitiveness' of definitions – has been challenged by the loosely postmodern notion that it is impossible to proclaim an objective truth about the thing being defined, because all meaning is relative, defined by experience and contingent on language and context. Despite this complication, definitions continue to be supplied in dictionaries, encyclopaedias, professional glossaries and standards in support of practice, alongside a general acceptance that there may be many readings and interpretations of specific terms and concepts. Analysis demonstrates that practitioners (as well as postmodern philosophers) have generated a range of different definitions, based on their own practical requirements; relativism at work in practice as well as theory.[3]

## 4.1 The variety of definitions

We must therefore accept that definitions are never 'definitive'. Accepting this premise, however, need not detract from the significance and usefulness of definitions: indeed it enables us to think more broadly about their interpretation. Interest in the characterization of records and archives exists both within and beyond the recordkeeping disciplines. Glossaries show that a 'record' to a computer scientist is a group of fields within a table and database; to a lawyer it is a financial document or an account of proceedings in a case; to a telecommunications officer it is the unit of data that is transmitted from sender to receiver. 'Archives' may be used to refer to anything (and not just documents) that is old or that needs to be saved: digital performance archives, linguistic archives, toys archives and peat bogs as biological archives are all in the frame. In the recordkeeping disciplines of records management, archives management and the allied areas of information management, data management, knowledge management, library management, museum and heritage management there may be some professional disagreement about what precisely is meant by a 'record'. Yeo (2007, 318) notes that

> those whose understanding has been shaped by an archival education are likely to emphasize the roles of evidence, contextual provenance, integrity and authenticity; those whose background is in information management see records primarily as information assets for government or corporate business; while those brought up in what may loosely be called the 'manuscript' tradition tend to view them as quasibibliographic materials.

Given that there are so many parties with an interest in definitions, it is not surprising therefore that they have been produced by individuals from a range of recordkeeping environments. The earliest published definitions were largely the products of national and state archives. Those of Muller, Feith and Fruin (1898) in the Netherlands, Hilary Jenkinson (1965) in England in 1922, Eugenio Casanova (1928) in Italy, Adolf Brenneke (1953) in Germany and Theodore Schellenberg (1956) in the USA focused largely on records as products of governance.[4]

### 4.1.1 Professional and academic contributions

From the 1960s professional associations began to produce definitions, an indicator perhaps of their developing maturity. The Society of American Archivists, Association of Records Managers and Administrators, the ICA and the UK Information and Records Management Society (IRMS) continue to produce definitions and glossaries to support members and practitioners.

Towards the end of the twentieth century, as recordkeeping became a subject of (largely graduate) study, academics, many of whom had practical experience, challenged the rather pragmatic assumptions that had been made to date. David Bearman and Richard Cox in the USA, Luciana Duranti, Terry Cook and Tom Nesmith in Canada, Chris Hurley, Sue McKemmish, Frank Upward and Adrian Cunningham in Australia and Michael Cook in the UK are representatives of early discussions in Anglophone countries. Here definitions were derived from conceptual underpinnings – that is, observations based on the analysis of a range of examples and uses – rather than resulting directly from a single practical instance.

A recent example of an academic contribution is that of Yeo (2008), who turns to other disciplines – in this case psychology and sociology – for insights into the nature of records. Here the concepts of prototypes and 'boundary objects' have been used to conceptualize records. A prototype is envisaged as a mental mapping of the typical features of something: typical features of a bird might be feathers, beak, ability to fly and build nests, and any candidate claiming membership of the 'bird' category might, in simple terms be expected to display these features: a non-prototypical one might not be able to fly, while still being admissible to the category, for example. A prototypical record may display attributes recognized in different degrees by different communities, while non-prototypical ones may align to a greater or lesser extent.

Having explored these ideas, Yeo (2008, 122) concludes: 'in Western culture in the twenty-first century, such a prototype might be a written document, created for business purposes with some pretensions to objectivity and maintained in a formal recordkeeping system'. This would allow the acceptance of non-prototypical records: a voice recording created for literary purposes, or personal papers, for example. As well as being 'atypical', non-prototypes may, according to Yeo, be 'boundary objects', that is, have attributes that straddle different disciplines and communities of practice. Yeo (2008, 131) cites reports, procedure manuals and websites as boundary objects: the last mentioned might be interpreted by different communities 'as (among other things) a record, a computing resource, a sales platform, a corporate management tool, and a manifestation of contemporary culture'.

Despite acceptance of many common assumptions between scholars, however, consensus with regard to definitions remains elusive, and this scholarly trend continues.

Finally, the output of collaboration between academics and practitioners, for example on national and international standards bodies and the ICA provides the best opportunity, perhaps, for providing a 'prototype' definition acceptable to all core recordkeeping disciplines: the widespread practical application of these is evidence that this is the case (Finnell, 2011). While internationally records managers use definitions provided by ISO 15489 (ISO, 2001), so do archivists derive their practices from the standards produced by the ICA, noted above.

## 5 Definitions of records and archives: two approaches

From the beginning of the twentieth century, therefore, definitions have been developed from a range of contexts, including national archives, professional associations, university departments and international standards organizations. The definitions that have been produced tend to fall broadly into two categories: exclusive and inclusive. The 'exclusive' category is quite prescriptive and permits only those records that individually display very specific attributes to be defined as such, and excludes all others. The 'inclusive' category takes a more flexible approach which permits, under certain conditions, a range of aggregated information resources to be brought into scope.

## 5.1 'Exclusive' definitions

The first category is broadly the product of national archives, academics and standards organizations. It offers a strict and exclusive interpretation and is based on the need for records to provide authentic, reliable and auditable evidence of activities and events for the individuals and organizations creating them. As such, the emphasis is on current rather than archival records. Records have been described historically as 'written documents, drawings and printed matter' (Muller, Feith and Fruin, 1898), 'accumulation of documents' (Casanova, 1928), 'whole of the papers and documents' (Brenneke, 1953), 'documents' (Jenkinson, 1965) and 'books, papers, maps, photographs, or other documentary materials' (Schellenberg, 1956). (More recent descriptions bring digital formats into scope.) In terms of the context of their creation and use, records were required to have been created or accumulated in the conduct of (official) business and used for administrative, legal or other business purposes (Casanova includes 'cultural' purposes and Brenneke evidence of the past) by the creating body or official (Schellenberg, 1956 12–16). Jenkinson's definition (1965, 11) continues to be cited, supported and challenged:

> A document which may be said to belong to the class of Archives is one which was drawn up or used in the course of an administrative or executive transaction (whether public or private) of which itself formed a part; and subsequently preserved in their own custody for their own information by the person or persons responsible for that transaction and their legitimate successors.

The sharp-eyed will spot that Jenkinson (as do the others noted above) is referring here to *archives* and not to *records*, although the attributes he describes more readily align with what today in the Anglophone area would be called records. Jenkinson saw no distinction between archives and records, and it was Schellenberg's definitions, published in 1956, which provided different definitions for each category, that started a new debate. Schellenberg (1956, 16) declared that while 'records' referred to the material that an organization generated as evidence of its activities or for informational purposes, archives were

> Those records of any public or private institution which are adjudged worthy of permanent preservation for reference and research purposes and which have been deposited or have been selected for deposit in an archival institution.

This counters both Jenkinson's requirement for an unbroken line of custody (which, he argued, was necessary in order to provide authenticity, and which assumes that records remain in-house and are not collected by external archival organizations) and his opposition to the selection or appraisal of records for historical research purposes. Schellenberg's is the first in a line of definitions that are more inclusive in nature, discussed further below.

Pursuing the Jenkinsonian legacy, some academics writing in the 1990s and 2000s adhered strongly to his principles, importing them into the new discussions that focused on the management of electronic, born-digital records. Academics at the universities of Pittsburgh and British Columbia (Duranti), while undertaking projects to establish functional requirements for the management of born-digital records, disagreed between themselves about how this might be done in practice, but did agree about the restricted nature of a record.[5] As paraphrased by Greene et al. (2004, 4,) they argued that to qualify as such, *records* are created by business activities and are 'by nature only evidence of activities and actions (transactions); must be demonstrably authentic (inviolate), reliable ... and complete'; while *archives* 'are records and only records, not simply created but maintained for the purposes of the creator/parent unit'.

Such a definition excludes such things as diaries, maps, data in databases, information and most non-textual material, as these were not produced as a result of transactions or activities and do not therefore possess the attributes necessary for 'recordness'. It also disregards any archival records not maintained by their creating body.

Since 1997, when the ICA Committee on Electronic Records (1997, 22) produced a series of studies, it has generally been accepted that

> A record is recorded information produced or received in the initiation, conduct or completion of an institutional or individual activity and that comprises content, context and structure sufficient to provide evidence of the activity.

This was a new way of expressing what was already recognized: Schellenberg (1965, 120–1), for example, included in his descriptive diagram of record attributes 'subject matter', 'structure' and 'provenance' – further described as the 'provenance of a unit, the time and place of its production, its functional origins, the subjects to which it relates, its types and its composition'.

Such attributes have been validated in the international standard ISO 15489-1:2001 *Information and Documentation: Records management* mentioned above (ISO, 2001). This defines records as:

> Information created, received, and maintained as evidence and information by an organization or person, in pursuance of legal obligations or in the transaction of business.

By confining records to evidence of 'business' transactions the standard appears very restrictive: and although the term 'business' might be interpreted more broadly to encompass more general activities this does not appear to be the intention. The standard further requires that, as well as containing content, a record should include such structure and business context that would enable it to persistently document a transaction; and that it should display the further characteristics of authenticity, reliability, integrity and usability.

Possession of these attributes undoubtedly results in records of high quality. Compliance with the standard reduces the risks of generating incomplete and unreliable evidence and of failures of audit and accountability. A key argument is that only by demonstrating compliance might legal admissibility (the acceptance of records as evidence in a court of law (BSI, 2008), perhaps the ultimate benchmark and key test of recordness) be assured in practice. The ISO 15489 standard (ISO, 2001) acts as a core document for records managers; it does not, however, provide a definition of archives per se.

## 5.2 'Inclusive' definitions

The second category of definitions, supported predominantly by professional associations, is a more inclusive one, providing a broader categorization of records and archives. It recognizes that in practice organizations generate and depend on large amounts of information and data for the efficient and accountable management of their affairs. These are not all strictly records as defined either by the University of Pittsburgh and the University of British Columbia or the ISO 15489 standard (ISO, 2001), but may be indispensable for ongoing business management. While e-mail and documents saved in records management systems might comply, sets of data in human resources, financial and other business systems, relational databases, content management systems, publications, the content of websites and intranets, and Web 2.0 content in wikis, blogs and so on would be open to challenge.[6] This has significant implications for records managers, for whom familiarity with the processes of information management, data management and knowledge management is also required alongside an understanding of such boundary objects as information, data and knowledge.

Definitions of records provided by professional recordkeeping associations contribute to this broader category. In the UK the IRMS maintains that records are information assets:

> Information and records management is, in a nutshell, all about an organisation's control and utilisation of its information assets. These in turn are defined as all the various records and information resources held by an organisation. Information assets comprise all written records as well as data, images, sound recordings and information held in other formats. They include information held in paper, electronic and other media as well as staff knowledge relating to their employment within the organisation.
>
> (IRMS, 2011)

As far as legal admissibility is concerned it might be argued that the courts will in practice consider non-'record' material. In the USA, for example, law commissioners challenge the admissibility of a record less on the basis of its inherent recordness than on the fact that 'the sources of information or the method or circumstances of preparation indicate a lack of trustworthiness' (Greene et al., 2004, 11). Greene et al. also note that the organization's retention decisions are based on degrees not of recordness but of utility of the material to that organization.

In terms of archives, the broader approach acknowledges that those undertaking archival research may be less concerned with recordness, or the structure, context and provenance, of the material at hand than with its content. Schellenberg's definitions recognize this, as do those provided by professional associations. Canadian Terry Cook's (2000) response to the 'exclusive' definition explains why:

> There seems little space in this new discourse that is dominated by talk of business transactions, evidence, accountability, metadata, electronic records and

> distributed custody of archives, for the *traditional* discourse of archivists centered around history, heritage, culture, research, social memory and the curatorial custody of archives.

According to the Society of American Archivists (2012) *Glossary*:

> 'Record' connotes documents, rather than artifacts or published materials, although collections of records may contain artifacts and books. To the extent that records are defined in terms of their function rather than their characteristics, the definition is stretched to include many materials not normally understood to be a record; an artifact may function as a record, even though it falls outside the vernacular understanding of the definition.

And archives are defined as:

> Materials created or received by a person, family, or organization, public or private, in the conduct of their affairs and preserved because of the enduring value contained in the information they contain or as evidence of the functions and responsibilities of their creator, especially those materials maintained using the principles of provenance, original order, and collective control; permanent records.

## 5.3 Some further refinements

A selection of scholarly definitions can be added to those provided by professional organizations, associations and national archives. Reference has already been made to David Bearman's approach: for him, the role of records is to provide evidence of transactions; records themselves are identified as 'metadata encapsulated objects':

> Metadata encapsulated objects may contain other metadata encapsulated objects, because records frequently consist of other records brought together under a new 'cover', as when correspondence, reports and results of database projections are forwarded to a management committee for decision.
>
> (Bearman and Sochats, c.1995)

Brien Brothman (2001, 51–2) challenges this narrow outlook, perceiving records as 'cognitive memory artifacts':

> The conviction that evidence is central to archival practice may have merit, but it is one that needs to be tested on several counts … This essay proposes that the construal of records as cognitive memory artifacts, rather than merely as legal, evidence-bearing artifacts, opens up a potentially endless field of possibilities for institutional and professional growth that only a failure of imagination can limit.

Tom Nesmith (2006, 262), in denying that records and archives were simply the static objects of traditional definition, re-emphasizes their role in a series of processes and with a number of contexts:

> A record is an evolving mediation of understanding about some phenomenon – a mediation created by social and technical processes of inscription, transmission, and contextualization …

He perceived archiving

> as the multifaceted process of making memories by performing remembered or otherwise recorded acts, transmitting such accounts over time and space, organizing, interpreting, forgetting, and even destroying them, [which] produces constructions of some prior activity or condition.

Geoffrey Yeo (2007, 337; 2008, 136) defines records as representations of activities, taking care not to be too prescriptive about the nature of that representation:

> Records can be characterized as persistent representations of activities created by participants or observers of those activities or by their authorized proxies.

While definitions will continue to evolve and the debate will clearly endure, there is general agreement that a real shift in thinking has occurred as a result of many technological, philosophical, social and other factors. This has been described as a paradigm shift, something that occurs when existing principles no longer fit newly developed practical situations and new ideas, concepts and perspectives are developed. In recordkeeping this is well described by Terry Cook (2001b, 4):

> At the heart of the new paradigm is a shift away from viewing records as static physical objects, and towards understanding them as dynamic virtual concepts; a shift away from looking at records as the passive products of human or administrative activity and towards considering records as active agents themselves in the formation of human and organizational memory; a shift equally away from seeing the context of records creation resting within stable hierarchical organizations to situating records within fluid horizontal networks of work-flow functionality. For archivists, the paradigm shift requires moving away from identifying themselves as passive guardians of an inherited legacy to celebrating their role in actively shaping collective (or social) memory. Stated another way, archival theoretical discourse is shifting from product to process, from structure to function, from archives to archiving, from the record to the recording context, from the 'natural' residue or passive by-product of administrative activity to the consciously constructed and actively mediated 'archivalisation' of social memory.

This is by no means an exhaustive account of the definitions of records and archives that have been published over the past hundred or so years. However, I have tried to identify such key issues as the roles of evidence, activities, provenance, context, history and memory in relation to records and archives, and which contribute to the overall, complex picture.

The lesson to be taken from this discussion is that while there is a general understanding of the role, purpose and definitions of records, archives and the recordkeeping profession, the emergence of different contextual and perspectival approaches will ensure an ongoing debate.

## 6 The application of concepts in practice

What is the point of all these discussions about the conceptual aspects of the nature, characteristics and roles of records and archives? Is there not a risk that in devoting too much time and attention to theories, principles and concepts we might lose sight of their relevance to and impact on practice?

It undoubtedly helps if theory and concepts can be seen to be relevant in practice, although at the extremes their relevance may not always be immediately obvious. At the same time it is unproductive to attempt to separate theory from practice: we know that the relationship between the two is interactive and iterative. According to Foucault (Williams, 2006b, 81–2), 'practice is a set of relays from one theoretical point to another, and theory is a relay from one practice to another', and recordkeepers have accepted this contention.

It can, for example, be difficult to see the immediate relevance of the overarching concept of postmodernism to recordkeeping. A theory that so explicitly rejects fixed definitions seems very difficult to pin down in practical terms. Hardiman (2009, 28, 31), however, explains that while 'postmodernism' 'resists definition because it is not a coherent philosophy but a "pervasive mindset"', a basic understanding of such core philosophies can provide a useful context for practical work. The postmodern mindset places in context the writings of some of the most influential recordkeepers – Cook, Harris, Nesmith, Schwartz and Ketelaar, for example – who certainly describe how postmodernism informs practice. If an understanding of postmodern approaches does no more than explain why our formerly traditional stances of neutrality, objectivity and passivity – the products of the positivist philosophy espoused by Jenkinson – are no longer tenable, it will have done its job.

All recordkeeping functions are based on concepts and principles. Conceptual discussions about the nature of records and archives must take place before any serious action can take place in managing them. The identification of content, context and structure and the assurance of authenticity, reliability and integrity in both paper and digital records provide the basic building blocks in the development of any recordkeeping system. We know that national and international standards intermediate between concepts and their application: so that anyone who is setting up or maintaining systems using these will already be applying such concepts in practice. In addition, the management of archival records depends on sufficient understanding of their attributes and characteristics to facilitate methods of ensuring that evidence of provenance and contextual relationships remains intact.

An understanding of the nature of records and archives will accompany a realization of how they 'behave' in different environments, since this too will affect their management. Customary approaches have identified the lifecycle (Williams, 2006a, 10–12; Parker, 1999, 12–13) as a model for behaviour, and indeed in a pre-digital environment this made sense. The notion that any record has a life – that, having been generated, it has an active life in maturity, a less active life in old age and at death is either destroyed or transferred to the archives – is useful in supporting a sequential series of processes such as creation, description, storage, retrieval, appraisal and destruction. It is less useful in that it pays scant attention to *archival* processes (i.e. after the end-of-life stage) and fails to recognize that many records do not follow this path, some being born 'archival', others born ephemeral, and others going into reverse by becoming current again.

The continuum model, in contrast, discards the notion of a series of linear stages and processes because it recognizes that actions on records do not occur sequentially, particularly in a digital environment, where records are essentially intangible and many are dynamic (Atherton, 1985–86). The processes of record creation, classification, appraisal, control, maintenance and retrieval are seen as multidimensional, and so interrelated, overlapping and integrated that one has to view records/archives holistically (Cook, 2000). The continuum model's Australian creators (Piggott and McKemmish, 1994; Standards Australia, 1996, Clause 4.22; Upward, 2005, 202) see 'a consistent and coherent regime of management processes from the time of creation of records (and before creation, in the design of recordkeeping systems), through the preservation and use of records as archives'. Although this model does not map neatly to a series of processes in the way that the lifecycle model does, in offering recordkeepers a more realistic understanding of how records actually behave it enables systems to be developed that recognize this complexity (Flynn, 2001).

## Conclusion

This chapter has considered the role of records and archives for individuals, organizations and society, the development of definitions of records and archives and the importance of the interplay between concept and practice. What has become clear is that thinking about records and archives is forever evolving. As technologies and business, organizational and social environments develop and change, so the potential – and need – for new theoretical and practical approaches becomes evident. Current challenges that the profession is proactively engaging with, for example, include the interrelated impacts of Web 2.0 and the volunteering movement. Developments in social media have reduced the barriers between professionals and non-professionals, experts and the crowd. This has enabled the skills and knowledge of a wider public to be actively brought into archival and other heritage resources via interactive wikis, blogs and so on. Volunteering is having a similar effect: there is a huge human resource now being tapped whose contribution to recordkeeping has yet to be measured. At the same time its impact on the role of the profession and professional bodies needs to be considered. For the future, contributions to the literature about such issues as the development and implications for recordkeeping of cloud technologies, crowd sourcing and the Semantic Web should be anticipated. All such developments will necessarily refer back to the fundamental concepts, natures and attributes of records and archives, and the processes associated with recordkeeping in diverse environments.

## Notes

1 In the UK the Data Protection Act 1998 protects personal data. Implementation guidance for archivists and records managers issued in 2007 by professional societies and The National Archives is available at www.nationalarchives.gov.uk/documents/information-management/dp-code-of-practice.pdf. The Freedom of Information Act 2000 and the supporting 'Section 46 Code of Practice' issued by the Lord Chancellor (Ministry of Justice, 2009) provide guidance in 'connection with the keeping, management and destruction of … records'. The British Standards Institute publishes guidance such as PD0010 *Principles of Good Practice for Information Management* (BSI, 1997), and on legal admissibility in BSI (2008). See also ISO/IEC (2005); HM Government (2008).

2 The 'archival turn' is described by Buchanan (2011, 40) as 'an inter- or cross-disciplinary trend as scholars look outside the discipline with which they normally identify, to adopt techniques or approaches from another'.

3 T. R. Schellenberg (1956, 15), as a pragmatist rather than a postmodernist, noted that 'it is obvious, therefore that there is no final or ultimate definition of the term "archives" that must be accepted without change and in preference to all others'.

4 S. Muller, J. A. Feith and R. Fruin produced their manual *Handleiding voor het Ordenen en Beschrijven van Archieven* in 1898 in co-operation with the State Archives of the Netherlands and the Ministry of the Interior for the Dutch Association of Archivists; it was translated into English in 1940 as *Manual for the Arrangement and Description of Archives.* Eugenio Casanova, Superintendent of the Archivio di Stato in Rome and Director of the Archivio del Regno, published *Archivistica* in Siena in 1928. Adolf Brenneke, director of the Prussian State

Archives, published *Arkivkunde* in 1953. Theodore R. Schellenberg published *Modern Archives: Principles and Techniques* in 1956 while Director of Archival Management at the National Archives and Records Service in Washington, DC, and *The Management of Archives* in 1965, shortly after his retirement.

5 Bearman and Sochats (c.1995); Luciana Duranti at the University of British Columbia heads the InterPARES Project. The InterPARES 1 Project ran from 1994 to 1997, www.interpares.org/ip1/ip1_index.cfm.

6 A typical definition of information and data, used by Bantin, is 'information is not just data collected; rather it is data collected, organized, ordered, and imbued with meaning and context. Information must inform while data has no such mandate. Information must be bounded, while data can be limitless' (Bantin, 2008, 67).

## References and further reading

Adami, T. and Hunt, M. (2010) Reconciliation in Regions Affected by Armed Conflict: the role of archives. In Avery, C. and Holmlund, M. (eds), *Better off Forgetting? Essays on archives, public policy, and collective memory*, University of Toronto Press, 195–214.

Archives and Records Association (2012) *An ARA Framework of Competencies: report with findings and initial framework*, www.archives.org.uk/latest-news/competencies-work-welcomed-by-ara-board.html.

Atherton, J. (1985–86) From Life Cycle to Continuum: some thoughts on the records management–archives relationship, *Archivaria*, **21**, 43–51.

Avery, C. and Holmlund, M. (eds) (2010) *Better off Forgetting? Essays on archives, public policy, and collective memory*, University of Toronto Press.

Bailey, S. (2008) *Managing the Crowd: rethinking records management in the Web 2.0 world*, Facet Publishing.

Bantin, P. (2008) *Understanding Data and Information Systems for Recordkeeping*, Facet Publishing.

Bastian, J. (2003) *Owning Memory, How a Caribbean Community Lost its Archives and Found Its History*, Libraries Unlimited.

Bawden, D. and Robinson, L. (2012) *Introduction to Information Science*, Facet Publishing.

Bearman, D. and Sochats, K. (c.1995) 'Metadata Requirements for Evidence', Pittsburgh Project, www.archimuse.com/papers/nhprc/BACartic.html.

Bettington, J., Eberhard, E., Loo, R. and Smith, C. (eds) (2008) *Keeping Archives*, Australian Society of Archivists.

Blouin, F. X. Jr. and Rosenberg, W. (eds) (2007) *Archives, Documentation, and Institutions of Social Memory: essays from the Sawyer seminar*, University of Michigan Press.

Brenneke, A. (1953) *Arkivkunde: ein Beitrag zur Geschichte und Theorie des europäischen Archivwesens*, Koehler & Amelang.

BSI (1997) PD0010 *Principles of Good Practice for Information Management*, British Standards Institute.

BSI (2008) BS 10008:2008 *Evidential Weight and Legal Admissibility of Electronic Information*, British Standards Institute.

BSI (2009) PAS 197:2009 *Code of Practice for Cultural Collections Management*, British Standards Institute.

Brothman, B. (2001) The Past that Archives Keep: memory, history, and the preservation of archival records, *Archivaria*, **51**, 48–80.

Buchanan, A. (2011) Ideas of the Archive from Outside the Discipline. In Hill, J. (ed.), *The Future of Archives and Recordkeeping*, Facet Publishing, 37–62.

Casanova, E. (1928) *Archivistica*, Stab. arti grafiche Lazzeri.

Choksy, C. (2006) *Domesticating Information: managing documents inside the organisation*, Scarecrow Press.

Cook, T. (2000) Beyond the Screen: the records continuum and archival cultural heritage. Paper delivered at Australian Society of Archivists Conference, www.mybestdocs.com/cook-t-beyondthescreen-000818.htm.

Cook, T. (2001a) Fashionable Nonsense or Professional Rebirth: postmodernism and the practice of archives, *Archivaria*, **51**, 14–36.

Cook, T. (2001b) Archival Science and Postmodernism: new formulations for old concepts, *Archival Science*, **1**, 3–24.

Cook, T. (2004) Macro-appraisal and Functional Analysis: documenting governance rather than government, *Journal of the Society of Archivists*, **25** (2), 5–18.

Craig, B. (2004) *Archival Appraisal: theory and practice*, K. G. Saur.

Craven, L. (2008) From the Archivist's Cardigan to the Very Dead Sheep: what are archives? What are archivists? What do they do? In Craven, L. (ed.), *What Are Archives? Cultural and theoretical perspectives: a reader*, Ashgate, 7–30.

Cunningham, A. (1996) Beyond the Pale? The 'flinty' relationship between archivists who collect the private records of individuals and the rest of the archival profession, *Archives and Manuscripts*, **24** (1), 20–6.

Data Protection Act (1998), www.legislation.gov.uk/ukpga/1998/29/contents.

Data Protection Act: guidance for archivists and records managers (2007), www.nationalarchives.gov.uk/documents/information-management/dp-code-of-practice.pdf.

Derrida, J. (1995) *Archive Fever: a Freudian impression*, University of Chicago Press.

Finnell, J. (2011) Records Management Theory's Dilemma: what is a record? *Library Philosophy and Practice*, e-journal, http://digitalcommons.unl.edu/libphilprac/567/.

Flinn, A. (2011) The Impact of Independent and Community Archives on Professional Archival Thinking and Practice. In Hill, J. (ed.), *The Future of Archives and Recordkeeping*, Facet Publishing, 145–69.

Flynn, S. (2001) The Records Continuum Model in Context and Its Implications for Archival Practice, *Journal of the Society of Archivists*, **22** (1), 79–93.

Foster, H. (2004) An Archival Impulse, *October*, **110**, 3–22.

Freedom of Information Act (2000), www.legislation.gov.uk/ukpga/2000/36/contents.

Greene, M., Boles, F., Bruemmer, B. and Daniels-Howell, T. (2004) The Archivist's New Clothes: or the naked truth about evidence, transactions, and recordness, IUPUI Indiana University-Purdue University Indianapolis Scholar Works, https://scholarworks.iupui.edu/handle/1805/42 and http://hdl.handle.net/1805/42, 1–30.

Hardiman, R. (2009) En Mal d'Archive: postmodernist theory and recordkeeping, *Journal of the Society of Archivists*, **30** (1), 27–44.

Harris, V. (2001) On the Back of a Tiger: deconstructive possibilities in 'evidence of me', *Archives and Manuscripts*, **29** (1).

Harris, V. (2002) The Archival Sliver: power, memory, and archives in South Africa, *Archival Science*, **2**, 63–86.

Harris, V. (2005) Archives, Politics and Justice. In Procter, M., Cook, M. and Williams, C. (eds), *Political Pressure and the Archival Record*, Society of American Archivists, 173–82.

HM Government (2008) *Managing Information Risk: a guide for accounting officers, board members and senior information risk owners*, www.nationalarchives.gov.uk/documents/information-management/information-risk.pdf.

Hobbs, C. (2001) The Character of Personal Archives: reflections on the value of records of individuals, *Archivaria*, **52**, 126–35.

Hobbs, C. (2010) Re-envisioning the Personal: reframing traces of individual life. In MacNeil, H. and Eastwood, T. (eds), *Currents of Archival Thinking*, Libraries Unlimited, 213–41.

Hunter, G. (2003) *Developing and Maintaining Practical Archives: a how-to-do-it manual*, Neal Schumann.

ICA (2000) *General International Standard Archival Description* (ISAD(G)), 2nd edn, International Council on Archives, www.ica.org/10207/standards/isadg-general-international-standard-archival-description-second-edition.html.

ICA (2004) *International Standard Archival Authority Record for Corporate Bodies, Persons, and Families* (ISAAR(CPF)), 2nd edn, International Council on Archives, www.ica.org/10203/standards/isaar-cpf-international-standard-archival-authority-record-for-corporate-bodies-persons-and-families-2nd-edition.html.

ICA (2007) *International Standard for Describing Functions* (ISDF), 1st edn, International Council on Archives, www.ica.org/10203/standards/isaar-cpf-international-standard-archival-authority-record-for-corporate-bodies-persons-and-families-2nd-edition.html.

ICA (2008) *International Standard for Describing Institutions with Archival Holdings* (ISDIAH), 1st edn, International Council on Archives, www.ica.org/10198/standards/isdiah-international-standard-for-describing-institutions-with-archival-holdings.html.

ICA Committee on Electronic Records (1997) *Guide for Managing Electronic Records from an Archival Perspective*, Study guide 8, International Council on Archives, 22.

ICA Section of Professional Associations (c.2011) *Shape Your Own Archivist: developing a competency model: guidance*, International Council on Archives, www.ica.org/9210/news-events/the-spaeurbica-handbook-on-competencies-is-now-available.html.

IRMS (2011) The Importance and Value of Effective Information and Records Management in Difficult Economic Times, www.irms.org.uk/resources/information-guides/514-irm_in_difficult_economic_times.

ISO (2001) 15489-1:2001 *Information and Documentation: Records management. Part 1: General, Part 2: Guidelines*, International Organization for Standardization.

ISO (2003) 14721:2003. *Space Data and Information Transfer Systems – Open Archival Information Systems – Reference Model*, International Organization for Standardization.

ISO/IEC (2005) 27002:2005 *Code of Practice for Information Security Management.*

Jenkinson, H. (1965) *A Manual of Archive Administration*, 2nd edn, Lund Humphries.

Jimerson, R. (2009) *Archives Power: memory, accountability and social justice*, Society of American Archivists.

Johnson, V. and Williams, C. (2011) Using Archives to Inform Contemporary Policy Debates: history into policy? *Journal of the Society of Archivists*, **32** (2), 287–303.

Kaplan, E. (2000) We Are What We Collect, We Collect What We Are: archives and the construction of identity, *American Archivist*, **63** (1), 126–51.

Ketelaar, E. (2001) Tacit Narratives: the meanings of archives, *Archival Science*, **1**, 131–41.

Ketelaar, E. (2002) Archival Temples, Archival Prisons: modes of power and protection, *Archival Science*, **2**, 221–38.

Lane, V. and Hill, J. (2011) Where Do We Come from? Where are we? Where are we going? Situating the archive and archivists. In Hill, J. (ed.), *The Future of Archives and Recordkeeping*, Facet Publishing, 3–22.

Lifelong Learning UK (2011) *National Occupational Standards: libraries, archives, records and information management services*, www.archives.org.uk/images/documents/ARACouncil/nationaloccupationalstandards.pdf.

Magee, K. and Waters, S. (2011) Archives, Artists and Designers, *Journal of the Society of Archivists*, **32** (2), 273–85.

Manoff, M. (2004) Theories of the Archive from Across the Disciplines, *Portal: Libraries and the Academy*, **4**, 9–25; http://dspace.mit.edu/bitstream/handle/1721.1/35687/4.1manoff.pdf?sequence=1.

McDonald, T. (1996) *The Historic Turn in the Human Sciences*, University of Michigan.

McKemmish, S. (1996) Evidence of Me, *Archives and Manuscripts*, **24** (1), 28–45.

McKemmish, S. (2005) Traces: document, record, archive, archives. In McKemmish, S. et al. (eds), *Archives: recordkeeping in society*, Charles Sturt University Press, 1–20.

McKemmish, S., Piggott, M., Reed, B. and Upward, F. (eds) (2005) *Archives: recordkeeping in society*, Charles Sturt University Press.

McLeod, J. and Hare, C. (2005) *Managing Electronic Records*, Facet Publishing.

Merewether, C. (ed.) (2006) *The Archive*, Massachusetts Institute of Technology.

Millar, L. (2010) *Archives: principles and practices*, Neal Schumann.

Ministry of Justice (2009) *Freedom of Information Act: Lord Chancellor's 'Section 46' Code of Practice*, www.justice.gov.uk/downloads/information-access-rights/foi-section-46-code-of-practice.pdf.

Muller, S., Feith, J. A. and Fruin, R. (1898) *Handleiding voor het Ordenen en Beschrijven van Archieven*, English tr. 1940 *Manual for the Arrangement and Description of Archives*, H. Wilson Company.

Nesmith, T. (2006) Reopening Archives: bringing new contextualities into archival theory and practice, *Archivaria*, **60**, 259–74.

Nesmith, T. (2010) Archivists and Public Affairs: towards a new archival public programming. In Avery, C. and Holmlund M. (eds), *Better off Forgetting? Essays on archives, public policy, and collective memory*, University of Toronto Press, 169–91.

Parker, E. (1999) *Managing Your Organization's Records*, Library Association Publishing.

Pearce-Moses, R. (2005) *A Glossary of Archival and Records Terminology*, Society of American Archivists, www2.archivists.org/glossary.

Peterson, T. (2005) *Final Acts: a guide to preserving the records of truth commissions*, Johns Hopkins University Press.

Piggott, M. and McKemmish, S. (eds) (1994) *The Records Continuum: Ian MacLean and Australian Archives' first fifty years*, Ancona Press.

Procter, M., Cook, M. and Williams, C. (eds) (2005) *Political Pressure and the Archival Record*, Society of American Archivists.

Schellenberg, T. R. (1956) *Modern Archives*, University of Chicago Press.

Schellenberg, T. R. (1965) *The Management of Archives*, Columbia University Press.

Schwarz, J. and Cook, T. (2002) Archives, Records and Power: the making of modern memory, *Archival Science*, **2**, 1–19.

Shepherd, E. and Yeo, G. (2003) *Managing Records: a handbook of principles and practice*, Facet Publishing.

Spieker, S. (2008) *The Big Archive: art from bureaucracy*, MIT Press.

Standards Australia (1996) Australian Standard AS 4390, *Records Management*, part 1.

Steedman, C. (2001) *Dust*, Manchester University Press.

Steedman, C. (2007) 'Something She Called a Fever': Michelet, Derrida, and dust (Or, in the archives with Michelet and Derrida). In Blouin, F. X. and Rosenberg, W. (eds), *Archives, Documentation, and Institutions of Social Memory: essays from the Sawyer seminar*, University of Michigan Press, 4–19.

Upward, F. (2005) The Records Continuum. In McKemmish, S., Piggott, M., Reed, B. and Upward, F. (eds), *Archives: recordkeeping in society*, Charles Sturt University Press, 197–222.

Upward, F. and McKemmish, S. (2001) In Search of the Lost Tiger, by Way of Sainte-Beuve: re-constructing the possibilities in 'Evidence of Me …', *Archives and Manuscripts*, **29** (1), 22-43.

Williams, C. (2006a) *Managing Archives: foundations, principles and practice*, Chandos Publishing.

Williams, C. (2006b) The Application of Theory in an Aspect of UK Practice, *Archivaria*, **62**, 77–101.

Williams, C. (2008) Personal Papers: perceptions and practices. In Craven, L. (ed.), *What are Archives? Cultural and theoretical perspectives: a reader*, Ashgate, 53–67.

Yeo, G. (2007) Concepts of Record (1): Evidence, information, and persistent representations, *American Archivist*, **70** (2), 315–43.

Yeo, G. (2008) Concepts of Record (2): Prototypes and Boundary Objects, *American Archivist*, **71** (1), 118–43.

CHAPTER 2

# Archival appraisal: practising on shifting sands

Anne J. Gilliland

## 1 Introduction

American archivist F. Gerald Ham provocatively asserted in his 1974 Society of American Archivists presidential address that, 'Our most important and intellectually demanding task as archivists is to make an informed selection of information that will provide the future with a representative record of human experience in our time ... Is there any other field of information gathering that has such a broad mandate with a selection process so random, so fragmented, so uncoordinated, and even so accidental?' (Ham, 1975, 5). Appraisal, which has been described as 'the most difficult of archival challenges' (Cook, 1991, 181), is the process whereby archivists and others involved in recordkeeping, such as records creators, records managers and curators of special collections, make that selection. Although Ham uses the term 'information' unqualifiedly, appraisal primarily targets very specific kinds of information: bureaucratic, community and personal records and other forms of media and documentation[1] that serve as primary, and frequently unique, evidence of the acts and experiences of organizations, groups and individuals. Making appraisal choices involves weighing the qualities inherent in such evidence and deciding whether it is sufficiently valuable to preserve. Unlike bibliographic selection, archival appraisal prioritizes context rather than content (although, in practice, many archivists may indeed make their – often pragmatic – decisions primarily based on content). An appraisal decision has long-term and often irrevocable consequences, in that archives commit to enduring or permanent preservation of selected material, while material not selected is often destroyed or otherwise lost to society.

## 1.1 Archivists and appraisal

Ever since it was first professionally proposed in the early twentieth century as a necessity for coping with problems posed by modern records and recordkeeping, archivists have had a conflicted relationship with the notion of appraisal, as well as with their role in appraisal decisions. As discussed further in section 4, the original aims of appraisal were to address the archival implications of a reduction in the use of registry systems by records creators, as well as to reduce volume of and redundancies in records needing to be kept permanently, while still retaining the insights that they collectively could provide into the decision-making and other activities of their creators. While today these remain major motivations for many archival organizations, the goals of appraisal have expanded since the 1970s to include ensuring that there is adequate and systematic documentation of societal experiences and phenomena that might otherwise be under-represented in or excluded from the historical record (Peace, 1984; Menne-Haritz, 1994), and a heightened consideration of the privacy of individuals mentioned in the records that might be compromised in inappropriate ways through archival accessioning and subsequent description and access. Since the 1980s, electronic records archivists have been preoccupied with ensuring that preservable records of long-term value are generated by digital recordkeeping systems and increasingly complex, networked and trans-jurisdictional bureaucracies (Bearman, 1994; Eastwood, 2004; Duranti, 2010). In the twenty-first century, however, the use of appraisal as a mechanism for reducing the bulk of born-digital records (which soon will comprise the majority of all existing records), or for selecting those deemed most valuable for long-term retention, has been criticized as no longer being viable or relevant, especially when it is implemented on an institution-by-institution basis through records retention and disposition scheduling. In an era of digital recordkeeping, of digital curation, with its focus on reuse, multiversioning and asset management, of mass digitization and cloud storage, the central question underlying appraisal has shifted from *how* do we appraise digital materials to *should* we appraise digital materials?

With all of this conceptual and practical expansion, other parties besides archivists have increasingly been drawn into the appraisal process, including records creators, subject experts, community members, systems analysts, documentarians and digital curators. Some appraisers, such as those in complex bureaucracies, have recommended a top-down conceptual approach to appraisal, while others, especially those working with community archives, have argued in favour of appraisal of extant documentation from the bottom-up. As Canadian archivist Barbara Craig observes:

> Historians, sociologists, anthropologists, philosophers, communication theorists, and cultural analysts have each tackled issues in the general area of records. Scholars who are interested in the life of organizations and bureaucracies have most consistently addressed records in their work. But a small group has chosen to approach the present using the past as a context that is an active player being neither a neutral background for current actions nor a restricting dead hand to escape from in the future. This historical-contextual research supports a better understanding of the archives that survive, and, consequentially, of the instrumentality of appraisal in shaping, concealing, liberating or altering the past.
>
> (Craig, 2004, 149)

## 1.2 Appraisal theory and practice

Appraisal, therefore, covers an extensive and divergent historical, theoretical and practical territory. This chapter aims to provide practising archivists with a broad overview of what they need to know in terms of background, and what they need to reflect upon regarding appraisal in the constantly shifting sands of modern recordkeeping and information technology. It will first provide a brief review of how thinking about appraisal has evolved over the past century, including underlying propositions, major rationales and prominent models or approaches. It will then summarize several enduring and emergent questions that have implications for current and future archival practice. It concludes by arguing that appraisal developed out of necessity to address problems of the modern paper era (Cook, 1994). It is no longer viable or environmentally sound, in an era dominated by born-digital material and highly networked recordkeeping, to attempt to segregate and preserve only certain kinds of records. Instead, archival efforts traditionally invested in appraisal should be transmuted into developing greener storage and preservation infrastructures and more sophisticated and reflexive ways of describing, compartmentalizing, retrieving and transforming massive quantities of preserved digital materials to support the needs of ever-wider ranges of audiences, uses and reuses (Lee and Tibbo, 2011).

## 2 The evolution of appraisal thinking

Appraisal is the facet of modern archival practice that has been the most contemplated and critiqued in the course of the past century, especially in North America. Critiques of appraisal have also influenced archival thinking in other areas such as description (Duff and Harris, 2002, 265). Many models, both theoretical and applied, have been proposed and many approaches have been tried. It bears underscoring, however, that appraisal is not understood or practised in the same way in every country in the world, and conceptually it is integrally tied to the personal, institutional, technological, disciplinary and socio-political contexts and values of archivists and archival theorists, and the archival institutions and traditions within which these people operate. As Hugh Taylor (1980, 9) observed regarding how archivists should approach the ideas of two of the most influential twentieth-century theorists, Englishman Hilary Jenkinson and American Theodore Schellenberg, 'Above all, they wrote from their own very different archival traditions and this should always be taken into account.'

## 3 Underlying propositions, key rationales and prominent approaches

Several propositions have been central to evolving archival ideas about appraisal (although these are not always co-present or in accord with each other):

- There is an overabundance of available documentation.
- Not everything that is created merits being retained.
- Certain phenomena remain under-represented in archives, and possibly under-documented overall in society.
- It is appropriate for archivists to make choices about what should be preserved and possibly also about what additional documentation should be created.
- It is possible and desirable to develop appraisal frameworks and value principles that provide the 'how,' 'why' and 'what' for those faced with making appraisal decisions.

Although it has always been the case that the creators of records made choices about which records to retain, or indeed the corollary has held – that records were destroyed or lost because such actions were not taken by their creators – appraisal did not surface as a formal, archives-driven practice until the twentieth century (Duranti, 2007). Many of the most prominent appraisal approaches employed since then have been articulated by government or university archivists in Europe or North America. The institutional rationales within which such archivists have worked have included *administrative* (the preservation of records that support the administrative, fiscal and legal needs of the institution that created them); *public* (the promotion of institutional transparency and accountability to its public); *research* (the support of scholarly and other types of secondary use of archives) rationales; and *documentary* (ensuring that a documentary record of diverse communities and social and political movements is created and preserved). A fifth rationale that is becoming increasingly prevalent is *human rights* (the preservation and utilization of records as key instruments that can be employed in circumstances such as war crimes tribunals, truth commissions and reparations, reconciliation and recovery efforts).

## 3.1 Appraisal frameworks and methods

Responding to different recordkeeping contexts as well as to prevalent exigencies in different time periods, the range of frameworks and methods for appraisal differ in various respects, for example, in the kinds or definitions of records being appraised; the point in the life of records when appraisal might be carried out; whether or not appraisal is carried out by means of records retention schedules; whether the archivist is working within a records continuum, life-cycle or digital curation model; who is responsible for making appraisal decisions; whether an appraisal process addresses a single or multiple institutions; and whether a custodial or a post-custodial approach is being taken. Most, however, can be grouped under one or more of the following rubrics (these are loosely ordered according to the points in a record's life when an appraiser first becomes engaged):

1 Letting the creator decide what, if anything, should be preserved. Such a stance, Hilary Jenkinson (1965) argued, maintains the naturalness of how records accumulate, thus supporting their authenticity, as well as emphasizing that the records were created to meet the creator's needs, not those of secondary users. Contemporary variants on this are a

diversity of self-archiving strategies being employed for personal archives; and archival accessioning of entire digital accumulations without any attempt at appraisal. An example of the latter is the daily ingestion of tweets into the Twitter Archive at the Library of Congress. Rather than selecting from among the tweets, the Library is concentrating on the development of new search and retrieval methods for mining the archive (Fear, 2011; Tweet Archivist, n.d.).

2 Implementing functionality within new or existing recordkeeping systems to ensure that essential, sufficient and reliable evidence of actions and transactions is created and is preservable (e.g. InterPARES Conceptual Framework for the Requirements for Assessing and Maintaining the Authenticity of Electronic Records; Designing and Implementing Recordkeeping Systems-DIRKS (InterPARES 2, n.d.; State Records of New South Wales, 2007)). Such an approach might involve, for example, an analysis of how important business functions are or should be carried out or communicated digitally according to juridical and administrative requirements, and then adding into the software of the business or communications systems being used the ability to recognize, record and potentially export to an archive or preservation environment any digital transactions that were associated with those functions.

3 Analysing the substantive functions and activities of an organization or type of organization such as a government or university, of a geographic region, or of a disciplinary field or sector in order to identify key activities that should be documented, the existing records that are generated and those that should be generated, as well as which should be preserved and, in some cases, what other documentation might need to be created, how and by whom (e.g. macroappraisal; documentation strategy) (Ham, 1975; Hackman and Warnow-Blewett, 1987; Samuels, 1992; Warnow-Blewett, 1992; Cox, 1994; Bantin and Bernbom, 1996; Ericson, 1991–92 and 1997; Greene and Daniels-Howell, 1997; Library and Archives Canada, 2000). A similar approach has been taken to documenting phenomena historically under-represented in archives, although actual implementations may differ (Chodorow, 2006; Flinn et al., 2009; Daniel, 2010; Flinn, 2010).

4 Assessing the kinds and degrees of bureaucratic, legal, research, cultural, community, personal and intrinsic values that are present in

extant records in order to arrive at a decision about their eventual disposition – what Schellenberg referred to as 'evidential' and 'informational' values (Brooks, 1940; Schellenberg, 1956a and 1956b); and overtly factoring pragmatic considerations into that assessment, such as space requirements, preservation costs and potential future use of preserved records, as well as the political implications of appraisal decisions and the growth of the reputation of the archival repository (Bauer, 1946; Fishbein, 1970; Brichford, 1977; Pinkett, 1981; Boles and Young, 1985; Greene, 1998).

5 Sampling voluminous case files and sensitive personal information contained in records (Steinwall, 1986; Cook, 1991; Ketelaar, 1995).

6 Automatically analysing or comparing extensive aggregations of digital materials by applying large-scale computational capabilities to identify salient structural and sometimes content similarities of those materials in order to arrive at an understanding of their nature and predominant characteristics, as well as anything that might be noticeably different or distinctive in the midst of the analysed corpus. Another approach involves visualizing large and complex digital bitstreams, datasets, records (for example, database content or electronic mail) and collections in order to delineate their content and context (especially procedural context and documentary inter-relationships), to assess the kinds of evidential and informational values they might exhibit, and to illustrate potential future uses (for example, expert appraisal systems; Persistent Archives Technology; appraisal of a Natural Electronic Archive) (Gilliland-Swetland, 1995; Horsman, 1997; Moore et al., 2000a and 2000b; Esteva, 2007).

7 Incorporating additional parties into appraisal decision making in order to make the process more representative and participatory (Booms, 1987; Shilton and Srinivasan, 2007; Huvila, 2008).

8 Projecting and programming for the level and types of potential future reuse of digitized and born-digital records (e.g. data curation; digital curation; digital asset management) (Akmon et al., 2011; Conway et al., 2011; Faniel and Zimmerman, 2011).

## 4 The history of appraisal

### 4.1 The emergence of appraisal as an idea and as a discourse

In the nineteenth century, European archivists responsible for government records had been preoccupied with ensuring that records of historical interest would be preserved indefinitely and not be illegally destroyed. In the early twentieth century, however, they began to acknowledge in their writings the need for a professional mechanism for coping with the impact of new office technologies (for example, the adoption of the typewriter and carbon paper, that together facilitated the production of multiple copies of records), the growth in bureaucracies and in the volume of records since the beginning of World War 1 and the deterioration of the registry systems that had controlled government recordkeeping in modern nation-states (Jenkinson, 1965; Müsebeck, 1929).

The first formal enunciation of appraisal criteria was made in 1901 by Heinrich Otto Meisner, head of the Prussian Privy State Archives. Meisner's criteria had a heuristic turn to them (in other words, they were more like rules of thumb than heavily codified rules). They embraced the primacy of provenance that was a fundamental of Muller, Feith and Fruin's 1898 *Manual for the Arrangement and Description of Archives*, thus ensuring that records were assessed in their documentary context rather than item by item.[2] Records that were created for a temporary purpose could be discarded once their object had been achieved and records that documented permanent activities could also be discarded. Meisner argued pragmatically: 'respect old age', 'avoid extremes' and 'too great an abstraction is an evil'. In the United Kingdom's Public Records Office, Hilary Jenkinson conceded that some selection was probably inevitable, but not preferable. He was concerned about preserving the objectivity of the record and ensuring that archivists did not introduce their own biases into what was kept for posterity. He was also concerned that selectively eliminating records from a fonds would result in damaging the evidential integrity of its collectivity. He argued, therefore, that records creators, and not archivists, were the 'competent authority' to make decisions about what should be transferred to the archives for preservation, a stance that Kolsrud argues has had a lasting legacy on how records creators have behaved with their own records (Jenkinson, 1965; Kolsrud, 1992).

When the US National Archives was founded in 1934, its inexperienced and largely untrained staff was quickly overwhelmed by the massive volumes of idiosyncratically maintained records that the federal government had generated in a dispersed and expanding bureaucracy that had never adopted registry systems or otherwise regulated record flow or elimination. European discussions of appraisal had taken place with reference to the role traditionally played by *pré-archivage* or registry systems, and the absence of such systems in the USA marks an important point of difference between the circumstances in which American archivists found themselves and those of their colleagues in European countries and their colonies and former colonies. It also helps to explain why American archivists played such a central and often creative role in addressing appraisal issues in the twentieth century, as well as why an approach that is developed in one national context may not translate so well into another. Several US National Archives staff members, including Philip Brooks, G. Philip Bauer and Emmett Leahy, argued that everything could not possibly be retained by the archives and that there needed, therefore, to be a systematic way to identify and schedule for transfer those records that needed to be retained permanently by the archives, and to eliminate and dispose of those that did not. Brooks and Bauer in particular suggested various approaches that addressed the tripartite administrative, public and research role of the National Archives. In fact, the criteria proposed by Brooks, namely value to the agency of origin, value for administrative history and value for historical research, were adopted in England in 1943, with the addition of one other criterion: records that could answer technical questions about the operations of the agencies should be preserved (Kolsrud, 1992). In 1952, however, the Grigg Committee, which was established in England to address problems associated with the growing volume of modern records, reversed this approach and again took a Jenkinsonian approach to appraisal by requiring a two-stage appraisal process based upon administrative and historical criteria. The records creator was to make the initial appraisal decision based upon administrative considerations, and 25 years later whatever remained was to be appraised by an archivist for its historical value, presumably with the added perspective of historical hindsight.

## 4.2 T. R. Schellenberg and beyond

The arguments presented within the US National Archives culminated in Schellenberg's influential articulation of a value-based appraisal framework for bureaucratic records in which the archivist, rather than the records creator, is actively engaged in making selection decisions (Schellenberg, 1956a and 1956b). At the time, Schellenberg was Director of Archival Management for the National Archives and was supervising the appraisal and archival deaccessioning of federal records under the 1950 Federal Records Act. The Act mandated that each federal agency, with records management guidance from the National Archives, should make and preserve records that documented the organization, functions, policies, decisions, procedures and essential transactions of the agency and provide the information necessary to protect the legal and financial rights of the government and of persons directly affected by the agency's activities (US Government, 1950).

Like other National Archives colleagues such as Leahy and Solon J. Buck, Schellenberg had come to realize that, for a variety of reasons, principles and practices articulated by European archivists could not translate exactly as stated or practised into the American federal context. Schellenberg saw Jenkinson's ideas as dated, given the accelerated changes in bureaucratic recordkeeping and information technologies, and overly passive with regard to the role of archivists in shaping the historical record. His framework was based on the notions of primary and secondary values, where secondary values were further divided into evidential and informational values. Primary values were those that reflected the record creator's 'administrative, fiscal, legal, [or] operating' actions (i.e. administrative use), while secondary values referred to additional research uses for records that might emerge after records became inactive. The two kinds of values were not envisaged as being mutually exclusive. A precursor to later appraisal theories that emphasized the analysis and ranking of organizational functions and activities, evidential value referred to the ways in which the records provided evidence of the organizational structure, functions, hierarchical relationships and activities of the creating body. Informational value, on the other hand, resonates more closely with some of the more data-centric preoccupations of other information fields over the past several decades: 'Records containing data about persons (individual or corporate bodies), things (places, buildings and other material objects) and phenomena (the interaction between persons and things).' Informational value emphasized the characteristics of uniqueness, form and importance (Schellenberg, 1956a and 1956b).

Not surprisingly, Schellenberg's framework was roundly and publicly criticized by Jenkinson (1955). For over 20 years, however, it was the only American appraisal framework available to the young American archival profession, which comprised an eclectic assortment of government archivists at federal, state and local levels, increasing numbers of academic and corporate archivists and an important contingent of manuscript librarians and curators from historical manuscript repositories and academic special collections. As the numbers and holdings of non-governmental repositories swelled and as collecting repositories began to be influenced in the 1960s and 1970s by the new social history and also by public history initiatives, it became evident that Schellenberg's framework, designed as it was with the federal government in mind, needed to be reframed, or at least extended, to address other types of institutional archives, and was even less suitable for collecting repositories that tended to select their holdings thematically, according to their collecting interests, rather than on the basis of their primary values to the institution that created them. In 1977 Maynard Brichford, a university archivist, authored the Society of American Archivists' first manual on appraisal. Brichford based the manual on Schellenberg's ideas but attempted to broaden their relevance to a wider range of repositories that did not necessarily have a legally defined mandate for what they were required to preserve or the kinds of resources available to the National Archives. He reintroduced the constraint of costs and considerations of different types of use that had first been enunciated by Bauer (1946), emphasizing that records that were unusable or difficult to use for various reasons were a poor investment of archival resources. He expanded Schellenberg's criteria for secondary value to encompass uniqueness, credibility, understandability, time span, accessibility, frequency of use and type and quality of use (Brichford, 1977).

The 'black box' approach of Frank Boles and Julia Marks Young, both also American university archivists, further built upon these criteria, proposing a more replicable, transparent and measurable process where all the elements of appraisal decision making, and potentially any weights accorded to them, are made explicit (Boles and Young, 1985). Boles and Young's model has three components. The first two, while they were spelled out in more detail, essentially drew from prior articulations: value of information and costs of retention. The use of the term 'information' rather than a more archival term such as 'records' or 'evidence' probably reflected, as with F. Gerald Ham's work, the preoccupation of the late 1970s and the 1980s with the Information Age and Boles' situation in a repository that was both a university archives and a historical collection (a fairly typical combination in US universities). The third component, implications of the appraisal recommendation, was an innovation that, while relevant in all contexts, in particular provided a reality check for archives that did not acquire records by means of a legal or regulatory mandate. This third component was subdivided into external political considerations (the authority and influence of records creators and others, and records assessment discrepancies) and internal procedural precedents (internal policies). Nowhere in these appraisal ideas was there a strong sense of a documentary mission for archives. They all emerged as ways of approaching records created within a particular institution.

## 4.3 The Minnesota Method

In 1997 Mark Greene and Todd Daniels-Howell of the Minnesota Historical Society proposed the Minnesota Method for the appraisal and reappraisal of business records collected by archives. The Minnesota Method is a fusion that Greene and Daniels-Howell deemed to be 'pragmatic' and 'proactive' of aspects of several approaches (Greene and Daniels-Howell, 1997). They argue that use and the growth in reputation of the archives are the 'surest proof of sound records appraisal' (Greene, 1998, 127). Like the Black Box, the Minnesota Method offers the potential for data-based decision making and the measurement of outcomes. It outlines a process for identifying, prioritizing and ranking records creators and suggesting various levels of documentation appropriate for creators at each rank. In terms of creators, it examines businesses by industry, sector and then four tiers based on economic impact, extant documentation, identification with the state and the degree to which the industry was unique to Minnesota. It then lays out five documentation levels from 'do not collect' to 'document thoroughly', and compares the levels, social value and purposes of use to volume and resources expended on keeping collections and repository mission, arguing also that large collections should be sampled or microfilmed (Greene, 1998).

Although Greene provides data on how this was implemented in Minnesota, more data needs to be published by other repositories that are implementing this approach, in order for it to be possible to arrive at an assessment of how widely it is being used and how effective it might be.

## 4.4 Documentation strategy and macroanalysis

### 4.4.1 Hans Booms

A controversial sea change in appraisal thinking came in the 1980s as the appraisal ideas of Hans Booms began to spread outside Germany, especially after his landmark 1972 article was translated into English and published in *Archivaria* in 1987. While appraisal is one of the most prominent examples in the archival field of how conceptual frameworks can and should both inform and develop out of practice, it is at the same time an example of the ways in which the archival field, consciously and subliminally, has responded to wider intellectual and social movements and the value systems they have promoted. Since the mid-1960s and the rise of the new social movements that emphasized identity, culture and lifestyle, there has been pressure on archives to include additional voices and narratives in the historical record. Postmodern and, more recently, postcolonial critiques have also urged archivists to become more reflexive about the values and experiences that they personally, as well as their institutions, bring to their activities. Such critiques have, for example, drawn attention to the ways in which archives can act as instruments in the promotion of nationalist agendas or, consciously or unconsciously, impose grand narratives on societal memory (Booms, 1987; Cook 1997; Peterson, 2001; Cook, 2011; Cook, 2013).

On this latter point, concerned about the incursion of statist values and ultimately totalitarian control in archives, Booms argued that 'in the context of the ideological battles waged between different social systems in the modern world' it was essential that archivists approach appraisal within a framework of critically and analytically derived value principles and theoretically formulated objectives (discussed further in the following section) (Booms, 1987, 73). Booms, an archivist at the West German Federal Archives, was responding not only to what he referred to as the 'authoritarian ideas of the 20s and 30s in Germany' that continued to be promulgated in West Germany by those trained in the earlier Prussian school of archival practice, but also to critiques levelled by East German archivists who asserted the superiority of archival science based upon Marxist-Leninist principles. Randolph Head, citing East German scholars of the 1950s and 1960s such as Ingo Rösler and Helmut Lötzke, and their influence on Peter Rück, notes that, 'Drawing on Marxist theories of base and superstructure ... [they] had proposed that the order found in archival accumulations necessarily constituted a reflection (*Wiederspiegelung*) of class relations and power structures in the society that produced the records involved' (Head, forthcoming; Lötzke, 1967; Rösler, 1967; Rück, 1975).

Booms emphasized the societal embeddedness and social responsibility of the archivist and called for co-operation across government and also non-governmental archives, as well as for the broader participation of other parties in appraisal decision making: 'within the pluralistic structure of our modern industrial society, the purpose and goal of the archival formation of the documentary heritage can only be to document the totality of public life as manifested in communities formed by common interests or other ties' (Booms, 1987, 106). Perhaps the close identification of Booms' argument with Cold War Germany resulted in archivists elsewhere failing to pay sufficient attention to its broader and enduring relevance. However, today's burgeoning community archives movement, as well as recent research of scholars in postcolonial studies, ethnic studies and science and technology studies, has further exhorted archival practitioners and theorists alike to contemplate the nature of archives, the political orientation and applications of archival science in different national and community contexts and the effect (that is, the anticipated and unanticipated outcomes, implications and consequences) and affect (that is, the emotional impact, such as dis/trust, surprise, wonder, joy, relief, frustration or grief) of archival practices and processes (Stoler, 2009; McKemmish et al., 2011; Caswell, forthcoming 2014).

### 4.4.2 Documentation strategy in North America

Ham, who was State Archivist and head of the Division of Archives and Manuscripts at the State Historical Society of Wisconsin, was among the first North American archivists to be influenced by Booms' ideas. He was also influenced by the political, social and intellectual movements that had been occurring in the USA in the 1960s and 1970s. His 1974 presidential address to the Society of American Archivists in many ways anticipated the documentation strategy movement in the United States in the later 1980s, but it also responded to developments in information technology and adopted an information orientation that provided an early bridge between archival science and information science (Ham, 1975 and 1981).

Terry Cook credits Helen Samuels, archivist for the Massachusetts Institute of Technology, with pioneering the documentation strategy or plan 'formulated to assure the documentation of an ongoing issue, activity or geographic area' (Samuels, 1991–92). This approach, which is often a collaborative one engaging archivists from multiple institutions as well as other experts and users, involves arriving at an understanding of what is to be documented, identifying what records (in any form or format) already exist and then making a plan for who will collect or create records to fill documentary gaps, and how. Along with fellow documentation strategists Richard Cox, Larry Hackman, Joan Warnow-Blewett and Tim Ericson (Hackman and Warnow-Blewett, 1987; Ericson, 1991–92; Cox, 1994), Samuels opened up the possibility of institutional archives acquiring non-bureaucratic records, or even of creating archival materials through documentary initiatives such as oral and video histories. Archivists who were more oriented toward institutional recordkeeping and evidentiary concerns criticized the thematic approach as being an artificial rather than an organic and provenancial method for identifying and acquiring archival materials.

Enthusiasm for collaborative documentation strategies waned in the 1990s, in part because of a renewed focus on more classically defined records and evidence that emanated from electronic records management. More importantly, in an era of declining resources, it was a casualty of the high investment in collaboration that was required (for example, in reaching agreement on planning and strategic priorities, identifying and sharing resources, surveying existing documentation outside one's own institution) and of the competition between repositories that led them to prioritize their own collections (Ericson, 1997). The documentation strategy approach has seen a revival in the twenty-first century and some new twists as a mechanism for community archives to identify and collect documentation (which can take on multiple forms, especially audiovisual and social media) and for more traditional collecting repositories to diversify their holdings with documentation relating to communities that have, historically, been under-represented in the historical record (Bastian and Alexander, 2009; Flinn, 2010). In this context, collaboration in the appraisal process has focused on consensus building and innovative participative approaches between communities and archivists (Shilton and Srinivasan, 2007; Huvila, 2008). Counter to much of the history of appraisal thinking, a major consideration in community archiving is often how to assess and address the paucity rather than the abundance of extant documentation. Under these circumstances, the documentation strategy's focus on working with community experts to identify all available documentation, as well as on conducting documentary initiatives such as oral histories, can be highly relevant.

### 4.4.3 Cook and macroappraisal

Cook himself espoused approaching appraisal through a conceptual analysis of the record creator, its mandate and functions, its structure and decision-making processes, the way it creates records and changes to these processes over time. Rather than examining the actual, and often voluminous, records that exist 'at the bottom' within organizations, this top-down approach identifies the functions and characteristics likely to generate records that will be of high value (Cook, 1992). Reminiscent of Booms' exhortations that appraisal first had to be theoretically conceived, Cook's macroanalysis framework has four aspects: theory, strategy, methodology and practice (Cook, 2005). In 1990 the Canadian Archivists Association scheduled a debate on appraisal between Cook and Samuels that positioned them to address what were envisioned to be the polarities in their respective approaches to appraisal. Cook was to argue for no role for the user in forming appraisal decisions and an institutional or provenancial focus, and Samuels for a strong role for the user as well as a thematic or subject focus for appraisal (Cook, 1992, 181). The debate did not transpire as envisioned, however. In their exchanges prior to the debate, Samuels, in what was to become the hallmark of her book on the subject, *Varsity Letters* (1992), melded the notion of institutional functional analysis with documentation strategy (i.e., identifying the major administrative and societal functions of the institution or institution type, and then also identifying what records would be necessary to ensure that each function would be adequately documented), thus effectively rendering moot the central tenets of the proposed debate.

During the same period, it had also become clear to many archivists that existing appraisal practices had to undergo a profound re-orientation if they were to cope with the impact of electronic recordkeeping and changing organizational structures. Macroanalysis and, specifically, the analysis of key business functions and the records that they do or should create, was proposed as being a new way to approach the appraisal of records created by digital recordkeeping systems. The particular concern that this approach was able to address was that of what constitutes a record in a distributed and virtual recordkeeping environment, as well as its completeness and reliability in terms of its relationship to the business process through which it is generated (Bantin and Bernbom, 1996; State Records of New South Wales, 2007). Bantin and Bernbom's research at the University of Indiana, however, demonstrated how time- and labour-intensive such a strategy can be when undertaken thoroughly – a significant limitation of this approach for many institutions.

## 4.5 Postcustodiality

Another major shift signalled by Ham in 1981 and reinforced by documentation strategists and macroappraisal proponents was that toward the postcustodial role of the archivist. Ham argued that 'the revolution in information processing' was resulting in an unprecedented abundance of hard-to-preserve records, thus requiring archivists to take a more proactive and less proprietary role in making 'crucial decisions – or decide by not deciding – about the future of the historical record' (Ham, 1981, 207). He also noted several other ways in which this revolution was challenging traditional archival ideas such as provenance, uniqueness, authenticity and arrangement and description. Ham presented a five-point agenda for how archivists should proceed in the postcustodial era. His agenda emphasized the need for coherent and comprehensive programmes for acquiring and providing access to archival materials locally, regionally and nationally, even though these materials would be increasingly complex and dispersed. He also stressed the need to devise ways to appraise and preserve materials that were being created by information technology and also for archivists to become involved in resolving the conflicts between freedom of information and privacy in terms of how these affect the quality and content of the archival record and access to it. The latter conflicts have become of particular concern with digitally born records today, and although Cook proposed sampling as an important strategy for addressing privacy concerns in large series of case files, a comparable consideration of these issues in the appraisal of electronic records, digital datasets and social media has yet to be undertaken (Cook, 1991).

The postcustodial idea was picked up and developed further in the context of electronic records management by David Bearman. He argued that the archivist was not only no longer to be viewed as the passive recipient and custodian of records, but also potentially might never take physical custody of preserved records. Instead the archivist would articulate design requirements for electronic recordkeeping systems and set policy and preservation requirements for, and serve as a broker and mediator to, preserved records that remained with their creator or wherever the necessary technological infrastructure was available. Bearman's stance was influential on the Australian archives community as it restructured its entire theoretical and practice domain around the concept of the records continuum (Bearman, 1991 and 1993b; Upward, 1996). Australian archivist Glenda Acland exhorted the archival field in 1992, to the effect that:

> A change in the traditionally perceived archival mindset is needed here to manage the records and their continuum, not the relics at the end stage in the record life cycle ... With the spotlight clearly on the record rather than the relic, the equilibrium can be adjusted to provide efficient, effective and innovative public record management with an intellectual control not custody axis, safeguarding and making accessible archival resources for good government, public accountability and future research needs.
>
> (Acland, 1992, 58–9)

Although regarded as an inevitability by many archivists as the preponderance of records has become digital, postcustodialism remains controversial within the archival community. Citing Acland (1992), Duranti (1996) and Cunningham (1996), Barbara Craig argues that

> there is a tension between policy and standards or physical custody as better techniques for implementing appraisal and preservation of information artefacts. Standards and audits may be more in tune with the needs of today. The tension will most likely be resolved by another way that combines aspects of standards, reformatting and custody.
>
> (Craig, 2004, 147)

## 4.6 Appraising born-digital records

As already discussed, electronic records archivists have focused since the 1980s on the impacts of growing and complexifying bureaucracies and technological innovation on the volume, status and nature of records. Examples of some of the issues raised by these records include blurred distinctions between drafts and record copies, multiple simultaneous originals and derivative versions of records; the generation of records in new media or new forms; and changing conceptualizations of permanence.

Various experimental efforts at automated appraisal have been explored, but none has as yet been widely implemented (Bearman, 1993b; Gilliland-Swetland, 1995; Horsman, 1997; Moore et al., 2000a and 2000b; Esteva, 2007). A currently emergent area with important implications for the appraisal of born-digital materials is digital forensics. Digital forensics potentially extend archival options regarding the granularity at which appraisal is conducted beyond either the aggregation (e.g. a fonds, a collection or a series) or the individual item, to the recorded bitstream and its location on a storage medium. Digital forensic techniques allow archivists to assess evidence inscribed on digital media such as hard drives that can include changes, erasures, date and time sequences and authorship patterns that are not directly visible to the human eye (Lee et al., 2012).

However, current debates are not only about how, but also about whether to appraise born-digital materials. It remains a topic of speculation as to whether it is fruitful to continue to attempt appraisal, given the extraordinary volume of digital documentation being created today and the profoundly networked nature of organizational and personal activities in the digital realm that makes it difficult to identify points of decision making or to establish institutional boundaries around records. Certainly there are legitimate questions to be asked about whether records retention schedules devised by individual institutions are adequate to identify records and to implement appraisal decisions, given how most institutions and sectors interoperate in a highly networked way and predominantly use digital communications such as electronic mail to arrive at and communicate their business decisions. An alternative, in light of the ready availability of increasingly inexpensive digital storage locally and in the cloud, would be to revert to the pre-twentieth-century position of retention rather than elimination as the default. The latter strategy would certainly retain the documentary integrity of the fonds, even as that fonds increasingly straddles provenancial and jurisdictional boundaries, but it would also multiply privacy concerns and make the ability to compartmentalize sensitive data or otherwise restrict access, and to conduct complex information retrieval, much more central to appraisal considerations than has previously been the case (Neumayer and Rauber, 2007). Neumayer and Rauber propose another strategy that is reminiscent of some of the earlier sampling approaches – random selection, backed up by traditional manual appraisal and restrictions on access to protect privacy (Neumayer and Rauber, 2007). Fuel is added to these debates by the accelerating development in data archiving and digital asset management of innovative techniques for mining, recovering and reusing digital materials and their traces that previously might not have been considered useful or viable for such purposes.

In addition to considering what can be complex legal ramifications of what is not only postcustodial but often extra-jurisdictional records retention, dependence on cloud storage also raises new concerns for archivists about environmental impact. As green consciousness becomes an increasing priority for archives and their parent institutions, archivists may find themselves evaluating not only the mechanisms of appraisal and the cost implications of appraisal decisions. They may also be weighing the respective environmental footprints of employing traditional archival storage for selected physical materials against using digital storage to retain much greater volumes of digital materials in less physical space, but on devices such as large server arrays that require large amounts of electricity and that release significant amounts of heat into the atmosphere (Bailey, 2008).

## 5 Reappraisal

A major concern with appraisal in any form is that discursive or political shifts, changes in institutional agendas and evolving notions of value constantly occur, as do community upheavals, transitions in custodial responsibilities and seismic changes in technologies. Appraisal, usually occurring at one specific moment in the life of a record, tends to be inflexible in responding to such dynamics (with the exception of electronic recordkeeping, discussed below). Although this limits its susceptibility to passing trends – a not insignificant consideration – it raises the importance of reappraisal as a mechanism for checking the effectiveness of the original appraisal decision and reassessing whether preserved records continue to merit retention. The approach taken by the Grigg Committee is an early, if ultimately ineffective, example of building a mechanism for reappraisal into records retention that incorporated not only a measure of hindsight but also two different perspectives (the creator's and the archivist's) into the process (Committee on Departmental Records Report, 1954). While there is always the possibility of reappraisal in most of the above-discussed approaches, few specifically emphasize appraisal as an iterative and recursive process. The most prominent of these is appraisal within the records continuum. Framed within the philosophy that all recordkeeping is situated within ever-evolving social, cultural and political contexts, appraisal occurs at multiple points across the continuum's dimensions of create, capture, organize and pluralize, and along its axes of evidence, recordkeeping, transactionality and identity (Reed, 2005). This provides archivists with the desired conceptual rationale for reappraisal, but does not give them the tools for carrying it out.

With the exception of approaches based in functional and transactional analyses, most of appraisal thinking to date has been dominated by concerns associated with analogue media. By the 1990s, however, archivists had realized the extensive preservation commitment involved in maintaining electronic records and had begun to move away from the rhetoric of the permanence of archived records to that of periodically reappraising the 'continuing value' of preserved records. Assessment of continuing value is essentially a reappraisal activity and is most likely to occur when preserved digital records are scheduled for refreshing or migration. This replacement of 'permanent' with 'continuing value' in the archival psyche has gradually been extended to archival holdings in all media.

## 6 Conclusion

Although research suggests that they believe appraisal to be the most important of all archival activities (Craig, 2007), archival practitioners often resist its 'modelization', arguing that appraisal is more of an art than a science. Some also object to the proposition that archivists wield significant power in shaping historical narratives and therefore should operate within an overt conceptual framework. A consistent and compelling motivation for archivists has been the ever-increasing abundance of documentation and the resulting fear of being overwhelmed by the management of an increasingly voluminous, multimedia and documentarily complex, yet qualitatively diluted, record. In response, many archivists are persuaded that local context, expediency, cost-effectiveness and indications of future use should be the most important considerations in deciding what materials should be retained by archives, rather than consciously articulating and acting upon imperatives to support remembering and forgetting, accountability and transparency, and completeness and authenticity that are central to the archival role in society (Williams, 2006).

This stance would seem at first glance to be at odds with the excitement in other information fields over the ability, thanks to ever-evolving information technology, to generate and capture more documentation about more aspects of human lives than ever before. Although it aligns more closely with privacy and human rights experts and scholars in areas such as communication and policy studies, who are emphasizing 'forgetting' or the elimination of digital documentation as a societal good (Gross, 2000; Ricoeur, 2004; Bannon, 2006), this is more often an accidental rather than a conscious alignment. Many archives also shy away from acquiring records that relate to activities or perspectives that are unpopular, distasteful or controversial or that otherwise do not represent mainstream values (Neumayer and Rauber, 2007), even when they are committed to a broad-based approach to documenting society (which might mean acquiring records of aspects of society that many would prefer to conceal or forget, and which potentially might receive less use).

What is more, the effectiveness and long-term impacts of appraisal ideas and practices remain woefully under-documented and under-assessed, and thus it is impossible to evaluate in any rigorous or replicable fashion the relative merits of all of the various arguments and approaches discussed in this chapter. The very terminology associated with appraisal, for example, 'identifying', 'assessing', or 'determining', begs important questions about which appraisal processes and evaluation techniques might be the most effective in the short and also the long term, for which constituencies and under what circumstances.

## 6.1 Key questions

The discussion in this chapter has highlighted a number of enduring and emerging questions that twenty-first-century archivists should reflect upon when contemplating archival appraisal and identifying an approach that will work in their particular context:

- *The continuing centrality of appraisal as an archival practice*: Is appraisal only a tool of the physical world? Is appraisal still necessary or indeed even feasible in a global digital society?
- *Appraisal in a networked world:* Is there a way to conduct appraisal that mirrors the networked and increasingly global ways in which organizations and individuals today conduct their affairs and create and circulate documentation?
- *Appraisal within a paradigm of abundance:* Is appraisal relevant or necessary only when/where there is an abundance of documentation?
- *Appraisal and the construction of historical narratives and identities:* What effect does appraisal have upon what is remembered by society, and how can we assess that? In what ways might appraisal construct group identity?
- *Who, if anyone, should make appraisal choices?* Should archives be chosen? If choice is necessary, then who should choose what is preserved and what is not?
- *Appraisal and representativeness:* Is a representative record a desirable goal for appraisal? If so, how can the archival profession work towards that? Should different cultural values and memory practices be taken into account by appraisal? If appraisal is subject to the perspectives, values, motivations and constraints of the institution and, potentially, even of the individual undertaking the appraisal, in what ways can we be assured that a plural record will be preserved for the future?
- *Appraisal of 'difficult' materials:* In what ways do current appraisal practices address the selection and preservation of controversial materials or those related to contentious, unpopular or otherwise difficult histories?
- *Changing values of records:* Do records change in meaning and/or value when they become part of an archive or special collections or as a result of intervening events after their accessioning? On what basis, if at all, should reappraisal be conducted?
- *Environmental responsibility:* What are the environmental implications of archival appraisal choices?

## 6.2 A diversity of ideas and practices

Although this chapter has laid out a multiplicity of approaches that archivists might consider, as already stated, each has been developed within a particular experiential, institutional or social context and, even if it claims to be universally applicable, it will probably work best within that context. As Eric Ketelaar has argued, 'Before we decide on "sameness" before we can codify global theories and principles, and before we can afford to build and implement universally applicable models, we have to study the differences' (Ketelaar, 1997, 4). Many archives are, after all, an integral part of the legal, bureaucratic and cultural infrastructure of nations and communities and their practices take their lead as much from their contexts as from external professional theories. Moreover, although there has been a progression of ideas over the past decades, that does not mean that earlier ideas have been replaced. As Terry Cook has argued, we can identify several phases in archival science over this period, resulting in a layering and diversity of ideas and practices, rather than in the emergence of one as the single best (Cook, 2013). In the final analysis, there remains a very real difference between articulating a model and being the person who is faced with making choices about records on the ground. What is more, now more than ever, the records on the ground will not wait for an ideal approach to emerge.

More consequential to ponder and debate at this moment is the very real possibility of the death of appraisal with regard to born-digital records. Appraisal was an idea of its time. It is not an idea of this time. We exhibit much hubris in thinking that we can actually eliminate all traces of networked digital material. At the same time, information leaks, ubiquitous security cameras, satellite photography and drones have already compromised so much of citizen privacy. Instead, we should focus on the benefits of retaining and securing digital evidence and becoming the lead agents in its intellectual and physical control. The only supportable rationales for selective elimination should be based on forgetting – when important emotional and human rights issues are at stake – and on promoting green archival management. Keeping everything better supports new research modes and enfranchises a greater diversity of user groups and uses. By replacing archival efforts at appraisal with a much stronger emphasis on compartmentalizing digital materials and on other forms of privacy controls, and on truly investing in more nuanced and reflexive description and sophisticated information retrieval technology, archives and the archival field have the potential to make a contribution that is truly of this time.

## Notes

1 Because of the diversity of types of documentation that are the focus of institutional, collecting, media, community, personal and online archives, the term 'records' (in its broadest documentary sense) will be used in this chapter to refer generically to the objects of appraisal processes. As discussed in Chapter 1, the definitions of what is considered to be a record and the values that it might exhibit may vary across different legal, institutional, documentary and technological contexts, but a solid delineation of how records and their associated values are understood in a given context is an essential part of making informed and transparent appraisal decisions.

2 The impact of the Manual will be explored further in Chapter 3.

## References and further reading

Acland, G. (1992) Managing the Record rather than the Relic, *Archives and Manuscripts*, **20** (1), 57–63.

Akmon, D., Zimmerman, A., Daniels, M. and Hedstrom, M. (2011) The Application of Archival Concepts to a Data-intensive Environment: working with scientists to understand data management and preservation needs, *Archival Science* **3–4**, 329–48.

Bailey, S. (2008) *Managing the Crowd: rethinking records management in the Web 2.0 world*, Facet Publishing.

Bannon, L. J. (2006) Forgetting as a Feature, Not a Bug: the duality of memory and implications for ubiquitous computing, *CoDesign*, **2** (1), 3–15.

Bantin, P. C. and Bernbom, G. (1996) The Indiana University Electronic Records Project: analyzing functions, identifying transactions, and evaluating recordkeeping systems: a report on methodology, *Archives and Museum Informatics: Cultural Informatics Quarterly*, **10**, 246–66.

Bastian, J. (2002) Taking Custody, Giving Access: a postcustodial role for a new century, *Archivaria*, **53**, 76–93.

Bastian, J. A. and Alexander, B. (eds) (2009) *Community Archives: the shaping of memory*, Facet Publishing.

Bauer, G. P. (1946) *The Appraisal of Current and Recent Records*, Staff Information

Paper 13, National Archives and Records Service.

Bearman, D. A. (ed.) (1991) *Archival Management of Electronic Records*, Archives and Museum Informatics Technical Report no. 13.

Bearman, D. A. (1993a) The Implications of Armstrong v. Executive Office of the President for the Archival Management of Electronic Records, *American Archivist*, **56**, 674–89.

Bearman, D. A. (1993b) Record-keeping Systems, *Archivaria*, **36**, 16–37.

Bearman, D. A. (1994) *Electronic Evidence: strategies for managing records in contemporary organizations*, Archives and Museum Informatics.

Blanton, T. S. (1995) *White House E-Mail: the top-secret messages the Reagan/Bush White house tried to destroy/book and disk*, The New Press.

Boles, F. and Greene, M. (1996) *Et Tu Schellenberg?* Thoughts on the dagger of American appraisal theory, *American Archivist*, **59** (3), 298–310.

Boles, F. and Young, J. M. (1985) Exploring the Black Box: the appraisal of university administrative records, *American Archivist*, **48** (2), 121–40.

Booms, H. (1972[1987]) Society and the Formation of a Documentary Heritage: issues in the appraisal of archival sources, *Archivaria*, **24**, 69–107. Trans. H. Joldersma and R. Klumpenhouwer. Originally published as: Gesellschafsordnung und Überlieferungsbildung: Zur Problematik archivarischer Quellenbewertung, *Archivalische Zeitschrift*, **68** (1972), 3–40.

Brichford, M. (1977) *Archives and Manuscripts: appraisal and accessioning*, Society of American Archivists.

Brooks, P. (1940) The Selection of Records for Preservation, *American Archivist*, **3** (4), 221–34.

Caswell, M. (forthcoming 2014) *Archiving the Unspeakable: silence, agency and the photographic record in Cambodia*, University of Wisconsin.

Chodorow, S. (2006) To Represent Us Truly: the job and context of preserving the cultural record, *Libraries & the Cultural Record*, **41** (3), 372–80.

Committee on Departmental Records Report (1954) Cmd. 9163, HMSO (The Grigg Report).

Conway, E., Giaretta, D., Lambert, S. and Matthews, B. (2011) Curating Scientific Research Data: a preservation analysis method in context, *International Journal of Digital Curation*, **2** (6), 38–52.

Cook, T. (1991) *The Archival Appraisal of Records Containing Personal Information: a RAMP study*, UNESCO.

Cook, T. (1992) Documentation Strategy, *Archivaria*, **34**, 181–91.

Cook, T. (1994) Electronic Records, Paper Minds: the revolution in information management and archives in the post-custodial and post-modernist era, *Archives and Manuscripts*, **22**, 300–29.

Cook, T. (1997) What is Past is Prologue: a history of archival ideas since 1898, and the future paradigm shift, *Archivaria*, **43**, 17–63.

Cook, T. (2005) Macroappraisal in Theory and Practice: origins, characteristics, and implementation in Canada, 1950–2000, *Archival Science*, **5** (2–4), 101–61.

Cook, T. (2011) 'We Are What We Keep: We Keep What We Are': archival appraisal past, present and future, *Journal of the Society of Archivists*, **32** (2), 173–89.

Cook, T. (2013) Evidence, Memory, Identity and Community: four shifting archival paradigms, *Archival Science*, **13** (2–3), 95–120.

Cox, R. J. (1994) The Documentation Strategy and Archival Appraisal Principles: a different perspective, *Archivaria*, **38**, 11–36.

Craig, B. (2004) *Archival Appraisal: theory and practice*, de Gruyter.

Craig, B. (2007) Doing Archival Appraisal in Canada: results from a survey of practitioners' experience, practices, and opinions, *Archivaria*, **64**, 1–45.

Cunningham, A. (1996) Commentary: Journey to the End of the Night: custody and the dawning of a new era on the archival threshold, *Archives and Manuscripts*, **24** (2), 312–21.

Daniel, D. (2010) Documenting the Immigrant and Ethnic Experience in American Archives, *American Archivist*, **73**, 82–104.

Duff, W. and Harris, V. (2002) Stories and Names: archival description as narrating records and constructing meanings, *Archival Science*, **2**, 263–85.

Duranti, L. (1996) Archives as a Place, *Archives & Manuscripts*, **24** (2), 242–55.

Duranti, L. (2007) 'Rethinking Appraisal': conference overview. Paper presented at the DELOS Conference, 2007, www.interpares.org/display_file.cfm?doc=duranti_delos_2007_overview.pdf.

Duranti, L. (2010) Structural and Formal Analysis: the contribution of diplomatics to archival appraisal in the digital environment. In Hill, J. (ed.), *The Future of Archives and Recordkeeping: a reader*, Facet Publishing.

Eastwood, T. (1996) Should Creating Agencies Keep Electronic Records Indefinitely? *Archives and Manuscripts*, **24**, 256–67.

Eastwood, T. (2004) Appraising Digital Records for Long-term Preservation, *Data Science Journal*, **3**, 202–8.

Ellis, R. H. and Walne, P. (eds) (2003) *Selected Writings of Sir Hilary Jenkinson*, Society of American Archivists.

Ericson, T. L. (1991–92) At the 'Rim of Creative Dissatisfaction': archivists and acquisition development, *Archivaria*, **33**, 66–77.

Ericson, T. L. (1997) 'To Approximate June Pasture': the documentation strategy in the real world, *Archival Issues*, **22** (1), 5–20.

Esteva, M. (2007) Text and Bitstreams: appraisal and preservation of a natural electronic archive. In Pearce-Moses, R. and Davis, S. (eds), *Proceedings of the Colloquium New Skills for the Digital Era. Washington DC, 31 May–2 June 2006*, Society of American Archivists.

Evans, F. B. (1967) Archivists and Records Managers: variations on a theme, *American Archivist*, **30**, 45–58.

Faniel, I. M. and Zimmerman, A. (2011) Beyond the Data Deluge: a research agenda for large-scale data sharing and re-use, *International Journal on Digital Curation*, **1** (6), 58–69.

Fear, K. (2011) 'You Made It, You Take Care of It': data management as personal information management, *International Journal of Digital Curation*, **2** (6), 53–77.

Fishbein, M. H. (1970) A Viewpoint on Appraisal of National Records, *American Archivist*, **33**, 175–87.

Flinn, A. (2010) Independent Community Archives and Community-Generated Content: writing, saving and sharing our histories, *Convergence: The International Journal of Research into New Media Technologies*, **16** (1), 39–51.

Flinn, A., Stevens, M. and Shepherd, E. (2009) Whose Memories, Whose Archives? Independent community archives, autonomy and the mainstream, *Archival Science*, **9**, 71–86.

Foote, K. (1990) To Remember and Forget: archives, memory, and culture, *American Archivist*, **53** (3), 378–92.

Gilliland-Swetland, A. J. (1995) Development of an Expert Assistant for the Archival Appraisal of Electronic Communications: an exploratory study. PhD dissertation, University of Michigan.

Gilliland-Swetland, A. J. and Kinney, G. T. (1994) Uses of Electronic Communications to Document an Academic Community: a research report, *Archivaria*, **38**, 79–96.

Greene, M. A. (1998) 'The Surest Proof': a utilitarian approach to appraisal, *Archivaria*, **45**, 127–69.

Greene, M. A. (2010) MPLP: it's not just for processing any more, *American Archivist*, **73**, 175–203.

Greene, M. A. and Daniels-Howell, T. J. (1997) Documentation with 'An Attitude': a pragmatist's guide to the selection and acquisition of modern business records. In O'Toole, J. M. (ed.), *The Records of American Business*, Society of American Archivists.

Gross, D. (2000) *Lost Time: on remembering and forgetting in late modern culture*, University of Massachusetts Press.

Hackman, L. J. and Warnow-Blewett, J. (1987) The Documentation Strategy Process: a model and a case study, *American Archivist*, **50**, 12–29.

Ham, F. G. (1975) The Archival Edge, *American Archivist*, **38** (1), 11–22.

Ham, F. G. (1981) Archival Strategies for the Post-custodial Era, *American Archivist*, **44** (3), 207–16.

Head, R. C. (forthcoming) Historical Case Studies of Pre-Modern European Archives: a comparative approach. In Gilliland, A. J., Lau, A. J. and McKemmish, S. (eds), *Research in the Archival Multiverse*, Monash University Press Social Informatics Series.

Higgins, S. (2011) Digital Curation: the emergence of a new discipline, *International Journal of Digital Curation*, **2** (6), 78–88.

Horsman, P. J. (1997) *The Application of Knowledge Engineering in Archival Appraisal.* Thesis, University of Amsterdam.

Huvila, I. (2008) Participatory Archive: towards decentralised curation, radical user orientation, and broader contextualisation of records management, *Archival Science*, **8** (1), 15–36.

InterPARES 2 (n.d.) *Preserving Digital Records: guidelines for organizations*, www.interpares.org/ip2/display_file.cfm?doc=ip2(pub)preserver_guidelines_booklet.pdf.

Jenkinson, H. (1955) Modern Archives: some reflections on T. R. Schellenberg, *Journal of the Society of Archivists*, **1**, 147–9.

Jenkinson, H. (1965) *A Manual of Archive Administration*, 2nd edn, Lund, Humphries.

Kaplan, E. (2000) We Are What We Collect, We Collect What We Are: archives and the construction of identity, *American Archivist*, **63** (1), 126–51.

Ketelaar, E. (1995) The Right to Know, the Right to Forget? Personal information in public archives, *Archives and Manuscripts*, **23**, 8–17.

Ketelaar, E. (1997) The Difference Best Postponed: cultures and comparative archival science, *Archivaria*, **44**, 142–8.

Kolsrud, O. (1992) The Evolution of Basic Appraisal Principles – Some Comparative Observations, *American Archivist*, **55**, 26–38.

Lee, C. A. and Tibbo, H. (2011) Where's the Archivist in Digital Curation? Exploring the possibilities through a matrix of knowledge and skills, *Archivaria*, **72**, 123–68.

Lee, C. A., Kirschenbaum, M., Chassanoff, A., Olsen, P. and Woods, K. (2012) BitCurator: tools and techniques for digital forensics in collecting institutions, *D-Lib Magazine*, **18** (5–6), www.dlib.org/dlib/may12/lee/05lee.html.

Library and Archives Canada (2000) *Appraisal Methodology: macro-appraisal and functional analysis*, www.collectionscanada.gc.ca/government/disposition/007007-1035-e.html.

Lötzke, H. (1967) Methodologische Probleme der marxistischen Archivwissenschaft, *Archivmitteilungen*, **17** (6), 216–22.

McKemmish, S., Faulkhead, S. and Russell, L. (2011) Dis-trust in the Archive: reconciling records, *Archival Science*, **11**, 211–39.

Menne-Haritz, A. (1994) Appraisal or Documentation: can we appraise archives by selecting content? *American Archivist*, **57** (3), 528–42.

Moore, R., Baru, C., Rajasekar, A., Ludaescher, B., Marciano, R., Wan, M., Schroeder, W. and Gupta, A. (2000a) Collection-based Persistent Digital Archives: Part 1, *D-Lib Magazine*, **6**, www.dlib.org/back2000.html.

Moore, R., Baru, C., Rajasekar, A., Ludaescher, B., Marciano, R., Wan, M., Schroeder, W. and Gupta, A. (2000b) Collection-based Persistent Digital Archives: Part 2. *D-Lib Magazine*, **6**, www.dlib.org/back2000.html.

Müsebeck, E. (1929) Der Einfluss des Wetkriegs auf die archivalische Methode, *Archivalische Zeitschrift*, **38**, 138–50.

Neumayer, R. and Rauber, A. (2007) Why Appraisal Is not 'Utterly' Useless and Why It's not the Way to Go Either: a provocative position paper (PPP), *Digital Preservation Europe*, www.digitalpreservationeurope.eu/publications/appraisal_final.pdf.

Peace, N. (ed.) (c.1984) *Archival Choices: managing the historical record in an age of abundance*, Lexington Books.

Peterson, T. H. (2001) The Nasty Truth about Nationalism and National Archives, *Proceedings of the 5th General Conference of EASTICA*, 19 September, www.trudypeterson.com/downloads/Nasty%20Truth%20Korea2.pdf.

Pinkett, H. T. (1981) American Archival Theory: the state of the art, *American Archivist*, **44**, 175–87.

Reed, B. (1994) Electronic Records Management in Transition, *Archives and Manuscripts*, **22** (1), 164–71.

Reed, B. (2005) Reading the Records Continuum: interpretations and explorations, *Archives and Manuscripts*, **33** (1), 18–43.

Ricoeur, P. (2004) *Memory, History, Forgetting*, Chicago University Press.

Rösler, I. (1967) Zu einigen Fragen der marxistischen Archivwissenschaft, *Archivmitteilungen*, **17** (6), 222–9.

Rück, P. (1975) Zur Diskussion um die Archivgeschichte: die Anfaenge des Archivwesens in der Schweiz (800–1400), *Mitteilungen der Vereinigung*

*Schweizerischer Archivare*, **26**, 3–40.
Samuels, H. (1991–92) Improving Our Disposition: documentation strategies, *Archivaria*, **33**, 125–40.
Samuels, H. (1992) *Varsity Letters: documenting modern colleges and universities*, Scarecrow Press.
Schellenberg, T. R. (1956a) *The Appraisal of Modern Public Records: National Archives Bulletin 8*, National Archives and Records Service.
Schellenberg, T. R. (1956b) *Modern Archives: principles and techniques*, University of Chicago Press.
Shilton, K. and Srinivasan, R. (2007) Participatory Appraisal and Arrangement for Multicultural Archival Collections, *Archivaria*, **63**, 87–101.
State Records of New South Wales (2007) *Strategies for Documenting Government Business: the DIRKS manual*, www.records.nsw.gov.au/recordkeeping/dirks-manual/.
Steinwall, S. D. (1986) Appraisal and the FBI Files Case: for whom do archivists retain records? *American Archivist*, **49** (1), 52–63.
Stoler, A. L. (2009) *Along the Archival Grain: epistemic anxieties and colonial common sense*, Princeton University Press.
Taylor, H. A. (1980) *The Arrangement and Description of Archival Materials*, K. G. Saur.
Tweet Archivist (n.d.), www.tweetarchivist.com.
Upward, F. (1996) Structuring the Records Continuum Part One: postcustodial principles and properties, *Archives and Manuscripts*, **24**, 268–85.
Upward, F., McKemmish, S. and Reed, B. (2011) Archivists and Changing Social and Information Spaces: a continuum approach to recordkeeping and archiving in online cultures, *Archivaria*, **72**, 197–238.
US Government (1950) *Federal Records Act of 1950, as amended, codified at 44 U.S.C. chapters 29, 31 and 33.*
Warnow-Blewett, J. (1992) *Science After '40. Documenting recent science: progress and needs*, Center for the History of Physics.
Williams, C. (2006) Studying Reality: the application of theory in an aspect of UK practice, *Archivaria*, **62**, 77–101.

CHAPTER 3

# Arrangement and description: between theory and practice

Jennifer Meehan

## 1 Introduction

Arrangement, description and preservation – the core activities involved in records processing – are aimed at safeguarding the context and authenticity of records as well as the physical and, increasingly, digital materials themselves in order to ensure their long-term availability and access. The archival function of processing is a key aspect of archives management: in preserving and providing access to records in a timely and effective manner, holding institutions discharge the responsibility that they undertake in selecting or acquiring the records in the first place. Often carried out at an earlier stage in the recordkeeping process, the records management function of classification is a key means of organizing and providing access to records during their active use. While this chapter will focus on archival processes, it is important to think holistically about archives management and recordkeeping in order to situate the function of processing in relation to both, and to understand the theory and practice of arrangement and description within the broader landscape of making and keeping archives/records. Processing is also closely tied to the other functions of archives management (appraisal, selection/acquisition, accessioning, reference/use, digitization), in that the decisions and actions taken in those other spheres impact upon and inform the function of processing, and vice versa. Processing, particularly arrangement and description, is also informed by the recordkeeping systems and behaviours of the organizations and/or individuals responsible for creating and maintaining the records, and thus there is a connection between the work of the recordkeeper and that of the archivist.

As with other archival functions, processing involves a continual mix of practical, conceptual and theoretical concerns. At any given time there are various forces (some of which may seem at cross-purposes) shaping what is or is not required, feasible and/or desirable in terms of processing. Such forces include: the needs of the records as both physical and intellectual objects; the needs of users; the demands of archival theory (the set of ideas about the nature of records); the practical limitations of archival methodology (the set of ideas about how to treat records based on their nature); and the even more practical limitations of available resources, systems and tools. In many, if not most, holding institutions, processing will be carried out at both macro and micro levels. At the macro level, processing entails developing a programme for preserving and providing access to an institution's holdings, which might involve determining priorities, developing local standards and best practices, implementing systems and tools for description and determining and advocating for needed resources. At the micro level, processing involves planning and carrying out an individual project to arrange, describe and preserve a given body of records. The work involved ranges from the analytical and speculative to the mundane, typically including both intellectual work aimed at *the mind* (analysing context and content, devising an arrangement scheme, describing records) and physical tasks directed at *the matter* (rehousing, physical organization of files, weeding). At both the macro and micro levels, processing can be viewed as a continuum of possible decisions and actions, ranging from minimal to optimal, undertaken by an institution and/or individual practitioner for the purpose of preserving the records and making them accessible to users. Regardless of one's standpoint in relation to processing (whether one is an administrator, manager or processor), it is important to understand the theoretical and methodological concepts of arrangement and description, and the continual interaction of archival theory and practice involved in both conceptualizing and carrying out this work.

In discussing the theory and practice of arrangement and description in the context of archival processing, this chapter will focus on the intellectual work of arrangement and description (as opposed to the tasks of physical preservation and organization), as well as on programmatic and conceptual approaches to processing. The points of discussion will include:

- an overview of archival concepts and principles and different approaches to arrangement and description, highlighting the critical aspects of thought and practice
- the practical application of archival concepts in arrangement and description, touching upon aims, actions and decisions, and the impact of arrangement and description
- the products or outcomes of arrangement and description
- evolving areas of thought and practice in the realm of arrangement and description and of processing more generally, and how these are leading to new ways of seeing and doing arrangement and description.

## 2 Theory and methodology of arrangement and description

### 2.1 Archival concepts and principles

Archival theory has specifically to do with the facts (observed or otherwise) of records creation, maintenance, transmittal and use, and how these facts determine the nature and characteristics of archives. Since records are created in the course of a specific activity, whether of a business or personal nature, they bear an important relationship to the creator, function and process that gave rise to them, as well as to the other records stemming from the same activity. As the by-products of activity, records can serve as evidence of that activity; at the same time, their value and meaning as sources of evidence and memory are derived solely from the external and internal relationships that place the records in context. To preserve the evidential character of archives, one must preserve the contextual relationships of a body of records.

These ideas about the nature of records have shaped and continue to shape the concepts and principles of archival methodology for arrangement and description. The principle of *respect des fonds,* first put forth by Natalis de Wailly in France in the 1840s, is historically defined as the dictate 'to group, without mixing them with others, the archives (documents of every kind) created by or coming from an administration, establishment, person, or corporate body' (Duchein, 1983, 64). Other early articulations of the principle of *respect des fonds* can be found in the German *Provenienz Prinzip* (applied as early as 1816) and the Dutch *herkomstbeginsel* (applied as early as 1826) (Horsman, 1994, 53). In the German formulation, the principle was extended to also address the internal organization of a body of records (*Registraturprinzip*). The modern articulation of what became known as the principle of provenance and the principle of respect for original order can be found in the *Manual for the Arrangement and Description of Archives* (first published in Dutch in 1898 and in English in 1940) (Muller, Feith and Fruin, 1968). Based on the notion of an archival collection (*archief* in Dutch, *fonds d'archives* in French) as 'an organic whole', the Dutch authors outlined rules aimed at respecting the boundaries and structure of an archival collection. These include rules for systematic arrangement which dictate that '[t]he system of arrangement must be based on the original organization of the archival collection, which in the main corresponds to the organization of the administrative body that produced it' (Section 16) (Muller, Feith and Fruin, 1968, 52) and that 'in the arrangement of an archival collection … the original order should first of all be reestablished as far as possible' (Section 17) (Muller, Feith and Fruin, 1968, 59–60). While the specific rules are somewhat rigid and limited in their formulation and have at times been subject to narrow interpretation, the *Manual* can be regarded as 'a starting point of archival theory and methodology' (Horsman, Ketelaar and Thomassen, 2003, 243), giving expression to certain key ideas informed by the nature of archival collections (such as the significance of the connection between records and functions and the significance of their original context for interpreting the records) and meant to inform the practice of arranging and describing such organic bodies of records.

For the sake of clarity, one can unpack the archival concepts and principles of arrangement and description as follows:

- The concept of **provenance** refers to the origin or source of the records. The **principle of provenance**, simply stated, dictates that 'records of different origins (provenance) be kept separate to preserve their context' (Pearce-Moses, 2005). Provenance can usefully be thought of as the external structure of a body of records and as comprising the various possible sets of external relationships, including the relationships between the creator and the records, the relationships between functions/activities and the records to which they give rise and/or the relationships between and amongst multiple creators and multiple bodies of records. These and other relationships of external structure typically relate to socio-historical context, juridical-administrative context ('the legal and organizational system in which the creating body belongs'), provenancial context ('the creating body, its mandate, structure, and functions'), and certain aspects of technological context ('the characteristics of the technical components of an electronic computing system in which records are created') (The InterPARES Glossary, 2001). Further glosses on the concept of provenance are provided by writers such as David Bearman and Richard Lytle, who highlight the power of the principle of provenance in the management of all information within an organization (Bearman and Lytle, 1985); Tom Nesmith and Laura Millar, among others, who argue for broader notions of provenance beyond that of creatorship (Nesmith, 2005; Millar, 2002); and Jennifer Douglas, who traces the evolution of the principle of provenance as organizing principle, physical and intellectual construct and socio-historical context (Douglas, 2010).

- The concept of **original order** refers to 'the organization and sequence of records established by the creator of the records'. The **principle of respect for original order** dictates maintaining records in their original order for the purposes of 1) preserving existing relationships and evidential significance and 2) exploiting the record creator's mechanisms to access the records (Pearce-Moses, 2005). Original order can usefully be thought of as the internal structure of a body of records and as comprising the various possible sets of internal relationships between the records and the development of the activity giving rise to them and the relationships between and amongst the records related to the same activity. These and other relationships of internal structure typically relate to procedural context ('the business procedure in the course of which the record is created'), documentary context ('the archival fonds to which a record belongs, and its internal structure') (The InterPARES Glossary, 2001) and certain aspects of technological context. Brien Brothman, among others, critiques traditional notions of original order, challenging both the naturalness and the possibility of preserving any such order (Brothman, 1991).

Two points are worth making to highlight the relevance and applicability of archival concepts and principles. First, while many equate the principle of *respect des fonds* with the principle of provenance, Peter Horsman and others argue that the principles of provenance and respect for original order are outward and inward applications of the same principle – *respect des fonds* (Horsman, 1994, 51). In this view of things, one must always consider both the external and internal aspects of provenance when arranging and describing a body of records. Second, while the archival concepts and principles of arrangement and description were first formulated with regard to administrative records and before the advent of computing technologies, it is important to remember that the methodological ideas are based first and foremost on theoretical ideas about the nature of records as by-products of activity. As such, archival theory and methodology is and continues to be relevant for arranging and describing records in all formats (whether physical or digital) and across recordkeeping environments (whether organizational or personal, public or private, etc.).

## 2.2 Levels of arrangement and description

Proceeding from archival concepts and principles, one can unpack the processes and products of arrangement and description as follows:

- **Arrangement** is 'the intellectual and physical processes and results of analyzing and organizing documents' (International Council on Archives, Committee on Descriptive Standards, 2000). To put it another way, arrangement is 'the process of organizing materials with respect to their provenance and original order, to protect their context and to achieve physical or intellectual control over the materials; and the organization and sequence of items within a collection' (Pearce-Moses, 2005).
- **Description** is 'the creation of an accurate representation of a unit of description and its component parts, if any, by capturing, analyzing, organizing and recording information that serves to identify, manage, locate and explain archival materials and the context and records systems which produced it. The term also describes the products of the process' (International Council on Archives, Committee on Descriptive Standards, 2000).

In arrangement and description the elements of analysis and representation are, generally speaking, the **content**, **context** and **structure** of a body of records. In managing records during their active use, a recordkeeper might seek to organize or impose a structure (see discussion of classification in section 4.1) in order to provide access to the records (content) in a context that is useful to the creator. In arranging and describing a body of archival records, an archivist will analyse the contents and any existing structure or organization and how these relate to the activities and functions of the creator, in order to preserve and describe the contextual relationships. The products of arrangement and description result in a structure that purports to represent the contents and contexts of a body of records. The resulting structure is, to one extent or another, hierarchical in nature, with different levels representing subordinate groupings and vertical relationships of records within a larger body. That said, increasing attention is being paid to representing parallel groupings and horizontal relationships between and amongst different bodies of records, due to the impact of administrative and technological change on recordkeeping (see discussion of the series system in section 2.3.2).

The levels of arrangement and description, and their definitions, are as follows:

- **Fonds:** 'The whole of the records, regardless of form or medium, organically created and/or accumulated and used by a particular person, family, or corporate body in the course of that creator's activities and functions' (International Council on Archives, Committee on Descriptive Standards, 2000). In theory, the fonds is a conceptual unit referring to a totality ('the whole of the records') that in most cases does not exist as such within a given repository; however, in practice this term is often used to refer to the physical unit of records held by a repository.
- **Collection:** 'A body of archival material formed by or around a person, family group, corporate body, or subject either from a common source as a natural product of activity or function, or gathered purposefully and artificially without regard to original provenance' (Hensen, 1989). As a term of practice, collection refers to the physical unit of materials held by a repository and may be applied to organic bodies of records and artificial collections of material; in regard to organic bodies of records, fonds and collection are often used synonymously in practice, if not in theory.
- **Record group:** '[A] major archival unit established somewhat arbitrarily with due regard to the principle of provenance and to the desirability of

making the unit of convenient size and character for the work of arrangement and description and for the publication of inventories' (Schellenberg, 1956, 181).

- **Series:** 'Documents arranged in accordance with a filing system or maintained as a unit because they result from the same accumulation or filing process, or the same activity; have a particular form; or because of some other relationship arising out of their creation, receipt, or use. A series is also known as a records series' (International Council on Archives, Committee on Descriptive Standards, 2000).
- **Subseries:** 'A body of documents within a series readily distinguished from the whole by filing arrangement, type, form, or content' (Pearce-Moses, 2005).
- **File:** 'An organized unit of documents grouped together either for current use by the creator or in the process of archival arrangement, because they relate to the same subject, activity, or transaction. A file is usually the basic unit within a record series' (International Council on Archives, Committee on Descriptive Standards, 2000).
- **Item:** 'The smallest intellectually indivisible archival unit, e.g. a letter, memorandum, report, photograph, sound recording' (International Council on Archives, Committee on Descriptive Standards, 2000).

In practice, arrangement and description will typically proceed from the top down, starting with the topmost level (fonds, collection, record group, series) and then proceeding to subordinate levels (series, subseries, file, item). Arrangement and description will also typically proceed from the general to the specific, starting with a representation of the whole and then proceeding to representations of the component parts. Beyond the necessity of representing the whole first, there are no agreed levels to which arrangement and description must be carried out, nor are there agreed levels of detail which must be provided in the resulting products. However, local or other standards, such as the International Standard for Archival Description (General) (ISAD(G)), may offer guidance, such as which fields of information should be included in the different levels of description (International Council on Archives, Committee on Descriptive Standards, 2000) (see discussion of descriptive standards in section 4.2).

## 2.3 Models of arrangement and description

In theory, different record units provide the basis for different approaches to arrangement and description. While still adhering to archival principles, each approach is shaped by and likewise gives shape to different ideas about archival control, the multifaceted nature of provenance, the fixity of and relationship between arrangement and description and the role of description in recordkeeping. In this sense, the different approaches represent different conceptual models for theorizing and carrying out arrangement and description. Much has been written elsewhere about the history, context and development of these different approaches (Millar, 2010); what follows is a brief overview and comparative analysis of the main components of each.

### 2.3.1 Record group

The notion of the record group as a unit of arrangement and description, first put forth by T. R. Schellenberg, stands in contrast to the notion of 'the whole of the records' (*archief* in the Dutch Manual, archive group in Hilary Jenkinson's Manual) (Muller, Feith and Fruin, 1968; Jenkinson, 1965). While the archive group was suitable for dealing with closed, stable bodies of historical records (or 'dead records'), it was deemed insufficient for dealing with the records of modern government bureaucracy. The record group can be seen as a pragmatic way of dealing with: the records of active agencies; the records created by units of various status and authority; and the challenges posed by dynamic and constantly changing organizations and functions (Schellenberg, 1956, 181). It has been widely implemented in organizational settings ranging from government to corporate to academic, and is still in wide use today. Many practitioners may, in practice, refer to a record group as a fonds or collection.

The main departure from archival orthodoxy is in terms of where the outer limits or boundaries are drawn in defining the record unit; provenance, in terms of origins, is a determinative factor, but other factors, such as number, size and distinctness, are also considered. For example, Schellenberg suggested that in establishing record groups 'there should be neither too few nor too many record groups' (the factors of number and size) and the records of one administrative body need only be 'readily distinguished from other record groups on the basis of their relation to a distinct function or distinct subject field' (the factor of distinctness) and not on the basis of the completeness or independence of the administrative body (Schellenberg, 1956, 188). The arrangement of components within the record group typically follows the traditional model of hierarchical representation of the parts comprising the whole:

Record group
  Subgroup
    Series
      File.

The record group does not address or properly allow for series with multiple provenance, for instance, the records stemming from one function that has been carried out over time by multiple different agencies; rather, this approach requires that one series be arranged within or associated with one record group (although it is possible to make cross-references through description). The record group approach focuses as much on physical arrangement and control as it does on intellectual control; in doing so, it conflates what are two distinct aspects of archival control. Moreover, in imposing and describing a singular arrangement into and within record groups, this approach typically provides for only one view of the records, a snapshot of the records at one point in time (usually at the end of their active life).

The conceptual model underpinning the record group approach situates the function of arrangement and description solely in the realm of archives management, and in doing so reinforces the distinction between records management and archives management. In other words, it adheres to a life-cycle view of recordkeeping and a custodial view of archives making. In practice, records schedules and file classification schemes will likely inform the identification and arrangement of archives within record groups. However, despite this, the work of arrangement and description is conceptualized as a set of *post hoc* activities aimed at establishing control over archives after they have been selected or acquired for retention. Critics of the record group concept, including P. J. Scott among others, note its limitations for dealing with the impact of administrative and technological change and for representing the multifaceted nature of provenance (especially in the form of multiple-provenance series).

### 2.3.2 Series

The series system, first devised by Scott and his colleagues at the National Archives of Australia, was devised as a 'solution' to the problems of the record group concept (Scott, 1966). Based on the record series as the primary unit of physical arrangement, the series system separates the description of records ('record control') from the description of creators ('context control') and allows for individual series to be linked to as many creators as were involved in creating, maintaining and using the records over time. In effect, this model separates control of the physical record unit of the series (physical control) from the control of administrative context (intellectual control) and abandons notions that relationships between series and creators are strictly hierarchical (Yeo, 2010, 93). As Scott argues, the series system offers a more effective means of respecting provenance and original order because:

> (a) items are kept in their administrative context and original order by physical allocation to their appropriate series, and (b) series are no longer kept in any original physical order in a record or shelf group (if there is any such order) but simply have their administrative context and associations recorded on paper.
>
> (Scott, 1966, 497)

In separating the description of records and creators, the series system addresses the diachronic and synchronic changes in administration, technology and recordkeeping (for instance, a single function being carried out by a succession of different offices over time, or the adoption of a new technology or system for keeping records) that result in multiple-provenance series and allows for representing the evolving contexts of records throughout their active life and not just as a snapshot at the end. The documentation and representation of records in the series system moves away, in theory, from the static, hierarchical representation of the parts comprising the whole (although it is still possible to create a hierarchical representation by combining records and context descriptions in a single-access tool) and instead emphasizes and codifies the relationships between and amongst the parts, thus allowing, again in theory, for different views of the parts and the various possible wholes that they comprise. Bob Krawczyk offers a practical example of this in his discussion of the 'cross reference heaven' of describing one series of Ontario Government records (community information service correspondence files) that was created by five agencies over time. Separating the descriptions of the series and agencies and then showing the many links ('cross-references') between them affords views of the parts (the part of the series created by each agency) and the various wholes they comprise (the whole of the series created by the five agencies, as well as the wholes of each agency's records) (Krawczyk, 1999).

In addition to providing a different model for representing bodies of records, the series system also suggests a different conceptual model for theorizing and carrying out the work of arrangement and description. In emphasizing description as intellectual control and distinguishing this from physical arrangement (in effect, decoupling intellectual and physical control), the series model offers a different perspective on the relationship between the activities of arrangement and description, challenging the notions that description always reflects arrangement and that description necessarily proceeds from the general to the specific (in other words, from the top down). Moreover, in emphasizing the centrality of recordkeeping systems, the series model posits description as a function of recordkeeping and not just of archives management, and accordingly embraces a postcustodial view of archival description and a commitment to integrated records management. As Chris Hurley argues, 'records description must be capable of dealing with all records, at any stage in the continuum, not just an archival remnant which has passed out of current use' (Hurley, 1994, 152). Along these same lines, Scott suggests that '[t]he role of the archivist, as an analyst of recordkeeping systems of the past, may also be developed to include current systems' (Scott, 1966, 500). The proposals of Scott and others have led to further debate, particularly in Australian literature, and to the adoption of the Commonwealth Record Series System in the National Archives of Australia, a clear example of a conceptual approach being applied in practice (Biskup and Australian Society of Archivists, 1995).

### 2.3.3 Fonds

While both the record group concept and series system are based on a physical unit of arrangement and description, the fonds approach is in effect based on a conceptual unit of arrangement and description. The concept of the fonds derives from earlier conceptions of 'the whole of the records' as expressed in the Dutch Manual and writings of Hilary Jenkinson. But whereas earlier notions equated 'the whole of the records' with a physical record unit and earlier criteria for identifying fonds reflected a belief that records should have a single final resting place within a larger whole (Duchein, 1983; Cook, 1992, 67), the fonds is increasingly conceived of as a conceptual entity that is based on the idea of 'creatorship' and the act of creation and accumulation (Cook, 1992; Eastwood, 2000). In this view, the fonds is an imagining of the conceptual whole of which the physical records on hand (series, files, items) form part. Moreover, the fonds is not necessarily co-extensive with the physical records in archival custody, since a repository will rarely, if ever, hold 'the whole of the records' of an organization or individual (Yeo, 2012); for instance, other physical parts of one conceptual fonds might be held by different repositories, while yet others might be retained or destroyed by the creator. In its focus on conceptual creator(s) rather than physical records, the fonds approach has the potential to support postcustodial models of practice and relational models of description by providing a framework that is compatible with integrated records management, authority control systems and object-oriented modelling (Cook, 1992; Yeo, 2012). In this regard, one can trace possible areas of convergence between fonds and series models of arrangement and description, as Terry Cook does in describing the fonds as:

> the conceptual summary of descriptions of physical entities at the series level, or lower, and descriptions of the administrative, historical, and functional character of the records creator(s).
>
> (Cook, 1992, 73–4)

As a conceptual unit of arrangement and description, the fonds is a broad idea (or 'theoretical construct', to use Eastwood's term) (Eastwood, 2000, 108) that has for the most part been narrowly applied in practice. As the basis of international archival descriptive standards, the fonds has served to codify archival description as a multi-level and hierarchical representation of records and as proceeding from the general to the specific; in other words, it has codified archival description as a singular, fixed representation of a whole and its parts and as a linear, top-down process, which doesn't adequately reflect or address the complex realities of recordkeeping. Similarly, in practice, the fonds is usually applied in a limited fashion to the records in archival custody within a single repository, while ignoring and/or distorting the relationship between current and inactive records, the complexities of creatorship and the effects of change over space and time. Laura Millar and Peter Horsman note the limitations of the fonds concept as a model for arrangement and description based on a too-narrow conception of creation (Millar, 2002; Horsman, 2002). In theory, the fonds suggests a conceptual model of arrangement and description that focuses on intellectual control. When the fonds is viewed merely as a unit of physical control, its usefulness as a theoretical construct is diminished, at which point practitioners are dealing with constructed record 'groupings' rather than with organic wholes (Horsman, 2002, 22). One way to overcome the practical limitations of the fonds is to draw a distinction between the conceptual fonds and the physical collection in order to encompass both custodial and postcustodial models of practice (Yeo, 2012).

## 2.4 Conceptualizing arrangement and description

While the different conceptual models reflect different approaches to dealing with the impact of administrative and technological change, a commonality across these approaches (as well as across archival thought and practice generally) is an increased focus on the conceptual aspects of arrangement and description. The units of arrangement and description are viewed as comprising both conceptual and physical (and increasingly digital) entities. And the work of arrangement and description, while still involving some amount of physical control and physical arrangement of records in archival custody, is viewed first and foremost as establishing intellectual control by identifying, preserving and representing contextual relationships. Moreover, critiques of provenance and original order have served to both problematize and expand the notions of 'creatorship' and 'order(s)' so as to allow for multiplicity, thereby introducing another possible level of abstraction to the work of arrangement and description. Finally, in addition to highlighting the constructed nature of archives (whether record group, fonds or collection), postmodern critiques of archival practice have also highlighted the constructive nature of the activities associated with arrangement and description. In this view of things, practitioners don't so much *identify* as *create* the contextual relationships of a body of records in the course of arrangement and description; which is to say, in the course of interpreting and representing provenance and original order, practitioners are in effect creating the external boundaries and internal ordering of a body of records.

In focusing on the conceptual aspects of arrangement and description, one can begin to comprehend the possible role and scope of this function across various recordkeeping and archives-making environments – from organizational to personal, public to private, custodial to postcustodial and so on. It is also possible to distinguish the critical components of any approach to arrangement and description as:

- separating administrative/physical control from intellectual control
- preserving and representing content, context and structure
- identifying/creating the external and internal relationships (or the relationships of external and internal structure)
- representing functional and other aspects of provenance
- representing the relationships of parts to whole(s).

Conceptualizing arrangement and description also necessitates a reframing of archival concepts and principles in the context of both thought and practice. Rather than serving as hard and fast rules to be followed or implemented, the concepts of provenance and original order, broadly conceived, serve instead as a conceptual framework for analysing, understanding and creating the contextual relationships (both external and internal) that give records their meaning. This repositioning of archival concepts and principles firmly underscores the constructive nature of arrangement and description as well as the mediating role of the practitioner, and thus necessitates a further broadening of archival theory to also encompass ideas about the nature of archival processes and their impact upon the records (Meehan, 2009).

## 3 The practical application of archival concepts and principles

One approach to putting theory into practice involves clarifying and elaborating on the aims, decisions and actions, and impact of arrangement and description.

## 3.1 The aims of arrangement and description

As has already been discussed, the broad aims of arrangement and description are to establish intellectual and physical control over a body of records in order to preserve and provide access to the records now and in the future. In the context of records management, the function of arrangement and description is largely focused on meeting the needs of creators with regard to their active or semi-active records, and might encompass such control tools as file classification schemes, records schedules and/or recordkeeping plans or systems. In the context of archives management, the function of arrangement and description is largely focused on meeting the needs of users and facilitating the work of the holding institution, and might encompass such control tools as accession records, catalogue records, finding aids and/or collection management systems.

Although practices may diverge to a certain extent, based on the record-making or archives-keeping environment, the needs related to control, preservation of and access to records will converge around the need for trustworthy records. The dimension of authenticity, especially as it relates to the identity and integrity of the records, is of most concern in arrangement and description. The need to preserve the identity and integrity of records requires placing and preserving the records *in context* or, to put it another way, preserving the contextual relationships between the records and the functions of the creator as well as between and amongst the records. The work of arrangement and description, especially within the context of archival processing, is aimed at contextual preservation as much as physical preservation. The practical application of provenance and original order as a conceptual framework for analysing the external and internal relationships of a body of records will serve to achieve the contextual preservation aims of arrangement and description. In safeguarding the authenticity of records, arrangement can be viewed as 'the moral defence of the archive' (Cook, 1986, 103, citing Jenkinson) and description as 'the apparatus of authenticity' (MacNeil, 2005).

## 3.2 Decisions and actions

From a practical point of view, the work of arrangement and description entails a series of points where decisions are made and actions are taken with regard to both contextual and physical preservation and the provision of control and access. To better understand the general nature and impact of the various decision and action points, it is useful to consider the different levels of practice within a given institution – (1) the (macro) level of institutional context and (2) the (micro) level of individual process.

### 3.2.1 The institutional context of arrangement and description

The mission, history, organization and values of the holding institution play a significant role in shaping the practice of arrangement and description. Some of the different factors that determine the overall institutional framework for processing and providing access to holdings include: the types of records held (whether created, selected or acquired by the institution), the types of users served and types of services provided, the needs and priorities for preserving and providing access and the resources available for processing. To the extent that an institution has an established processing programme – for instance, in terms of resources, policies, procedures, systems and/or tools – certain decisions and actions will take place at the programmatic level. Macro-level decisions and actions might include:

- surveying the entirety of an institution's holdings and assessing physical condition and levels of intellectual and physical access
- establishing priorities and strategies for processing, in terms of what to process when, and the level or depth of processing required
- establishing local policies, procedures and standards for arranging and describing records
- implementing systems and tools for managing, describing and providing access to records, and so on.

These sorts of macro-level decisions and actions determine to one extent or another the broader institutional context within which arrangement and description is carried out, shaping both the local practice and the products stemming from that practice. It is important to be aware of the nature and impact of arrangement and description practice at an institutional level, and how an institution has transmitted and represented bodies of records (whether fonds, collections, record groups or series) over time.

### 3.2.2 The individual process of arrangement and description

Working within the broader framework of institutional practice, the individual process of arrangement and description entails a series of decisions and actions with regard to a specific body of records. At this level, the practice of arrangement and description is guided by the practitioner's understanding of archival concepts and principles and of the records themselves. As such, the subjectivity of the practitioner is a significant factor shaping both the processes and products of arrangement and description. Some of the main decision and action points at the level of individual process include:

- surveying the body of records (analysing content, context and structure; assessing physical condition, evidential and informational value, research strengths, etc.; identifying and analysing existing orders, relationships, structures)
- developing a plan for processing (determining level or depth of processing; preservation needs; arrangement scheme; descriptive tools)
- carrying out physical preservation (rehousing, reformatting, stabilizing and remediating as needed and/or as resources allow)
- carrying out arrangement (intellectual and/or physical arrangement; interpreting and representing existing orders; identifying/creating relationships between records and creator's functions/activities and between and amongst records; identifying/creating external and internal structures that best place and preserve records in context)
- carrying out description (representing content, context and structure; implementing descriptive standards; creating online access tools).

By deconstructing the individual process of arrangement and description as above, it is possible to grasp how the concepts of provenance and original order can be practically applied as a conceptual framework for analysing, understanding and creating the contextual relationships (both external and internal) that give records their meaning. In short, they allow for the framing of questions about content, context and structure and provide direction to the analysis or 'cross-examination' of sources (the records themselves as well as secondary sources) aimed at generating the knowledge necessary to place and preserve records in context (Meehan, 2009, 84–5; Meehan, 2010).

### 3.3 The impact of arrangement and description

In preserving and providing access to records, in safeguarding the authenticity of records, and in contextualizing records, the processes of arrangement and description effectively shape the records for users. These processes are not neutral or objective; rather, they are situated within specific sociocultural, professional, institutional and individual contexts. In devising an intellectual arrangement scheme for a body of records, the practitioner is imposing and creating order (one of many possible orders which ends up becoming *the* order of the records), thereby establishing value (Brothman, 1991). Moreover, the practitioner is, in effect, creating an imagined whole (whether a fonds, collection, record group or series) from the physical parts (Meehan, 2009; Yeo, 2012). In describing the content and context of the records, the practitioner is, in effect, constructing stories and names that highlight certain aspects of context, while downplaying or ignoring other aspects (Duff and Harris, 2002). At their core, archival arrangement and description are interpretive and representative acts. As Elizabeth Yakel argues,

> [t]he term 'archival representation' more precisely captures the actual work of the archivist in (re)ordering, interpreting, creating surrogates and designing architectures for representational systems that contain those surrogates to stand in for or represent actual archival materials.
>
> (Yakel, 2003, 2)

The conceptualization and practice of arrangement and description needs to account for the creative nature of archival processes, the constructed nature of archival products and the role of the individual practitioner and the holding institution in archival representation.

## 4 The products of arrangement and description

Another approach to putting theory into practice involves critically examining the products of arrangement and description. From a practical point of view, these typically include an intellectually organized body of records (whether physical, digital or both) and the descriptive outputs representing and providing access to those records. Underlying these practical products are the intellectual and often invisible categories, schemes and infrastructures that are devised, employed and imposed by the individual practitioner and the holding institution.

## 4.1 Classification and taxonomies

Geoffrey Bowker and Susan Leigh Star provide general definitions of classification as 'a spatial, temporal, or spatio-temporal segmentation of the world', and of classification system as 'a set of boxes (metaphorical or literal) into which things can be put to then do some kind of work' (Bowker and Star, 1999, 10). In the information world, classification is defined as 'the organization of materials into categories according to a scheme that identifies, distinguishes and relates the categories' or 'the process of assigning materials a code or heading indicating a category to which it belongs' (Pearce-Moses, 2005). In this definition, classification is viewed as distinct from arrangement. Yet the processes and products of both do a similar kind of work; they involve not only putting things into boxes but also, in effect, creating the boxes into which things can be put. Moreover, as classification relates to taxonomy, which is defined as 'a structure used for classifying materials into a hierarchy of categories and subcategories' (Pearce-Moses, 2005), so too does arrangement, particularly to the extent that it creates a hierarchical structure representing different levels of arrangement (fonds/collection/record group, series, file, item). Some examples of taxonomies that might be employed in the arrangement of records include: a file classification scheme, defined as 'a diagram or chart that describes standard categories used to organize materials with similar characteristics' (Pearce-Moses, 2005), for organizing active records in an office of origin; and standard or common series for organizing certain types of historical records, such as architecture and landscape design records (Shepherd and Lowell, 2000).

The work of creating boxes and putting things into boxes in the course of arrangement is at once informed by and intended to preserve and represent the contextual relationships of a body of records. That said, any such act of categorization and the categories themselves may in the end conceal as much as they reveal, especially in cases where records are conceived of as having one and only one place in the larger whole (for example, records are often represented as part of only one series, although they may relate to or overlap with several other series). As Bowker and Star point out, '[e]ach standard and category valorizes some point of view and silences another. This is not inherently a bad thing – indeed it is inescapable. But it is an ethical choice, and as such it is dangerous – not bad, but dangerous' (Bowker and Star, 1999, 5–6). It is important for practitioners to be aware of the danger implicit in the work of arrangement and to be mindful of how this plays out in the products of that work.

## 4.2 Standards for archival description

In the world of archival description, there are three categories of standards: data content standards, data structure standards and data value standards.

- **Data content standards** 'specify the content, order, and syntax of information to promote consistency' (Pearce-Moses, 2005). Examples include, at the international level, the International Standard for Archival Description (General) (ISAD(G)) and International Standard Archival Authority Record for Corporate Bodies, Persons and Families (ISAAR(CPF)); and at the national level, Describing Archives: A Content Standard (DACS), and Rules for Archival Description (RAD) (United States, and Canada, respectively).
- **Data structure standards** 'specify the elements into which information is to be organized' (Pearce-Moses, 2005). Examples include Encoded Archival Description (EAD), Encoded Archival Context (Corporate Bodies, Persons, Families) (EAC-CPF), and the Machine-Readable Cataloging (MARC) format.
- **Data value standards** consist of 'established list[s] of normalized terms used as data elements to ensure consistency' (Pearce-Moses, 2005). Examples include controlled vocabularies such as the Library of Congress Subject Headings (LCSH), thesauri such as the Art and Architecture Thesaurus (AAT), and authority files such as the Library of Congress Name Authority Cooperative Program (NACO).

In general, the aim of standardization in archival description is to promote consistency in descriptive information and terminology within and across institutions and to enable the transmission and communication of descriptive content between and amongst different systems. Under ideal circumstances, an institution will implement data content, structure and value standards in conjunction with each other to describe its holdings. For instance, a collecting repository in the United States will follow the format- and output-neutral guidelines of DACS for the description of archival materials and their creators; it will output multi-level archival descriptions in EAD and single-level (i.e. collection/record group) descriptions in MARC; and it will assign controlled name, subject and genre headings (NACO, LCSH and AAT, respectively) at the highest level of description. In practice, there can be many barriers to the implementation of archival descriptive standards, not the least of which are the technical barriers to implementing data structure standards that often require specialized tools or systems for authoring, encoding, storing and publishing files (Combs and OCLC Research, 2010). Even if it is not feasible for institutions to implement data structure standards and capitalize on national authority files and the like, the very least that can and should be done is to follow a data content standard in describing the content and context of archival holdings. Standards, such as ISAD(G), DACS and RAD, can variously be used to create accession records, database records, catalogue records, preliminary inventories, detailed guides and so on, whether in electronic or paper form. Adhering to standard data content elements not only promotes consistency but also offers the possibility of repurposing descriptive information by creating tools and/or systems that can be mapped to established standards.

In addition to the benefits and costs of standardization, there are also, as has already been suggested, certain risks or dangers. Wendy Duff and Verne Harris argue that archival descriptive standards function as 'metanames' or 'titular names' which force practitioners to describe very different material created in very different contexts in similar ways and which force users to use these 'names' in order to access particular holdings, thereby shaping their understanding of the records (Duff and Harris, 2002, 282). To address these and related concerns, Duff and Harris call for a liberatory descriptive standard (Duff and Harris, 2002, 284–5). For practitioners, there is the possibility of answering such a call through a liberatory approach to implementing existing archival descriptive standards, which might involve creating space for other voices and narratives and/or allowing for partial or multiple views in the products stemming from descriptive processes. Participatory approaches to description are being explored through the use of Web 2.0 technologies, with many archives soliciting user-generated description through sites such as Flickr or on their own websites (for example, the National Archives and Records Administration Citizen Archivist initiative, www.archives.gov/citizen-archivist/).

## 4.3 Access tools and systems

The products of archival description typically consist of tools and systems that provide for control, discovery and access. Access tools, such as finding aids, guides, inventories and bibliographic records, represent the content, context and structure of individual bodies of records (whether fonds, collection, record group and/or series). Access and discovery systems, such as finding aid and bibliographic databases, collectively store the individual tools describing one or more institutions' holdings and allow for searching and discovering descriptive information across and within those tools.

The standards-based, multi-level finding aid – in the United States broadly conceived of as a single tool comprising administrative and contextual information (biographical/historical note), content information (scope note, series descriptions, inventory) and structure information (arrangement note, inventory) – has become the canonical tool for describing historical records (Yakel, 2003, 16). A finding aid serves many purposes, both internal and external. One internal purpose of a finding aid is to establish physical control over a body of records; practitioners will often rely on finding aids to track, manage and locate the physical parts (i.e. containers) of individual holdings. As an access tool, the main purpose of a finding aid is to provide both physical and intellectual access to a body of records. Internal and external users will rely on finding aids to search for and find material that is relevant to their work or research. In making finding aids available online, institutions seek to provide wider access to their holdings and to promote discovery on the world wide web. Yet, finding aids as currently created in most institutions may not be ideally suited for online discovery and access; for instance, as Jennifer Schaffner argues, finding aids based on provenance primarily provide name access to records, whereas researchers are often browsing or searching for records by subject; and Michelle Light notes that finding aids do not typically include a sufficient number of keywords relating to the important aspects of the records (such as name, subject, genre, etc.) and are therefore not optimal for indexing by search engines (Schaffner and OCLC Programs and Research Division, 2009; Light, 2008). Moreover, these, as well as other tools and systems, may create barriers to use, since they employ terms, structures, schemas and codes of which users are largely unaware.

Beyond the practical purposes of control, discovery and access, the finding aid also effectively serves as a tool of contextual preservation or as 'an apparatus of authenticity' (MacNeil, 2005). By seeking to represent the connection between the creator and the records, the history of the records and the external and internal relationships of the records, the finding aid purports to maintain and preserve the contextual relationships that have been identified/created in the course of arrangement and description. In doing so, the finding aid serves to maintain and preserve the identity and integrity of the records, thereby ensuring their authenticity. How effective the finding aid is as a tool of contextual preservation remains an open question, however, given the inherent limitations of the content and structure of such tools imposed by the standards, schemas and codes used in their creation and by the systems used in their transmission.

## 4.4 Metadata

The data (content, structure, value) stemming from archival description is often thought of broadly as metadata, defined as 'data about data'. More specifically, it is descriptive metadata in that it 'refers to the intellectual content of material and aids in discovery of such materials' (Pearce-Moses, 2005). Descriptive metadata relates to but is distinct from other types of metadata that might be generated during the course of record making and archives keeping. On the record making end, such types might include administrative metadata, 'data that is necessary to manage and use information resources and that is typically external to informational content of resources' (Pearce-Moses, 2005), which could encompass both technical and preservation metadata stemming from electronic record management systems or digitization processes. On the archives keeping end, such types of metadata might include the preservation metadata (PREMIS) and structural metadata (MODS or METS) necessary to manage, preserve and provide access to digital assets.[1] The various metadata standards and schema are intended to facilitate interoperability between systems for creating, managing, storing, preserving and delivering digital information and/or content and are often implemented in conjunction with one another.

There are many points of overlap between the creation and representation of descriptive information and digital content, particularly in cases where a body of records consists of both paper and born-digital records or where parts of a body of paper records have been digitized. Such convergences might range from opportunities for streamlining descriptive workflow (i.e. repurposing data) to challenges of digital archival representation (i.e. representing 'hybrid' bodies of records online). Taking a data-centric view of archival description, as well as a critical view of its processes and products, will enable individual practitioners and institutions to more readily capitalize on available opportunities and address the challenges involved in archival representation.

## 5 Evolving areas of thought and practice in arrangement and description

The theory and practice of arrangement and description is continually evolving in response to the new and emerging realities of record making and archives keeping in the twenty-first century, leading to new ways of seeing and doing in the realm of archival representation.

### 5.1 Postmodern challenges to 'business as usual'

As already touched upon at various points above, the critical perspective afforded by the postmodern discourse on archives highlights the constructed nature of archival representation and the mediating role of the practitioner, in addition to problematizing core concepts (such as original order) and deconstructing the processes and products of arrangement and description. In advocating for greater inclusivity and transparency as a necessary corrective to the metanarrative of archival description and the dangers of standardization, the postmodern stream calls, in part, for rethinking what constitute the relevant contextualities of a body of records, and likewise what constitutes sufficient contextual information about records.

On a practical level, this stream of thought calls for documenting the *archival context* of a body of records, so that users are aware of and understand the decisions made and actions taken over time to select, preserve and make the records accessible. To better document archival context, specifically as it concerns arrangement and description, additional information might be included in the finding aid (or other access tool) and further documentation might be provided to users that sheds light on both the institutional context of arrangement and description practices and the process of the individual practitioner. Such institutional documentation, detailing the specific decisions made at the institutional or departmental level concerning the overall processing programme, might include:

- essays on the institution, its holdings and history
- the institution's processing manual
- an essay or timeline on the history of processing at the institution
- a statement on current processing priorities and strategies.

Documentation of individual process, detailing specific decisions made and actions taken for a particular body of records and the reasoning and rationale for doing so, might include:

- the processor's biography (for instance, as a 'colophon' to the finding aid) (Light and Hyry, 2002)
- the processing plan and/or file for a body of records, documenting what work was done and why, in terms of rehousing, physical organization, intellectual arrangement, the level of descriptive detail and what is highlighted in the narrative description
- digital photographs, documenting records in situ and before, during and after processing.

On a conceptual level, this critical stream of thought also calls for a certain rethinking of notions of trustworthiness and authenticity as they relate to arrangement and description. Given the mediating role of practitioners and the constructed nature of archival representations, it is necessary for users to trust *both* practitioners *and* the archival representations that they create *in order to* trust records. This in turn suggests that for practitioners to ensure the trustworthiness of records in their care they need to demonstrate their own trustworthiness as custodians and mediators. Documenting archival context and thereby accounting for archival mediation will address important aspects of identity and integrity that are key to trusting records and safeguarding their authenticity – the identity of the archival parties (institutions and individual practitioners) involved in the representation of the records and the integrity of archival methods geared toward interpreting and representing the records.

## 5.2 Pragmatic challenges to 'business as usual'

The pragmatic trend in processing, sparked in the United States by the 'More Product, Less Process' recommendations of Mark Greene and Dennis Meissner, challenges professional ideas about processing and calls for a rethinking of the processes and products of arrangement and description (Greene and Meissner, 2005). This trend responds to the real-world challenges of dealing with growing and seemingly insurmountable backlogs of contemporary records and growing user demand for online access to records (particularly in the form of online description but also, increasingly, in the form of online digital content). With an emphasis on efficiency in processing and more production-oriented approaches, the pragmatic stream advocates greater flexibility in minimally organizing records and producing sufficient descriptions of records, rather than unnecessarily perpetuating the tradition of uniformly detailed arrangement and description. In other words, it effectively argues against the one-size-fits-all approach to processing within a single institution and 'one-size-fits-all-finding aids' (Greene and Meissner, 2005, 217).

Practical responses to such pragmatic challenges might include:

- developing and implementing different levels of processing, ranging from minimal to standard to optimal
- establishing a programme to provide basic control for all holdings and to provide more detailed processing for select holdings only as warranted (in other words, taking an iterative approach to arrangement and description)
- conducting appraisal as part of processing in order to determine priorities for and appropriate levels of processing
- basing decisions and actions on the demonstrated needs of users
- matching the level of work done on individual holdings with the resources available to preserve and provide access to all holdings.

The pragmatic trend in processing also poses challenges on a conceptual level. It problematizes the notion of archival description – especially in the form of the standards-based finding aid – as a surrogate for or definitive representation of a body of records, a notion which stems from assumptions that equate a certain extent of processing with a finished and final product. It also challenges the notion of archival authority – in this instance, the authority to name, identify and describe what the body of records is, what is in it and what it is about. Finally, it questions assumptions about the nature of descriptive products – such as finding aids – as information objects, specifically with regard to how transparent, complete and fixed they are.

These practical and conceptual challenges to 'business as usual' can lead to new ways of seeing and doing arrangement and description. Recognizing the built-in limits and the fluid and iterative nature of archival representation can help to free practitioners from unrealistic expectations about what is possible in arrangement and description and can effectively open up the processes and products of arrangement and description to other possibilities. It will potentially grant practitioners more flexibility in envisioning and implementing scalable and sustainable approaches to processing; it also encourages practitioners to embrace their role as one of the many possible authors of (rather than having to be 'the authority' on) a body of records and to embrace the fact that archival representations are continually in the process of becoming (being added to, revised and/or enhanced). In the end, the purpose of arrangement and description is not to produce a final and finished product that will serve for all time (which is an impossibility); rather, it is to produce descriptive products that will serve for the time being and that will be revisited over time, as necessary.

## 5.3 Changes in the way people are creating and keeping records

The increasing use of computer technology by individuals, groups and organizations in their day-to-day personal and business activities impacts on what types of records are created and kept, how they are transmitted and used over time, how they are stored and maintained and whether they can be preserved over the long term. In many, if not most, cases, a body of records is comprised of both paper and digital records and is therefore hybrid in nature. In addition to the challenges of accessing, analysing and preserving born-digital content (whether acquired by file transfer or on removable storage media), arranging and describing hybrid bodies of records poses challenges to understanding, interpreting and representing content, context and structure.

Since the turn of the century a number of research projects have explored practical aspects of arranging and describing born-digital holdings, particularly in collecting repositories (AIMS Work Group, 2012; Paradigm project, 2005), and conceptual aspects of the application of archival principles to the organization and representation of digital archives (Zhang, 2012). By and large, current approaches to arranging and describing hybrid archives seem to involve extending the traditional archival concepts of provenance and original order by analogy (that is, by the way in which hybrid archives might be *like* traditional paper archives), rather than critically examining the concepts in the light of new and evolving realities. To move forward, an intellectual framework for the arrangement and description of hybrid archives is needed – one that is based on the distinctive character(s) of hybrid archives and one that sufficiently represents the analogue and digital contents, contexts and structures of hybrid archives.

An intellectual framework for arrangement and description of hybrid archives might encompass the following:

- *Technological context and digital materiality:* Broadly defined, technological context is 'the technological environment surrounding the record' (MacNeil, 2002, 33) and digital materiality is 'a curatorial sensitivity toward the uniqueness of individual instances of both hardware and data objects, coupled with an awareness of how the affordances of particular systems, environments, and technologies can all impact [on] the creative process' (Kirschenbaum et al., 2009, 110). These notions highlight the need to capture information not only about what systems and programmes the creator used but also about how and why the creator used them, and to analyse the hardware and software components in order to understand the affordances (and not merely the technical aspects) of these components. As such, technological context and digital materiality are important terms of practice that must be engaged when analysing the internal relationships of hybrid archives. They allow for the framing of important questions that will shed light on the various contents, contexts and structures of a given body of records, including the technical characteristics, the physical and digital environments and, potentially, the 'material conditions of computing' (Kirschenbaum et al., 2009, 110) associated with each of the component parts. Understanding the relative significance and meaning of the component parts will help to inform how the practitioner understands the relationships between and amongst the parts and between the parts and the whole.

- *Interplay of digital and paper materials:* As with 'traditional' arrangement and description, analysis of the interplay of digital and paper materials will focus on the relationships between and amongst records, but will likely entail multiple analyses of multiple sets of relationships – those between and amongst the paper materials and those between and amongst the digital materials. In cases where various computer media are present (for instance, one or more computers in addition to one or more removable storage devices), there will also likely be multiple sets of relationships between and amongst the digital materials.
- *Multiple internal structures:* Hybrid archives will, more likely than not, possess multiple internal structures, including different structures for the digital and paper materials as well as different structures across the different types of media comprising the digital component. The challenge for arrangement and description is not only how to identify and interpret the meaning and significance of the different structures and the possible relationships between them, but also how to ultimately represent the multiple structures or orders that reflect the multifaceted contents and contexts of hybrid archives. Current approaches – aimed at either integrating digital and paper materials by content (for instance, the James Welch Papers at the Beinecke Rare Book and Manuscript Library[2]) or separating by format (for instance, the Richard Rorty Papers at Special Collections and Archives, University of California, Irvine[3]) – result in a single order being imposed on potentially diverse sets of materials. Other approaches are needed that allow for both integration and separation in order to represent multiple orders within a given body of records as well as different views of those records. One promising example along these lines can be found in the Salman Rushdie Papers at Emory University[4] (Carroll et al., 2011).
- *Different levels of control for digital and paper materials:* Although the levels of control (series, file, item) may vary for paper and born-digital records (perhaps depending on the actions necessary for preservation and/or the amount of descriptive information that can be repurposed from existing media and systems), a flexible approach to arranging and describing hybrid archives is still possible and will in fact be necessary in order to

develop a sustainable programme. The challenge is to develop terms of practice specific to born-digital records, especially in hybrid archives.

## 5.4 Changes in the way people are seeking and using information

The increasing use of computer technology by individuals, groups and organizations in their day-to-day personal and business activities also impacts on the way in which record creators and users seek, find and use information and, by extension, on the way in which they discover and access records/archives. The changing expectations of creators and users who increasingly operate in an online and networked environment result in changing demands on institutions and practitioners in terms of describing and providing access to their holdings.

Increasingly, for creators and users alike, access to archival and record holdings means *online* access. If holdings cannot be found online, then for all intents and purposes they do not exist, especially for more casual and remote users. The expectation of online access to everything might pose challenges for an institution with limited resources or technological expertise or infrastructure, yet the demand is clear: in order to discharge the core responsibility of providing access to records, institutions need to the fullest extent possible to make descriptions of holdings available online. More than just online access to descriptive information, there is also a growing demand for online access to digital content (i.e. digitized versions of archival and record holdings). This poses additional practical challenges in terms of funding and technological support, as well as conceptual challenges in terms of representing the content, context and structure of digital content online, that is, in terms of *digital* archival representation.

Another reality behind the demand for online access is that the discovery of archival and record holdings is increasingly happening elsewhere, that is, at the network level rather than at the local or institutional level. Numerous studies have shown that most users start their information searches with search engines like Google or online resources like Wikipedia (Schaffner and OCLC Programs and Research Division, 2009, 5). Information professionals, including archival practitioners, have already recognized the need for creating structured metadata that can be shared across systems (that is machine readable) and that can effectively participate in the networked environment; and many are well on the way to doing so, whether creating bibliographic records (based on RDA and MARC), finding aids (based on ISAD(G) and EAD), or metadata for digital objects (based on MODS or METS) (as discussed in section 4.4). In order to make archival description more shareable, it is necessary for practitioners to move beyond a document-centric view of archival description and to embrace instead a data-centric view that conceptualizes archival descriptive metadata distinct from specific tools and systems and that supports greater flexibility in (re)use and (re)presentation of metadata at both the local/institutional and network levels. To the extent that greater sharing involves a loss of control, practitioners also need to be mindful of the challenges involved in providing context for the descriptive metadata and/or digital content made available online, and in balancing the need to promote online discovery and access with the need to preserve the contextual relationships of digital archives. Different approaches to digital archival representation include integrating digital content into existing descriptive tools such as finding aids (for instance, the Princeton University Library Finding Aids[5]) and repurposing archival descriptive metadata in the display of digital content (for instance, the Terra Foundation Center for Digital Collections at the Archives of American Art[6]), among others.

Jenn Riley and Kelcy Shepherd discuss the possibilities beyond enhanced discovery that might be afforded by shareable descriptive metadata, such as the reuse of descriptive metadata in visualizations and mash-ups and integration with existing online services and products, such as Google Earth, Wikipedia and the like (Riley and Shepherd, 2009, 94). Linked data, defined as 'data provided in RDF and linked to other data sources' (Stevenson, 2012, 15), is another emerging area that offers possibilities for extending the reach of archival description at the network level and 'connect[ing] archives more effectively to the wider information landscape, bringing them together with other resources to benefit researchers' (Stevenson, 2012, 14). Beyond sharing descriptive metadata, there are also possibilities for crowdsourcing archival description or soliciting user-contributed information through the use of Web 2.0 tools and technologies in archival access systems, allowing at once for the capture of more detailed contextual information about the records, and for the inclusion of more diverse perspectives on the records and their contents (Light and Hyry, 2002). For instance, the Polar Bear Expedition Digital Collections Project at the University of Michigan sought to design the next-generation finding aid by developing a dynamic interface with features and functionalities inspired by existing commercial and social applications, including a comments function which allows visitors to 'supply information about sources, ask questions, or participate in discussions' (Krause and Yakel, 2007, 285). As the project participants note, '[a]rchivists' incorporation of social navigation tools into descriptive systems has the potential to allow researchers to interact with archivists, collections and other users to validate, categorize and describe records in different and potentially more meaningful ways' (Krause and Yakel, 2007, 290).

Opening up archival description through greater sharing and inclusivity is a necessity for archival discovery and access in a networked environment; it is also emblematic of a movement within the profession towards an 'Archives 2.0' mode of thought and practice. As Kate Theimer explains, this mode involves openness, transparency, user-centeredness, facilitation, attracting new users, sharing standards, measuring results, iteration, innovation and flexibility, and embracing technology (Theimer, 2011, 61–3). In terms of archival description, 'Archives 2.0' potentially goes beyond 'Finding Aid 2.0' or mere crowdsourcing, in which 'the "original" or authoritative archive remains intact', as well as the dichotomy between 'user' and 'archival authority' (Palmer, 2009). Rather, an 'Archives 2.0' mode of description might encompass participatory archives, which 'posits a more radical user orientation, where both archivists and users collaborate to build the archive itself' (Palmer, 2009).

## 6 Conclusion

Putting theory into practice in arrangement and description involves the continual interaction of ideas and experience. The concepts of archival theory and methodology will guide and shape – without necessarily prescribing – practice; and the physical and conceptual realities of records and recordkeeping will likewise shape and guide the rethinking of archival concepts. As practitioners are continually called upon to open up the processes and products of arrangement and description, they will likewise need to be continually open to new ways of seeing and doing this work.

## Notes

1 PREMIS: Preservation Metadata Maintenance Activity has produced a data dictionary for preservation metadata, http://www.loc.gov/standards/premis/; MODS (Metadata Object Description Schema), www.loc.gov/standards/mods/; METS (Metadata Encoding and Transmission Standard), www.loc.gov/standards/mets/.
2 http://hdl.handle.net/10079/fa/beinecke.welch.
3 www.oac.cdlib.org/findaid/ark:/13030/kt9p3038mq/.
4 http://pid.emory.edu/ark:/25593/8zv36.
5 http://findingaids.princeton.edu/.
6 www.aaa.si.edu/collections/online.

## References and further reading


AIMS Work Group (2012) *AIMS Born-Digital Collections: an inter-institutional model for stewardship*, www2.lib.virginia.edu/aims/whitepaper/AIMS_final.pdf.

Bearman, D. A. and Lytle, R. H. (1985) The Power of the Principle of Provenance, *Archivaria*, **21**, 14–27.

Biskup, P. and Australian Society of Archivists (eds) (1995) *Debates and Discourses: selected Australian writings on archival theory*, Australian Society of Archivists.

Bowker, G. and Star, S. L. (1999) *Sorting Things Out: classification and its consequences*, MIT Press.

Brothman, B. (1991) Orders of Value: probing the theoretical terms of archival practice, *Archivaria*, **32**, 78–100.

Carroll, L., Farr, E., Hornsby, P. and Ranker, B. (2011) A Comprehensive Approach to Born-Digital Archives, *Archivaria*, **72**, 61–92.

Combs, M. and OCLC Research (2010) *Over, Under, Around, and Through: getting around barriers to EAD implementation*, OCLC Research, www.oclc.org/content/dam/research/publications/library/2010/2010–04.pdf?urlm=162938.

Cook, M. (1986) Archival Arrangement. In *The Management of Information from Archives*, 2nd edn, Gower.

Cook, T. (1992) The Concept of the Archival Fonds: theory, description, and provenance in the post-custodial era. In Eastwood, T. (ed.), *The Archival Fonds: from theory to practice*, 34–85, Bureau of Canadian Archivists.

Douglas, J. (2010) Origins: evolving ideas about the principle of provenance. In

Eastwood, T. and MacNeil, H. (eds), *Currents of Archival Thinking*, ABC-CLIO, 23–43.

Duchein, M. (1983) Theoretical Principles and Practical Problems of respect des fonds in Archival Science, *Archivaria*, **16**, 64–82.

Duff, W. and Harris, V. (2002) Stories and Names: archival description as narrating records and constructing meanings, *Archival Science*, **2**, 263–85.

Eastwood, T. (2000) Putting the Parts of the Whole Together: systematic arrangement of archives, *Archivaria*, **50**, 93–116.

Greene, M. and Meissner, M. (2005) More Product, Less Process: revamping traditional archival processing, *American Archivist*, **68**, 208–63.

Hensen, S. L. (1989) *Archives, Personal Papers, and Manuscripts: a cataloging manual for archival repositories, historical societies, and manuscript libraries*, 2nd edn, Society of American Archivists.

Horsman, P. (1994) Taming the Elephant: an orthodox approach to the principle of provenance. In *The Principle of Provenance: Report from the First Stockholm Conference on the Archival Principle of Provenance, 2–3 September 1993*, 51–63, Swedish National Archives.

Horsman, P. (2002) The Last Dance of the Phoenix, or the De-Discovery of the Archival Fonds, *Archivaria*, **54**, 1–23.

Horsman, P., Ketelaar, E. and Thomassen, T. (2003) New Respect for the Old Order: the context of the Dutch Manual, *American Archivist*, **66**, 249–70.

Hurley, C. (1994) The Australian ('Series') System: an exposition. In McKemmish, S. and Piggott, M. (eds), *The Records Continuum: Ian Maclean and Australian Archives' first fifty years*, 150–72, Ancora Press.

ICA (2000) *General International Standard Archival Description* (ISAD(G)), 2nd edn, International Council on Archives, www.ica.org/10207/standards/isadggeneralinternationalstandardarchivaldescriptionsecondedition.html.

The InterPARES Glossary (2001), www.interpares.org/display_file.cfm?doc=ip1_glossary.pdf.

Jenkinson, H. (1965) *A Manual of Archive Administration*, 2nd edn, Lund Humphries.

Kirschenbaum, M., Farr, E., Kraus, K., Nelson, N., Peters, C. S., Redwine, G. and Reside, D. (2009) Digital Materiality: preserving access to computers as complete environments. In *iPRES 2009: The Sixth International Conference on Preservation of Digital Objects, California Digital Library, UC Office of the President*, iPRES 2009: The Sixth International Conference on Preservation of Digital Objects, (October 5), 105–12.

Krause, M. G. and Yakel, E. (2007) Interaction in Virtual Archives: the Polar Bear

Expedition Digital Collections Next Generation Finding Aid, *American Archivist*, **70** (2), 282–314.

Krawczyk, B. (1999) Cross Reference Heaven: the abandonment of the fonds as the primary level of arrangement for Ontario government records, *Archivaria*, **48**, 131–53.

Light, M. (2008) The Endangerment of Trees. Presented at the *EAD@10: Symposium Celebrating the 10th Anniversary of Encoded Archival Description, August 31, San Francisco, CA*, http://files.archivists.org/pubs/proceedings/EAD@10/Light-EAD@10.pdf.

Light, M. and Hyry, T. (2002) Colophons and Annotations: new directions for the finding aid, *American Archivist*, **65**, 216–30.

MacNeil, H. (2002) Providing Grounds for Trust II: the findings of the Authenticity Task Force of InterPARES, *Archivaria*, **54**, 24–58.

MacNeil, H. (2005) Picking Our Text: archival description, authenticity, and the archivist as editor, *American Archivist*, **68**, 264–78.

Meehan, J. (2009) Making the Leap from Parts to Whole: evidence and inference in archival arrangement and description, *American Archivist*, **72**, 72–90.

Meehan, J. (2010) Rethinking Original Order and Personal Records, *Archivaria*, **70**, 27–44.

Millar, L. (2002) The Death of the Fonds and the Resurrection of Provenance: archival context in space and time, *Archivaria*, **53**, 1–15.

Millar, L. (2010) 'An Unnecessary Complication': international perspectives on the record group, the series and the fonds. In Cunningham, A. (ed.), *The Arrangement and Description of Archives Amid Administrative and Technological Change: essays and reflections by and about Peter J. Scott*, Australian Society of Archivists.

Muller, S., Feith, J. A. and Fruin, R. (1968) *Manual for the Arrangement and Description of Archives*, trans. Arthur H. Leavitt, H. W. Wilson Company.

Nesmith, T. (2005) Reopening Archives: bringing new contextualities into archival theory and practice, *Archivaria*, **60**, 259–74.

Palmer, J. (2009) Archives 2.0: if we build it, will they come? *Ariadne*, **60**, www.ariadne.ac.uk/issue60/palmer/.

Paradigm project (2005) *Workbook on Digital Private Papers*, www.paradigm.ac.uk/workbook.

Pearce-Moses, R. (2005) *A Glossary of Archival and Records Terminology*, Society of American Archivists, www2.archivists.org/glossary.

Riley, J. and Shepherd, K. (2009) A Brave New World: archivists and shareable descriptive metadata, *American Archivist*, **70** (1), 91–112.

Schaffner, J. and OCLC Programs and Research Division (2009) *The Metadata is the Interface: better description for better discovery of archives and special collections: synthesized from user studies*, OCLC Programs and Research, www.oclc.org/content/dam/research/publications/library/2009/2009=06.pdf.urlm=162923.

Schellenberg, T. R. (1956) Principles of Arrangement. In *Modern Archives: principles and techniques*, University of Chicago Press.

Scott, P. J. (1966) The Record Group Concept: a case for abandonment, *American Archivist*, **29**, 493–503.

Shepherd, K. and Lowell, W. (2000) *Standard Series for Architecture and Landscape Design Record: a tool for the arrangement and description of archival collections*, Environmental Design Archives, University of California, Berkeley.

Stevenson, J. (2012) Linking Lives: creating an end-user interface using linked data, *Information Standards Quarterly*, **24** (2/3), 14–23.

Theimer, K. (2011) What Is the Meaning of Archives 2.0? *American Archivist*, **74**, 58–68.

Yakel, E. (2003) Archival Representation, *Archival Science*, **3**, 1–25.

Yeo, G. (2010) Debates About Description. In Eastwood, T. and MacNeil, H. (eds), *Currents of Archival Thinking*, 89–114, ABC-CLIO.

Yeo, G. (2012) The Conceptual Fonds and the Physical Collection, *Archivaria*, **73**, 43–80.

Zhang, J. (2012) Original Order in Digital Archives, *Archivaria*, **74**, 167–93.

CHAPTER 4

# Ethics for archivists and records managers

Jeannette A. Bastian

## 1 Introduction: the ethical imperative

Ethics and ethical conduct lie at the heart of the archives and records profession, and the image of the ethical professional is axiomatic to the integrity of the record. The reliability, authority and power of records rests on the public's confidence in archives and records institutions as trusted repositories and in their belief in the trustworthiness of the individuals who work in those repositories. Ethical behaviour establishes public trust, safeguards that trust and maintains accountability. Supporting and practising high standards of ethical behaviour is core to the archives and records mission.

Building and retaining public trust through ethical behaviour, ethical standards and professional morality is a challenging mandate but an essential one for archivists and records managers. Without trust in the integrity of records, records lose much of their value. Without respect for rights, records have no meaning. Holding governments and organizations accountable, protecting people's rights, advocating for social justice and permanently affecting the ways in which communities and nations understand themselves and their histories requires that records themselves be trustworthy and reliable. Behaving ethically therefore is not only a core aspect of all archives and records activities, but one that must be imbued within all those activities.

Ethics always function at the level of the individual, even though ethical behaviours may be promoted by institutions or professional associations. Ethical positions may be expressed in protocols and codes, but in the end it is people who must make the often difficult determinations about right or wrong actions. An ethical approach may be company policy, but an ethical judgement is often a choice based as much on a personal morality as on institutional responsibility or public interest. Ethical conduct and ethical decisions are neither simple nor easy and have become infinitely more fraught with pitfalls in our digital age. Regardless, archives and records professionals must have a profound understanding of ethics and ethical behaviour in order to meet, establish and maintain the levels of trustworthiness that society places in them. Archives and records professionals need to understand themselves as ethical individuals.

What makes an ethical individual and an ethical profession? South African archivist Verne Harris suggests that 'the heart of the uncertainty, of the ethical struggle, is that no professional code of ethics provides a recipe, or blueprint for resolving competing rights. I would go further and argue simply that there is no such blueprint' (Harris, 2007, 204). At the same time, while no code of ethics can provide a recipe, it might provide a road map, because 'ethical persons, however strongly motivated to do what is ethically right, can only do so if they know what is ethically right' (Paul and Elder, 2013, 5). Ethical codes and codes of conduct, addressed in detail later in this chapter, in addition to broad understandings of moral and cultural issues, are central to facilitating a process of ethical reasoning that helps to guide and determine ethical behaviour.

## 1.1 Chapter overview

This chapter on ethics offers a brief overview of the ethical environment for archives and records professionals. The first section begins with the concept of the ethical perspective itself and why professionals need to have one. A brief review of the archives and records literature explores how the profession has grappled with establishing its own ethical perspective. It then discusses the primary ethical concerns for both archivists and records managers, including a range of issues that they may encounter. Considering and comparing national and international codes of ethics and codes of conduct will assist in distilling those elements common to all ethical codes.

The second section considers ethical issues that are particularly applicable to our current records environment at the beginning of the twenty-first century, including:

- ethics as a component of social justice
- consideration of the culturally sensitive codes of ethics and protocols being developed by indigenous groups, examining how these protocols challenge or complement the traditional codes of ethics
- ethics in digital environments, exploring how these environments are complicating the ethical landscape, where old issues turn up in new guises and new issues just turn up.

Ethics in an archives and records management context is a constantly evolving process. Protocols, statements of responsibility and codes of ethics are always works in progress, responding to the ethical needs of the moment while retaining and bolstering core principles. As the forms and formats of records shift, from paper records to e-mail to websites to tweets, instagrams and beyond, ethical situations arise that require imaginative and creative solutions that must be grounded in a firm understanding of ethical and moral imperatives. This chapter is only an overview of some of those basic imperatives, principles and considerations. It focuses on the ethics of the individual archives and records professional rather than on the institution, for ultimately it is individuals who must make choices and decisions.

## 2 Finding an ethical perspective

### 2.1 The literature

The literature on archives and records management ethics is substantial, offering an array of case studies, strategies and prescriptions. Useful and instructive, much of the literature is also questioning, seeking to offer guidance on ethical dilemmas but conceding that solutions are complex. Since the 1990s the ethical discussion has shifted, moving from an inward-looking focus to one that recognizes the increasingly significant roles of archivists and records managers in society.

In her book *The Ethical Archivist*, Elena Danielson (2010, 24–6) suggests a number of ways of understanding ethics: through the law, through professional standards and through social accountability. The archives and records literature also tends to fall into these divisions. The ethics of access has been a persistent concern for archivists and records professionals, one that involves both legal and professional issues. *Without Consent: the ethics of disclosing personal information* (MacNeil, 1992), brings these together as it analyses the ethical issues surrounding government-held personal information, balancing the individual right to privacy with the public's right to know. Similarly, Ketelaar (1995, 8–17) explores the legal and other ways in which the personal information held by governments is protected. Both MacNeil and Ketelaar approach access and privacy from the viewpoint of a government archives, but others have confronted similar access concerns in manuscript collections. Danielson (1989) and Becker (1993), for example, explore access problems associated with restricted personal papers in manuscript collections, balancing the conflicting claims of donors, researchers, heirs and institutions. In *The Ethical Archivist* Danielson explores the relationship of ethics to the practical work of archivists and records managers, concluding that 'the goal is to establish a standard of integrity that inspires confidence in the documentary record' (Danielson, 2010, 296).

In the early 2000s two watershed collections of case studies expanded the ethics discussion, redirecting the focus outwards, towards a wider societal arena. *Archives and the Public Good: accountability and records in modern society* (Cox and Wallace, 2002) brought the relationship between records and the wider society to the fore, tying ethics to the broader accountability responsibilities of records professionals. In their introduction, editors Cox and Wallace state: 'it is our contention that the chief value of records is, in fact, a broad accountability binding individuals with each other and with governments, organizations, and society across space and time'. The 14 compelling case studies underscore the significance of the role of records in society. *Political Pressure and the Archival Record* (Procter, Cook and Williams, 2005) brought accountability into even sharper focus with 20 essays, the result of an international conference in Liverpool, UK in 2003, that each presented examples of ethics and accountability issues that archivists confronted, including the use of records as a tool of government, records and secrecy in repressive societies and the destruction of records as a political act. More recently, the ethics of accountability specifically in relationship to social justice have been the central themes in Verne Harris' collection of essays, *Archives and Justice: a South African perspective* (Harris, 2007) and in a special issue of *Archival Science* on ethics and memory construction edited by David Wallace (2011a). Wallace's own article in that issue, 'Understanding the 9/11 Commission Archive: control, access, and the politics of manipulation', with its step-by-step analysis of the production and use of documents in that investigation is particularly instructive in illustrating the accountability issues inherent in that process (Wallace, 2011b).

Cases studies that address specific areas of archives and records practice have also proliferated since the turn of the century. Karen Benedict's *Ethics and the Archival Profession* (2003), analyses 40 short scenarios involving practical ethical problems that might be encountered in an archives or records workplace. *Privacy and Confidentiality Perspectives: archivists and archival records* (Wosh and Behrnd-Klodt, 2005) offers 16 case studies that explore the legal, ethical and administrative considerations of access to personal records. Donor agreements, appraisal, acquisitions and the balance between privacy and access are some of the issues presented.

Discussion and analyses of codes of ethics and their relationship to professionalism offer parallel narratives to the dilemmas posed by case studies as archivists attempt to find panaceas – but generally conclude that there is no 'magic bullet'. Tracing the histories and development of codes of ethics, archivists also generally conclude that not only are they unable to offer solutions, but they are not effective even when applied, and increasingly fail to address the real ethical and human rights concerns of today's world (Cox, 2010; Dingwall, 2004; Thomassen, 1999). This case is forcefully made by Mary Neazor in 'Recordkeeping Professional Ethics and their Applications', who concludes that not only are most codes of ethics contradictory or simplistic but also that 'few of the codes of ethics for professional recordkeepers developed in Anglophone or Francophone countries in the 1990's [*sic*] refer to any larger ethical frameworks, or indicate how the codes might support them' (Neazor, 2007, 82).

## 2.2 An ethical perspective

The term 'ethics', denoting a branch of moral philosophy originating with the ancient Greeks, comes from the Greek word *ethos*, meaning 'character'. Ethics has been variously defined as 'a set of moral principles' and 'a theory or a system of moral values', (Merriam-Webster, n.d.), and as 'a set of principles of right conduct' and 'the rules or standards governing the conduct of a person or the members of a profession' (The Free Dictionary, n.d.). However, 'mere verbal agreement on ethical principles alone will not accomplish important moral ends nor change the world for the better. Ethical principles mean something only when manifested in behavior. They have force only when embodied in action' (Paul and Elder, 2013, 5).

Ethical theories generally derive from two ways of moral thinking: teleological and deontological. Teleological ethical theories 'focus primarily on the consequences, results, ends, goals or purposes of agent's acts … they center either on the agents themselves or on the agents' actions' (Mason et al., 1995, 112). The moral 'rightness' of an action is judged in terms of an external goal or purpose. Deontological ethical theories 'center on the act taken by the agent and the duties, rights, privileges or responsibilities that pertain to that act' (Mason et al., 1995, 113). In this approach, it is the features of the action itself that determine the moral 'rightness'.

But, regardless of the ethical theory, as information management scholar Richard O. Mason suggests, 'every new age ushers in a new set of ethical challenges and problems for people to solve' (Mason et al., 1995, 1). The Information Age is no different. Rapid innovations in information technologies dramatically change the ways in which society acquires, creates, disseminates and uses information. Mason et al. point out that 'as the ascent of information accelerates and as we become more fully entrenched in an information society, our ability to become "good" citizens and contribute to a "good" society changes. It becomes increasingly dependent on our ability to make the right judgments when issues concerning information confront us' (Mason et al., 1995, 4). Nowhere is that truer than in the archival realm.

'Records involve complex notions of control, power, and the use of evidence. How can archivists, or anyone else working with records and recordkeeping systems, avoid facing ethical issues?' asks archival educator Richard Cox (2010, 26). Being an ethical archivist might mean adhering to a professional code of ethics, it might mean 'doing the right thing', it might mean looking out for the best interests of the organization, it might mean care of collections, it might mean providing equitable access. It will always mean behaving with integrity and according to a deep understanding of archival and records values – accountability, evidence and memory – and according to a personal moral compass. The obligation to adhere to ethical values is at the core of the relationship between archivists and records managers, on the one hand, and the records they care for and the communities they serve, on the other hand, simply because without integrity the records have little value to the organization and, without the trust of the organization, the archivist or records manager cannot function. But, on a cautionary note, Wallace writes:

> The archival profession's strivings for professional legitimacy via education, certification, research, publication, ethical codes, and other mechanisms will not in and of themselves increase public credibility. Such efforts have to be matched and demonstrated through actual practices and in how violations are dealt with by the concerned professional community.
>
> (Wallace, 2010, 177)

## 2.2.1 Ethics in practice

Although, from the viewpoint of the public, being an archivist or records manager may always seem synonymous with being ethical, documents and records are not ethical within themselves, and the probity of these materials, their societal worth, is dependent not only upon the circumstances and context of their creation, but upon the integrity with which they have been cared for, organized and described. Without these ethical characteristics archival materials will have little value over time. These core characteristics that are so critical to maintain were famously and clearly expressed in 1947 by Sir Hilary Jenkinson in his essay 'The English Archivist: a new profession':

> His Creed, the Sanctity of Evidence; his Task, the Conservation of every scrap of Evidence attaching to the Documents committed to his charge; his Aim, to provide, without prejudice or afterthought, for all who wished to know the Means of Knowledge.
>
> (Jenkinson, 2003, 258)

Although time and societal changes have brought many of Jenkinson's ideas into question, his statement on the mission of the archivist continues to ring true.

While maintaining integrity and authenticity for the purposes of evidence and accountability may be a primary ethical concern, there are other equally important values as well that speak to the acquisition of records and collections, appraisal policies, preservation, access and use. Maintaining the integrity of records within an organization or government by adhering to an unbiased records process, giving equal access to a wide variety of public users, respecting intellectual property rights, fully understanding cultural concerns and seeing records as instruments of social justice all entail ethical decisions that archivists and records managers may be called upon to make.

These decisions become infinitely more complex in virtual environments where determining copyright, authenticity or reliability is obfuscated by the affordances of the technology itself, including great participation by creators and users. What is important for archives and records professionals to understand from the outset is that essentially *all* archival and records procedures have ethical implications. A critical component in understanding and implementing these procedures is recognizing and adhering to ethical standards. One might argue that even establishing procedures and standards carries its own ethical implications.

At the same time, despite national and international codes of ethics, and despite codes of conduct and case studies, ethical situations are often complex and difficult, with no obvious right answers. Rather, their competing ethical claims challenge archivists to find equitable solutions. The following examples are drawn from actual cases:[1]

a. A government archives contains a report indicating serious public malfeasance on the part of the government. Government regulations mandate that the Archivist has the final say on retention and disposal of all government records. Officials strongly suggest that the Archivist consider appraising the materials in a way that legitimizes their destruction.
b. An archives in the western United States houses the well-known collection of an early twentieth-century anthropologist who had spent his life studying a particular Native American tribe. The collection's extensive field notes include photographs of rituals and ceremonies taken by the anthropologist as part of his observations but without the permission of the tribe. These photographs have been publicly available to users in the archives for many years. Recently, members of the tribe have asked that the photographs be removed from public use and that use be restricted and monitored by the tribe because public viewing of these ceremonies violates tribal tradition. Both the users of the archives and the Native American tribe have legitimate ethical claims to these images, the users on the grounds that materials in the archives should be accessible to all equally; the tribe on more complex grounds that include the violation of tribal laws, cultural sensitivity and intellectual property rights.
c. A university archives holds the audio tapes of oral interviews that faculty members had made with members of a radical organization.

Organization members had been promised complete confidentiality and that the tapes would be closed to access until the deaths of all members. However, the police believe that the tapes may lead them to the solving of a major crime, and are demanding access to the materials.

### 2.2.2 Personal and professional ethics

These situations with no easy answers represent clashes of values and constituencies as well as ethics. Recognizing the limitations of professional guidance, they may require archivists to look beyond professional codes of conduct and dig deep into personal morality. Codes of ethics and codes of conduct, as thoughtful as they may be, may be guides to professional behaviour but will not offer direct solutions to individual ethical dilemmas. The professional associations that promulgate these codes often feel unable to enforce them and may not even feel that they can provide the necessary public support, either from concern about litigation or from a perceived lack of power to influence decisions. Richard Cox points to a litany of current information concerns, all of which confront archives and records management professionals with a wide range of competing interests and colliding values that have no easy solutions. He writes that

> Scholars and commentators considering ethics in the modern Information Age argue that the rapid advances in information technologies are accelerating the density of ethical issues and even creating new ethical challenges. They point to matters such as the freedom of information; economics of information; privacy, secrecy, and confidentiality; intellectual property; control over the access to information; information security; and other issues such as intercultural information ethics.
>
> (Cox, 2010, 21–2)

In order to resolve these conundrums, being an ethical archivist or records manager may also require a personal ethic in addition to a professional one, a private moral compass as well as a workplace code of conduct. It is not impossible to envision that this personal code might occasionally be in conflict with an organizational culture, or with the mission of the corporation or institution, or even with a professional code of conduct. In these instances, how does an archivist or records manager decide to become a whistle-blower? What happens when both personal ethics and professional ethics conflict with institutional behaviour? In the Heiner Affair, briefly described in example (a) above, an archivist found himself in exactly that position. As the whistle-blower, he suffered the consequences by losing his job.

Many of these questions are not the purview of the archives and records profession alone, and in fact continue to be issues weighed by professions and philosophers alike. But in accepting responsibility for records, the caretakers of records assume complex ethical obligations. These commitments speak not only to the care of the records themselves, the safeguarding of their value as evidence and accountability, but also their protection against misuse.

## 3 Ethical issues

> The discipline of ethics, or moral philosophy, divides into several different branches some of which focus on the meaning and language of ethics (meta-ethics), on how people should behave (normative ethics), studying beliefs and morality (descriptive ethics), and others that focus on the practical (applied ethics).
>
> (Internet Encyclopedia of Philosophy, 2009)

'The proper role of ethical reasoning', write scholars of critical thinking Paul and Elder, 'is to highlight acts of two kinds: those which enhance the well-being of others – that warrant our praise – and those that harm or diminish the well-being of others – and thus warrant our criticism.' They add: 'the ultimate basis for ethics is clear: Human behavior has consequences for the well-being of others' (Paul and Elder, 2013, 4).

Danielson applies the term 'professional ethics' to those specific ethical concerns that practising archivists share. She defines professional ethics as 'the values appropriate to certain kinds of occupational activity, such as medicine or law, which have been defined traditionally in terms of a body of knowledge and an ideal of service to the community; and in which individual professionals have a high degree of autonomy in their practice' (Danielson, 2010, 3).

While archivists and records managers share many overarching professional ethical concerns, they may have different institution-specific perspectives and goals. They share concerns over compliance with regulations and best practices, safeguarding records as evidence, intellectual property rights, following professional standards and codes of conduct, observing privacy and confidentiality and maintaining the integrity of the institution through best practices. Defining, evaluating and understanding wrong and right behaviour and adhering to professional imperatives to behave ethically are overarching values common to both professions. And of course, in many institutions the care of archives and records are not separate functions but often reside with the same person or team. This section details some of the different and similar ethical issues that records managers and archivists face.

## 3.1 Records managers

As managers of active records, records managers focus particularly on meeting the institution's standards for compliance with internal and external regulations and on protecting the institution against present and future threats that may be relevant to recordkeeping. Records managers must respond to the immediate concerns of the organization, focusing on conformity with government or industry regulations, safeguarding classified information and responding correctly to freedom of information requests. Corporate records managers are particularly concerned with protecting the corporation, maintaining its financial and organizational integrity and risk management. ARMA International defines its *Generally Accepted Recordkeeping Principles* (*GARP*) as:

- Establishing policies/practices to ensure transparency AND appropriate confidentiality
- Conducting records retention and disposition actions in compliance with laws and regulations
- Integrating the organization's Code of Ethics into recordkeeping practices
- Auditing and measuring organizational recordkeeping practices; take specific corrective action if areas are not in compliance.

## 3.2 Archivists

Archivists, primarily dealing with inactive records in collecting institutions have a slightly different portfolio focused on executing the mission of their institution. Their activities include acquisition and appraisal of collections, negotiating and honouring donor agreements, managing privacy and confidentiality concerns and providing for access to and use of materials. Working ethically with archival materials combines issues of the physical stewardship of records with issues of their intellectual protection. How and where the institution houses the records, storage of the records themselves, protecting the contents of the records and equitably treating the users of the records all require ethical management. Specific issues include:

- *Ensuring equitable access, or fair and equal use of the records:* Opening collections to public use means minimizing the amount of time that a collection may be closed; processing collections and making them usable as quickly as possible; and not charging fees. Equitable access also includes physical accessibility (i.e. facilitating access for the disabled, providing sufficient reading room facilities, providing equipment for accessing non-text formats) and providing means of intellectual access, such as finding aids.
- *Protecting the physical or virtual records:* For physical records this includes maintaining climate controls, providing safe storage in acid-free boxes and folders, maintaining safeguards against fire and theft. In the case of digital records this would include an array of digital preservation standards, maintaining equipment and server space and making decisions about migration and storage.
- *Maintaining custody, ownership and evidence:* Ensuring the authenticity and reliability of the records requires the chain of custody to be maintained and recorded, and protection of the rights of the institution as the legal owner of the records, when appropriate.
- *Protecting copyright:* The copyright holder's rights must be protected, whether the holder is the institution or another party. Institutions can endeavour to obtain copyright to acquisitions through donor agreements.
- *Negotiating donor agreements; protecting privacy of content and third parties:* While donor agreements should protect donors' privacy and confidentiality wishes, they also need to allow maximum open access to the records. Sensitive information, particularly that of third parties who have no voice in the disposition of their records, needs to be protected.

- *Behaving ethically in the administration of records:* This involves compliance with institutional, professional and government records regulations, and following best practices and industry standards in archival procedures such as appraisal, acquisitions and processing.

Drawing from the set of ethical principles suggested by Karen Benedict in her book *Ethics and the Archival Profession: introduction and case studies* (2003), archival educator Randall Jimerson proposes 10 precepts of personal ethical behaviour for archives and records professionals. He argues that they:

1 should treat both users and colleagues fairly, without discrimination or preference.
2 must preserve the intellectual and physical integrity of their records.
3 may never alter, manipulate, or destroy data in records.
4 should discourage restricting access to records except for essential reasons of legality, privacy, or confidentiality; and must apply any such restrictions without preference or bias.
5 should protect the privacy of donors, users, and individuals who are the subject of records, and observe all legitimate access restrictions.
6 may never personally profit from privileged information in their records.
7 should use impartial judgment, rather than personal beliefs or biases, when appraising records.
8 should not publicly disparage colleagues or other archival institutions.
9 should not personally collect manuscripts or archival records in competition with their employers; nor appraise the fiscal value of materials donated to their own institutions.
10 should use their specialized knowledge and expertise for the benefit of society.

(Jimerson, 2006, 91–2)

## 4 Codes of ethics, codes of conduct

Most professions have codes of ethics. Archival educator David Wallace notes an online compendium of more than 850 codes of ethics from a vast array of 'professional societies, corporation, governments, and institutions of higher learning' (Wallace, 2010, 177). Codes of ethics, generally developed by professional associations, establish the ethical practices of a profession, defining what ethical behaviour means within that specific context. They are also designed to protect, support and guide members of the profession in their ethical decisions. Codes of ethics are critical to promoting the public trust that is an essential aspect of the archives and records mission. Glenn Dingwall observes that 'If the goal of such activities [archives and records keeping] is to buoy public faith in the trustworthiness of archival institutions and the people who work there, they must be able to make reference to codified ethics in order to proffer a justification for that faith' (Dingwall, 2004, 20).

Seldom as effective as they should be, primarily due to the difficulties of enforcement, codes of ethics nonetheless present the standard of ethical behaviour that is supported by a particular profession and proclaim a particular ethical set of principles to those outside the profession. Sociologist Eliot Freidson observes that 'A great many professional associations have a formal code of ethics, but few have any really viable machinery by which to search out violations and undertake effective actions to correct them' (Freidson, 1986, 187). This applies to archives and records as well, where the profusion of codes of ethics has not really lightened the ethical burden, despite the attempt to provide much-needed guidance. Commenting upon the tensions between the need for ethical guidance and the difficulties in providing it, Michael Cook, in a study of codes of ethics internationally, notes that

> The existence of tensions in the professional arena in some sense automatically generates such codes, in one form or another. Problems arise at every interface. These interfaces occur in every ARM [archives and records management] situation, whether in the public or in the private sector. The four-fold interface – employer-creator-user-data subject – seems to stand in the background in most cases. ARM professionals usually find themselves in the middle of this complex set of relationships.
>
> (Cook, 2006, 3)

## 4.1 Records

In addition to its *GARP*, referenced above, ARMA International, a not-for-profit worldwide professional association, also supports a professional *Code of Professional Responsibility* (ARMA, n.d.) that speaks to the basic underpinnings of ethical behaviour. Applying equally to archivists and records managers, and indeed to any information professional, the code is designed as 'a guide to reflection, decision making, and action in two broad areas of ethical concern: society and the profession'. Its precepts, looking inwardly at professional behaviour and outwardly at societal responsibility, speak to the overall obligations of archives and records professionals and to the totality of their ethical mandate. The Social Principles in ARMA's *Code* speak to the supporting of information systems, 'the creation, maintenance, and use of authentic, reliable, usable information and support the development and use of information systems that place a high priority on accuracy and integrity, which requires that records be complete and unaltered', in accordance with the International Organization for Standardization's (ISO) records management standards (ARMA, n.d). The Social Principles also include respecting the legal, moral and ethical use of information, the right to privacy and the 'free flow of publicly available information as a necessary condition for an informed and educated society'.

ARMA's Professional Principles in the *Code* address the relationship between the records manager and clients or employees and revolve around issues of compliance with regulations and protection of the organization. They include recognizing 'illegal or unethical [records and information management] RIM-related actions and inform[ing] the client or employer of possible adverse consequences', avoiding conflicts of interest and maintaining confidentiality. The *Code* seems to offer useful and even fundamental advice, importantly inviting records managers to think critically about their role in the workplace and society. Nonetheless, implementation in our current, complex information environment is not easy. Richard Cox observes that ARMA's *Code* may not be adequate to confront some of today's critical ethical challenges. He writes: 'we may now live in a time when complying with federal law may violate personal privacy or risk censorship through excessive secrecy' (Cox, 2006, 131). He, and others, explore these kinds of situations in 'A Different Kind of Archival Security: three cases' (Cox et al., 2009, 33–60), with cases ranging from the FBI's seizing of personal records protected by donor agreements to secret audiotapes of the US Supreme Court.

## 4.2 Archives

Dingwall notes that 'there are two fundamental impediments to the exercise of well-considered ethical action: a lack of sufficient guidance for practice, and a lack of autonomy in exercising ethical decisions. Archivists have overcome the first of these impediments through the construction of ethics codes' (Dingwall, 2004, 12).

Archives organizations in myriad countries have codes of ethics. Many are modelled on the universal code approved by the General Assembly of the International Council on Archives (ICA) in 1996. Providing both principles and commentaries, the ICA code succinctly states its purpose, 'A code of ethics for archivists should establish high standards of conduct for the archival profession. It should introduce new members of the profession to those standards, remind experienced archivists of their professional responsibilities and inspire public confidence in the profession' (ICA, 1996).

Although the code covers a wide range of archives and records issues, the emphasis is on protecting and maintaining the integrity of the record, clearly addressing and placing priority on a primary concern. Protecting and maintaining the integrity of the record in an international context often implies more than passive custody or stewardship, often involving pro-active measures that put archivists in conflict with their own employers. Item 1 of the ICA code reflects that concern:[2]

> Archivists should protect the integrity of archival material and thus guarantee that it continues to be reliable evidence of the past.
>
> The primary duty of archivists is to maintain the integrity of the records in their care and custody. In the accomplishment of this duty they must have regard to the legitimate, but sometimes conflicting, rights and interests of employers, owners, data subjects and users, past, present and future. The objectivity and impartiality of archivists is the measure of their professionalism. They should resist pressure from any source to manipulate evidence so as to conceal or distort facts.
>
> (International Council on Archives, 1996)

National codes of ethics take a variety of forms. While they tend to reflect the archival culture of the country, they all cover similar areas. They may be prescriptive, advisory or aspirational, such as the Society of American Archivists (SAA) code, revised in 2011, which is a complementary combination of a statement of core values and a code of ethics. The core values of the SAA code address the conduct of archivists themselves, 'both to remind archivists why they engage in their professional responsibilities and to inform others of the basis for archivists' contributions to society'. While emphasis is placed on access and use, personal papers and cultural heritage, all areas of the archival endeavour are covered. The SAA code emphasizes its aspirational nature. The introduction states that

> As advocates for documentary collections and cultural objects under their care, archivists aspire to carry out their professional activities with the highest standard of professional conduct. The behaviors and characteristics outlined in this Code of Ethics should serve as aspirational principles for archivists to consider as they strive to create trusted archival institutions.
>
> (Society of American Archivists, 2012)

The Archives and Records Association (ARA) of the UK and Ireland takes a slightly different approach. Its code is announced as a code of conduct rather than of ethics. Closely following the ICA's *Code*, it focuses on records protection and integrity. Taking a proactive approach to enforceability, the ARA code ties membership in the organization with observance of the code, stating that

> The Code of Conduct sets out certain, basic principles that are intended to help members maintain the highest standards of professional conduct. Should a case arise where a member is believed to have fallen short of the standards desired, procedures are defined within the Articles of Association of the Archives and Records Association (UK and Ireland) and within the Bye-Laws of the Association, which permit the convening of a Disciplinary Panel to consider the matter.
>
> (Archives and Records Association of UK and Ireland, 2012)

## 4.3 The limits of ethical codes

Ethical codes, as guides to the conduct of archives and records professionals, offer advice and even prescriptions for behaviour but do not offer specific solutions. And this is as it must be. The limitless landscape of ethical questions and dilemmas, the range of perspectives of different institutions and organizations, and even the variety of country contexts, suggest that ethical codes are paths to ethical behaviour rather than solutions in themselves. While codes function as much to build public trust as they do to create archival confidence, Dingwall cautions that 'merely assuring the public that a code of ethics exists is not sufficient to warrant that trust. It must be demonstrated that archivists are adhering to the standards embodied within the code. The code must also be accessible to the public so that the public can verify for itself that the standards and practices enshrined within truly do serve its best interests' (Dingwall, 2004, 29).

Having a professional code does not guarantee ethical behaviour and does not exempt archives and records professionals from continually questioning and analysing. In fact, professional codes are really just the beginning of the ethical process, stating general principles but not offering prescriptions or answers. Interpreting the principles and applying them to specific situations is left to the individual. And as Richard Cox, Michael Cook and others have suggested, ethical codes often are not adequate to address the complex ethical issues of today's records environment.

In addition, codes themselves might even suggest or require courses of action that in particular contexts could themselves be unethical, and so codes must be continually evaluated. Wallace counsels that 'codes need to be actively engaged and cross-examined, as opposed to implicitly accepted or explicitly pointed to, in order for them to be rendered meaningful' (Wallace, 2010, 178).

## 5 Ethics of social justice

The alliance of archival ethics with social justice is rapidly becoming a central focus of archival inquiry and concern in the twenty-first century. Social justice is a broad and ambiguous term with definitions ranging from the general understanding of a 'natural law that all persons, irrespective of ethnic origin, gender, possessions, race, religion, etc., are to be treated equally and without prejudice', (BusinessDictionary.com) to 'the view that everyone deserves equal economic, political and social rights and opportunities' (National Association of Social Workers, n.d.). In the archival context, social justice is still being defined. Archival educator Michele Caswell notes that 'while there has been a great deal of interest in incorporating a social justice perspective within archival practice, there is much confusion over the exact meaning of the term and its implications' (Caswell et al., 2012, 5). In her discussion of the applicability of social justice in archival education, she identifies four areas of focus:

> the more equitable distribution of economic opportunity; the empowering effects of self representation; the encouragement of dialogue between those with incommensurate ontologies; and an analysis of power and its abuses.
>
> (Caswell et al., 2012, 7)

More explicitly, 'Struggles for social justice are battlegrounds over values, priorities, resources, dignity and survival' (Wallace, 2010, 184). Ethics is intimately implicated. A multitude of well-known archival case studies over the past several decades dealing with the opening of secret files, displaced archives, the destruction of public records, truth and reconciliation commissions, secrecy in government and government malfeasance have highlighted the power of records to reveal or conceal the truth. They have also shone a light on the attempts of governments and institutions to be complicit in, if not initiators of, the concealment.[3]

The reluctance of governments and organizations to retain and to open records can place archivists and records managers in ethical and moral dilemmas that codes of ethics have little power to resolve. Archivists have placed their careers in jeopardy by becoming whistle-blowers – as in the destruction of public records in South Africa – more often than not losing their positions or being forced to resign (Harris, 2007). But archives and records professionals have also opened records, helping to reconcile and facilitate ethical/social justice solutions, as in the case of the *Stasi* files in the former East Germany (Danielson, 2004, 176–93), or exposing records of social injustice through organizations like the National Security Archive (National Security Archive, n.d.). Equally, archivists can inadvertently become complicit in unethical records behaviour, as in the case of the infamous Heiner Affair, described above. The fact that codes of ethics, codes of professional conduct or responsibility and statements of values have little impact in terms of enforcement or protection, but that nonetheless archives and records professionals may be confronted with ethically untenable situations, suggests that archivists need to go beyond codes of ethics and even beyond conventional perceptions of professional ethics in order to determine their own ethical behaviour. Verne Harris suggests that 'there is no knowing of right without giving account to personal morality. For each of us has the right, and the obligation, to be true to ourselves' (Harris, 2007, 211).

In attempting to resolve the conflicting rights and interests that make up ethical/social justice dilemmas, Harris (2007, 211) observes, 'for none of us

[is] impartial. We can neither stand outside process nor avoid bringing to process a pre-impression shaped by our experience as individuals'. The best that records managers and archivists can do is to make sure that the ethical decisions that they make are taken in an appropriate way so that ethical reasoning, moral imperatives and professional practice guide and drive decisions. How the decision is reached, the process of ethical determination, is crucial to the final decision. Harris offers a prescription for this process that is particularly applicable to those ethical issues that go beyond daily ethical behaviour and touch upon the larger societal dilemmas. He counsels:

> Getting the how right, I want to argue, always involves at least four elements. Firstly, an illumination of the web of rights as it applies to the interested parties at different levels. Secondly, an analysis aimed at weighing competing claims against one another in the specific circumstances confronting the archivist. Thirdly, a testing of one's views and feelings with respected colleagues and friends. And finally, paying heed to one's conscience.
>
> (Harris, 2007, 211)

## 6 Protocols and rights of indigenous peoples

Beginning in the late twentieth century, the ethics dialogue began to incorporate a new dimension. Revolving around cultural sensitivity, cultural property and the rights of the indigenous creators and (sometimes) holders of that property, the debate introduced elements that often conflicted with accepted ethical codes, suggesting that 'a commonly held understanding of the public good as being equivalent to unabridged access to public domain materials often blinds collecting institutions to non-Western systems of information management and circulation that work from and mobilize different understandings of "public," "private," and the like' (Christen, 2011, 189). The moral and ethical rights of indigenous peoples to control their own cultural and intellectual products, as well as their collective concepts of intellectual property, call many of the accepted ethical archival concepts surrounding such issues as 'privacy', 'access', 'public good', and the 'public domain' into question. Australian Aboriginal artwork, for example, continues to be a target of misuse through illicit merchandizing, in spite of advocacy efforts and laws protecting indigenous cultural and intellectual property rights (Janke, 1998; Aboriginal Art Online, 2007). At the very least, acknowledgement of these rights creates profound conflicts with these concepts. Archaeologist/archivist Kimberly Christen points out that

> Indigenous traditional knowledge systems and associated modes of knowledge circulation and access call into question standard notions of the public domain that overwrite histories of exclusion and injustice. Yet, because variations of the public domain are either poorly understood or romantically imagined, indigenous knowledge systems are usually discounted as viable alternatives to, or additions within, a conception of the public domain that allows for a continuum of access strategies.
>
> (Christen, 2011, 190)

But at the same time, given the recognition of these cultural differences, 'even archivists, librarians, and museum specialists who agree in principle that indigenous knowledge systems and culture-specific protocols undo the logic of the public as an undifferentiated mass often see no way around their professional obligations to make their collections "open" to the "public"' (Christen, 2011, 190).

Article 32 of the United Nations *Declaration on the Rights of Indigenous Peoples* specifically addresses those rights as they pertain to cultural heritage, intellectual property and access, stating that

> Indigenous peoples have the right to maintain, control, protect and develop their cultural heritage, traditional knowledge and traditional cultural expressions, as well as the manifestations of their sciences, technologies and cultures, including human and genetic resources, seeds, medicines, knowledge of the properties of fauna and flora, oral traditions, literatures, designs, sports and traditional games and visual and performing arts. They also have the right to maintain, control, protect and develop their intellectual property over such cultural heritage, traditional knowledge, and traditional cultural expressions.
>
> (United Nations, 2007, 11)

The *Aboriginal and Torres Strait Islander Protocols for Libraries, Archives and Information Services*, first introduced in 1995 by the Australian Library and Information Association and subsequently updated periodically, offer precepts that expand upon Article 32 with specific guidelines in areas such as content and culturally sensitive materials, intellectual property, access, use, management, repatriation and preservation. Similarly, the *Protocols for*

*Native American Archival Materials* developed in 2007 by the First Archivist Circle emphasize partnerships between repositories holding indigenous materials and the indigenous communities themselves. Such partnerships involve respecting the community, consulting with the community on all aspects of their materials and, above all, recognizing the intellectual property rights of the community. The Native American protocols state that

> Conditions under which knowledge can be ethically and legally acquired, archived, preserved, accessed, published, or otherwise used change through time. Some materials may have been collected or later restricted by a donor in contravention of community rights and laws or of contemporary federal laws or professional ethics. In all of these cases the rights of a Native American community must take precedence.
>
> (First Archivists Circle, 2007)

On a similar issue, the Aboriginal and Torres Strait Islander protocols state that

> The primary rights of the owners of a culture must be recognized. Organisations will:
>
> 3.1 Raise awareness of the issues surrounding cultural documentation and the need for cultural awareness training.
> 3.2 Develop professional recognition of cultural and intellectual property rights of Aboriginal and Torres Strait Islanders and consult with appropriate Aboriginal or Torres Strait Islander peoples on their application.
> 3.3 Develop ways, including the recognition of moral rights, to protect Aboriginal and Torres Strait Islander cultural and intellectual property.
>
> (Aboriginal and Torres Strait Islander Library, Information and Resource Network, 2012)

Reconciling the archives and records rights of indigenous peoples with many of the principles articulated in ethical codes will be a continuing challenge for archives and records professionals, in particular, where many legacy records that include material relating to indigenous peoples reside in archival collections, in the area of access and use. One solution is offered through the *Access Standard* promulgated by the National Archives of New Zealand, a code developed jointly with the indigenous Maori population. The *Standard* envisions a partnership between users and access providers, recognizing that

> *Access should be a partnership between access providers and all users of the records, and access providers should develop effective partnerships with Māori.*
> Accessing records is a collaborative task between those who care for the records and those who are interested in using them. This partnership should be taken into consideration in the development of access policies and practices, to ensure that they aim to meet the expectations and needs of both custodians and users.
> The diversity and knowledge of the user community should be recognised, welcomed and respected by access providers. Access providers should encourage and be responsive to different groups, especially those that are under-represented as users of records due to social, language or other barriers.
> (Archives New Zealand, 2006)

While many archives and records professionals may feel that indigenous records lie outside their purview, the standards and precepts suggested in these protocols must be read more subtly. Ethical questions relating to culturally sensitive material are not confined to indigenous groups but might equally apply to records from a wide variety of communities. Colonial records and the oral and written records of marginalized ethnic populations or immigrant groups might all potentially contain materials with disputed and contested claims that require reasoned and fair ethical decisions based on cultural sensitivity as well as sound archival practice. Codes and protocols, taken together, may challenge one another, but are not necessarily adversarial. Rather, read in a more nuanced fashion, they can be complementary, offering a rounded perspective that allows room for negotiating between rights and arriving at equitable solutions that recognize and respect all interests.

## 7 Ethics in a digital world

The malleable and dynamic nature of digital materials adds further layers of complexity to ethical concerns. Intellectual property, authenticity, copying, dissemination, capture and access are just a few of the rapidly evolving areas of ethical issues in digital environments. While this environment does not alter accepted professional ethical standards, it adds complexity to concepts such as copyright, privacy and third party protection, while revealing new issues of security, web archiving, digital preservation and social media. These issues are highlighted here but not explored in any depth. The effort, rather, is to point to further reading and resources.[4] The websites of the Center for Digital Ethics and Policy at Loyola University in Chicago and eResearch Ethics at Oxford University, for example, offer a wealth of resources and essays on current aspects of digital information, and there are many others on specific aspects of digital ethics such as copyright, privacy, confidentiality and open access and digital forensics.

Wikileaks, which has riveted people's attention worldwide, presents just one example of the ethical complexities surrounding digital information:

> Due to the explosion of digital information, the ubiquity of the web and social media, records issues that historically were primarily the purview of archivists and records managers, are now general societal concerns.
>
> (Wikileaks, n.d.)

For archives and records professionals in particular, the internet and its digital content creates new ethical issues that are peculiar to that medium and that have as much to do with the owners of the technology as the owners of the content. The authors of a case study on the digitization and ownership of cultural heritage sites suggest that, rather than ethical codes applying equally to analogue and digital materials, 'many, particularly in scholarly circles, consider the relationship between creators, rights holders, and users to have become distorted by the commodification of information', and that seen 'in this light, continued support of the current intellectual property regime raises moral issues' (Lor and Britz, 2012, 2160).

## 8 Conclusion

What are archivists and the records managers to do when faced with such an entanglement of moral imperatives, ethical codes and the old and the new? International records consultant Rick Barry (2007) suggests some general principles for understanding broadly how ethics and codes of ethics impact upon the archives and records profession. He points out that 'ethical cases are not rare phenomena, but occur in all countries and sectors, in governments at all levels, large and small businesses, universities, and religious groups', and that 'the importance of strong recordkeeping, freedom-of-information and whistleblower legislation offer strong defenses against improper political pressures upon recordkeeping'. He encourages archivists and records managers to support ethical conduct and whistle-blowers and to take strong action against those who disdain ethical principles. Barry points out that sound recordkeeping policies and practices are essential, and that 'the absence of sound recordkeeping policies and practices makes for a climate in which ethical violations will occur. The information and records management professional is a complicit partner of the violators in such cases for not having carried out necessary policymaking tasks.' And while Barry supports codes of ethics, he recognizes that they are not sufficient to 'address serious ethical violations in a timely manner that is credible to the public'.

Essentially, it comes down to the individual to determine 'right' from 'wrong' and to examine, understand and implement those ethical strategies and principles that not only gain or regain public trust but satisfy internal moral dictates. It is up to the individual archivists and records managers to employ ethical reasoning in decision making, to use ethical codes as guides while recognizing the limitations, and to trust in their own sense of personal morality.

## Notes

1 a. The Heiner Affair, www.heineraffair.info/; b. Adapted from an account in Brown (2004); c. Ongoing case involving the release of IRA tapes held by Boston College, http://bostoncollegesubpoena.wordpress.com/.

2 The reality of ethical conflict between archivists and the state was made clear in a 2003 conference on archives and political pressure. The proceedings are published in Procter, Cook and Williams (2005).

3 Cox and Wallace (2002), Procter, Cook and Williams (2005) present but a few of the case studies in this area. Added to that is Harris (2007).

4 There is a growing literature on many aspects of ethics in digital environments. Some useful publications include, Jessica Litwin, *Digital Copyright* (Prometheus Books, 2006); James Boyle, *The Public Domain, Enclosing the Commons of the Mind* (New Haven: Yale University Press, 2010). Richard J. Cox,

A. Middleton, R. G. Rohrbaugh and D. Scholzen, A Different Kind of Archival Security: three cases, *Library and Archival Security*, 22 (2009): 33–60; Christopher Lee, *I, Digital: personal collections in the digital era* (Society of American Archivists, 2011); Paul Conway, Preservation in the Age of Google: digitization, digital preservation, and dilemmas, *Library Quarterly*, 80 (January 2010): 61–79.

## References and further reading

Aboriginal Art Online (2007) *Copyright and Intellectual Property Protection for Indigenous Heritage*, www.aboriginalartonline.com/resources/debate.php.

Aboriginal and Torres Strait Islander Library, Information and Resource Network (2012) *Aboriginal and Torres Strait Islander Protocols for Libraries, Archives and Information Services*, http://aiatsis.gov.au/atsilirn/index.php.

Archives and Records Association of UK and Ireland (2012) *Code of Conduct*, www.archives.org.uk/membership/code-of-conduct.html.

Archives New Zealand (2006) *Access Standard*, http://archives.govt.nz/advice/continuum-resource-kit/continuum-publications-html/s4-access-standard.

ARMA (n.d.) *Code of Professional Responsibility*, www.arma.org/r2/who-we-are/code-of-professional-responsibility.

ARMA International (n.d.a) *Standards and Best Practices*, www.arma.org/r2/standards-amp-best-practices.

ARMA International (n.d.b) *Generally Accepted Recordkeeping Principles*, www.arma.org/r2/generally-accepted-br-recordkeeping-principles.

Barry, R. (2007) *Ethics Issues for Creators, Managers and Users of Records: key cases*, Barry Associates, www.mybestdocs.com/barry-r-eth-iss0307-lucas.htm.

Becker, R. (1993) The Ethics of Providing Access, *Provenance*, **11**, 57–77.

Benedict, K. (2003) *Ethics and the Archival Profession: introduction and case studies*, Society of American Archivists.

Brown, M. (2004) *Who Owns Native Culture*, Harvard University Press.

BusinessDictionary.com, Definition: *social justice*, www.businessdictionary.com/definition/social-justice.html.

Caswell, M. et al. (2012) Implementing a Social Justice Framework in an Introduction to Archives Course: lessons from both sides of the classroom, *InterActions, UCLA Journal of Education and Information Studies*, **8** (2), 1–30.

Center for Digital Ethics and Policy (n.d.), http://digitalethics.org/about/.

Christen, K. (2011) Opening Archives: respectful repatriation, *American Archivist*, **74**, 185–210.

Cook, M. (2006) Professional Ethics and Practice in Archives and Records Management in a Human Rights Context, *Journal of the Society of Archivists*, **27** (1), 1–15.

Cox, R. J. (2006) *Ethics, Accountability and Recordkeeping in a Dangerous World*, Facet Publishing.

Cox, R. J. (2010) Teaching, Researching, and Preaching Archival Ethics Or, How These New Views Came to Be, *Journal of Information Ethics*, **19** (1), 2–32.

Cox, R. J. and Wallace, D. (2002) *Archives and the Public Good: accountability and records in modern society*, Quorum Books.

Cox, R. J., Middleton, A., Rohrbaugh, R. G. and Scholzen, D. (2009) A Different Kind of Archival Security: three cases, *Library and Archival Security*, **22**, 33–60.

Danielson, E. (1989) The Ethics of Access, *American Archivist*, **52**, (Winter) 52–62.

Danielson, E. (2004) Privacy Rights and the Rights of Political Victims: implications of the German experience, *American Archivist*, **67**, 176–93.

Danielson, E. (2010) *The Ethical Archivist*, Society of American Archivists.

Dingwall, G. (2004) Trusting Archivists: the role of archival ethical codes in establishing public faith, *American Archivist*, **67**, 11–30.

eResearch Ethics (n.d.), http://eresearch-ethics.org/about/.

First Archivists Circle (2007) *Protocols for Native American Archival Materials*, www2.nau.edu/libnap-p/.

The Free Dictionary (n.d.), www.thefreedictionary.com/ethics.

Freidson, E. (1986) *Professional Powers, a Study of the Institutionalization of Formal Knowledge*, University of Chicago Press.

Harris, V. (2007) *Archives and Justice: a South African perspective*, Society of American Archivists.

International Council on Archives (1996) *Code of Ethics*, www.wien2004.ica.org/en/node/30046.

Internet Encyclopedia of Philosophy (2009) *Ethics*, www.iep.utm.edu/ethics/.

Janke, T. (1998) *Our Culture; Our Future*, Report on Australian Indigenous Cultural and Intellectual Property Rights, prepared for Australian Institute of Aboriginal Torres and Straits Islanders Studies and Torres Strait Islander Commission.

Jenkinson, H. (2003) The English Archivist: a new profession. Inaugural lecture for a new course in Archive Administration delivered at University College,

London, 14 October 1947. In Ellis, R. and Walne, P. (eds), *Selected Writings of Sir Hilary Jenkinson*, Society of American Archivists, 236–59.

Jimerson, R. C. (2006) Ethical Concerns for Archivists, *The Public Historian*, **28**, 87–92.

Ketelaar, E. (1995) The Right to Know, the Right To Forget? Personal information in public archives, *Archives and Manuscripts*, **23**, 8–17.

Lor, P. J. and Britz, J. J. (2012) An Ethical Perspective on Political-Economic Issues in the Long-Term Preservation of Digital Heritage, *Journal of the American Society for Information Science and Technology*, **63**, 2153–64.

MacNeil, H. (1992) *Without Consent: the ethics of disclosing personal information*, Scarecrow Press.

Mason, R. O. et al. (1995) *Ethics of Information Management*, Sage Publications.

Merriam-Webster (n.d.), www.merriam-webster.com/dictionary/ethics.

National Association of Social Workers (n.d.) *Social Justice*, www.socialworkers.org/pressroom/features/issue/peace.asp.

National Security Archive (n.d.), www.gwu.edu/~nsarchiv/.

Neazor, M. (2007) Recordkeeping Professional Ethics and their Applications, *Archivaria*, **64**, 47–87.

Paul, R. and Elder, L. (2013) *The Thinker's Guide to Understanding the Foundations of Ethical Reasoning*, Foundation for Critical Thinking Press.

Procter, M., Cook, M. and Williams, C. (eds) (2005) *Political Pressure and the Archival Record*, Society of American Archivists.

Society of American Archivists (2012) *SAA Core Values Statement and Code of Ethics*, www2.archivists.org/statements/saa-core-values-statement-and-code-of-ethics.

Thomassen, T. (1999) Archivists between Knowledge and Power: of the independence and autonomy of archival science and the archival profession, *Archiviski Vjesnik*, **42**, 149–67.

United Nations (2007) *Declaration on the Rights of Indigenous Peoples*, www.un.org/esa/socdev/unpfii/documents/DRIPS_en.pdf.

Wallace, D. A. (2010) Locating Agency: interdisciplinary perspectives on professional ethics and archival morality, *Journal of Information Ethics*, **19** (1), 172–89.

Wallace, D. A. (ed.) (2011a) *Archival Science*, Special Issue: Archives and the Ethics of Memory Construction, **11** (1/2).

Wallace, D. A. (2011b) Understanding the 9/11 Commission Archive: control, access, and the politics of manipulation, *Archival Science*, Special Issue: Archives and the Ethics of Memory Construction, **11** (1/2), 125–68.

Wikileaks (n.d.), http://wikileaks.org.

Wosh, P. and Behrnd-Klodt, M. L. (eds) (2005) *Privacy and Confidentiality Perspectives: archivists and archival records*, Society of American Archivists.

CHAPTER 5

# Archives, memories and identities

Eric Ketelaar

## 1 Introduction

### 1.1 What are archives?

Archives, libraries and museums are all in the 'memory business', ensuring 'time future contained in time past' (Ketelaar, 2004). But what distinguishes archives from all other memory institutions is that the individual, organizational and collective memories they preserve are not defined primarily in terms of a cultural heritage: they have been created as 'process-bound information', that is, 'information generated by coherent work processes and structured and recorded by these work processes in such a way that it can be retrieved from the context of those work processes' (Thomassen, 2001, 374). Notwithstanding the importance of this definition for archival theory and methodology, in practice (as I will argue in section 4.7) it is often more important to ask: how does this particular individual or group perceive and understand an archive? Throughout this chapter the term 'archives' (or archive) is used to denote two concepts. As in the first sentence of this chapter archives is an organization that collects (and the building that houses) archives. Archives (or records)[1] also means 'information created, received, and maintained as evidence and/or as an asset by an organization or person, in pursuance of legal obligations or in the transaction of business or for its purposes, regardless of medium, form or format' (ISO 30300, 2011, 3.1.7).

Archivists are 'all those concerned with the control, care, custody, preservation and administration of archives' (International Council on Archives, 1996), which includes record managers.

## 1.2 Why this chapter?

Many archives call themselves the 'Memory of the city' or the 'Memory of the nation'. There is even a 'Memory of the world' – a UNESCO programme to promote 'the documented, collective memory of the peoples of the world – their documentary heritage' (UNESCO, 2002). That this is a misleading analogy (Brothman, 2010; Hedstrom, 2010, 174; Jimerson, 2009, 213–14) we discover once we have developed 'a more refined sense of what memory means in different contexts, but also a sensitivity to the differences between individual and social memory' (Hedstrom, 2002, 31–2). This in turn, as Margaret Hedstrom argues, will help to create a greater awareness of how collective memory operates.

'Whether conscious of it or not, archivists are major players in the business of identity politics' (Schwartz and Cook, 2002, 16). Many archivists claim that identities are constructed and reconstructed through the experience of archival documents (Craven, 2008, 17). All recordkeepers, particularly those involved with community archives and other memory institutions, rather than relying on conceptions of identity that 'were long ago rejected by serious scholars as a means of understanding or articulating ethnic, gender, national, or other differences' (Kaplan, 2000, 146), have to understand how identities are produced and – like memories and archives – are managed, contested, transmitted and recontextualized.

This chapter will first review some of the literature and research (including non-archival texts which have an impact on the archivists' discourse) on memory (section 2) and identity (section 3) and the role of archives in the formation of memory and identity (section 4). I have not attempted to paraphrase all the literature, but have instead tried to provide a reading of the authors' original statements. To avoid leading the reader onto many detours, I will only occasionally discuss views deviating from the mainstream literature. After the review of theories and concepts in the first four sections, section 5 provides some examples of and suggestions for archival policies and practices which would enhance the role of archives and archivists in the construction of individual and collective memories and identities. In a short conclusion (section 6) I tie the main strands of the chapter together.

## 1.3 Literature

The literature is abundant, especially because studies and practices using concepts of memory and identity are situated in numerous disciplinary domains and interdisciplinary discourses. Barbara Misztal (2003) provides a remarkable synthesis of some 500 monographs and articles on social memory (see also Erll, Nünning and Young, 2008; Elliott, 2011). In 2011, *Identity: An International Journal of Theory and Research* was founded 'as a publication venue for identity-related work across a broad range of fields including, but not limited to, psychology, sociology, anthropology, human development, education, gender studies, family studies, and psychiatry. Comparable consideration will be accorded to manuscripts looking at the expression of identity within the full range of cultures and cultural contexts.'[2] Since 2008 a journal *Memory Studies* has been examining 'the social, cultural, cognitive, political and technological shifts affecting how, what and why individuals, groups and societies remember, and forget'.[3]

Within the archivists' discipline one of the early publications is by a historian, Kenneth Foote (1990). His article (based on a paper presented at the Society of American Archivists in 1985) discussed archives as one of the resources for a society's memory and as a means to combat societal forgetting. Barbara Craig (2002) reviewed selected themes in the literature on memory and their pertinence to archives. Margaret Hedstrom (2010) wrote the most recent and comprehensive review of the challenges which archival theory and practice face from memory studies. Of the many other scholars in archivistics (or archival science) who have dealt with memory and archives, the most important are Schwartz and Cook (2002), Ketelaar (2002; 2005; 2008), Piggott (2005; 2012), Millar (2006), Jimerson (2009), Brothman (2002; 2010) and Josias (2011). Among the studies of particular cases of the nexus between archives, memories and identities are McIntosh (1998), Kaplan (2000), Bastian (2009a; 2009b), Tucker (2009) and Daniel (2010). Examining archives created by totalitarian regimes inevitably entails discussing their role in reshaping collective memories (Harris, 2002; 2007; Ketelaar, 2008 and 2009; Quintana, 2009; Nannelli, 2009; Caswell, 2010; Josias, 2011; Jump, 2012; Van Engen et al., 2012). Studies of community archives are important to understand the interplay between communities and their archives, memories and identities (Flinn, Stevens and Shepherd, 2009; Flinn, 2010; 2011; Moore and Pell, 2010; and Newman, 2011–12).

This summary shows that the literature in the archival domain dates mainly from this century. This is, I believe, because the archival profession (including the growing number of faculty and PhD students in archivistics) only recently came to revisit the agency of archives as societal resources and the agency of archivists as mediators for memories and identities. This fitted in the search, around the turn of the century,

> for the archivist's own identity as a conscious mediator aiding society in forming its own multiple identities through recourse to archival memory and as an active agent protecting evidence in the face of the blistering complexity of rapidly changing societal organizations and digital media.
>
> (Cook, 2013, 113)

Until recently, the archival literature on collective memory was fairly insular and self-referential, as Trond Jacobsen, Ricardo Punzalan and Margaret Hedstrom have demonstrated (Jacobsen, Punzalan and Hedstrom, 2013). They reviewed 165 articles on collective memory published from 1980 to 2010 in the four leading English-language archival journals. These articles referred to 1174 publications; among the 20 most influential only six were written by non-archivists: Derrida, Halbwachs, Lowenthal, Foote, Stoler, and LeGoff.[4]

## 2 Memories

### 2.1 Social frameworks of memory

The French sociologist Maurice Halbwachs was the first to study individual memory in its social context. His book *La Mémoire collective* was published posthumously in 1950. At the time of its writing, mainly during the years 1935 to 1938, it was not customary to speak, even metaphorically, of the memory of a group (Halbwachs, 1980, 50). Frederick Bartlett – the Cambridge psychologist and a contemporary of Halbwachs – wrote about memory *in* the group, rather than memory *of* the group. According to Halbwachs, each individual memory is a viewpoint on the collective memory.[5] In his earlier book, *Les Cadres sociaux de la mémoire* (1925), Halbwachs had developed the thesis that every memory is socially framed: 'no memory is possible outside frameworks used by people living in society to determine and retrieve their recollections' (Halbwachs, 1992, 43).

Collective memory is a metaphor, because a collectivity, a group of people, has no memory itself: the individuals, who make up the collectivity, have a memory. Halbwachs argued:

> While the collective memory endures and draws strength from its base in a coherent body of people, it is individuals as group members who remember.
>
> (Halbwachs, 1980, 48)

Nevertheless, Halbwachs laid 'what might seem excessive emphasis on the collective nature of social consciousness' (Fentress and Wickham, 1992, ix). Thus he paid hardly any attention to the question of how individual consciousness might relate to those of the collectivities that these individuals are members of. Individual memory becomes 'social' through transmission and sharing of experiences and emotions. This, as Halbwachs saw it, is a social process.

## 2.2 Individual memory

Individual memory (the autobiographical memory) fades if it is not supported and nourished in contact with other people or – as we will see – in contact with 'memory texts' (Halbwachs, 1992, 53). One's memory is, as it were, rooted in other people's remembrances, intertwined with the memories of other people. This is clear, even in what is mostly considered to be a reflection of the most personal way of remembering, the diary – particularly the modern blog, but also the traditional paper diary (Piggott, 2003; Van Dijck, 2007). As Annette Kuhn concludes, echoing Halbwachs:

> in all memory texts, personal and collective remembering emerge again and again as continuous with one another … All memory texts … constantly call to mind the collective nature of the activity of remembering.
>
> (Kuhn, 1995, 6)[6]

The first social framework of any individual's memories is constituted by his or her family. Personal memory (remembrance of what one has experienced) is not sealed off from other people's remembrances, from what Halbwachs called social or historical memory (1980, 52). The family, too, has a memory: as with any other collective group the family has 'its memories which it alone commemorates, and its secrets that are revealed only to its members'

(Halbwachs, 1992, 59). Through the family memory the individual is connected with a past that he or she has not experienced. This connectivity is the basis for any culture.

## 2.3 Group memory

Family memory, in turn, is embedded in (and permeated by) larger frameworks of kinship, local and regional memories, religion, nation, etc., even if, as in the case of (im)migrants, the family replaces the nation as the frame of memory and identity (Fortier, 2000). Halbwachs therefore discussed the collective memory of the family first, before he went on to describe religious collective memory and that of social classes.

The memory of a group is not merely the sum of the memories of its members, nor is the memory of an organization only the sum of the memories of its units. Group (or unit) members share memories, tacit knowledge and social cohesion. For example, members of different groups, even within the same organization, often inhabit different social and language worlds (King and Star, 1990). Once the group or unit's information is to be shared with other units within the organization, that information has to be made understandable for outsiders. This is done by formalizing the information, thereby stripping it of information that was meant to stay inside the group.

## 2.4 Collective memory

What we call collective memory is a cultural practice of constructing the self-image of a community. There is no single collective memory. Even if members of a group have experienced what they remember, they neither remember the same things nor do they remember in the same way. The collective memory of the Vietnam War is shared by people who have not experienced that war or the anti-war movement. It is what Alison Landsberg calls a prosthetic memory, a deeply felt memory of a past event through which one did not live but which has been constructed by reading and viewing books, movies and other media (Landsberg, 2004). But the people who did not take part, and even those who did, remember the events differently. Their memories differ according to the nature of the social frameworks in which they functioned then and function now, the groups of which they were a member then and are a member now. This has led Ann

Curthoys to state that 'particular social groups are constructing different "Vietnams"' (Curthoys, 1994, 114). In the same way different people (re)construct a different Holocaust (Rapaport, 1997). To a large extent these differences originate from differences in the way in which media transform the 'historical' Vietnam War and the 'historical' Holocaust into a represented and symbolic Vietnam War and Holocaust.

The collective memory distorts the past, just as the memory of an individual does not store an exact picture of the world. As the neurologist Antonio Damasio explains, the memory you have of someone you met is not stored as a lifelike copy, like a Polaroid picture, but rather as 'dispositions', a set of codings for reactivation or reconstruction that provide 'some kind of image that approximates the image that you actually had in perception' (Damasio and Mulder, 2003, 153).

Many studies of memory are content to describe the representation of the past without bothering to explore the transmission, diffusion and, ultimately, the meaning of this representation (Confino, 1997). However, as Paul Connerton argues, the social formation of memory can be understood only by studying 'those acts of transfer that make remembering in common possible' (Connerton, 1989, 39).

The collective memory is maintained and handed on by written and printed documents and oral traditions, through rituals, ceremonies and other performances (Connerton, 1989), but also in monuments, buildings and even in the landscape itself (Schama, 1995). Through these 'memory texts' the collective memory is construed and found, but also often 'invented', distorted and sometimes even falsified.

The German scholars Jan and Aleida Assmann introduced the term cultural memory (*das kulturelle Gedächtnis*), focusing on the cultural practices 'of transmitting and storing information deemed vital for the constitution and continuation of a specific group' (Assmann, 2010, 43). Sociologist Barbara Misztal defines cultural memory as

> the representation of the past, both that shared by a group and that which is collectively commemorated, that enacts and gives substance to the group's identity, its present conditions and its vision of the future.
>
> (Misztal, 2003, 7)

For Halbwachs, social identities precede collective memories, whereas Benedict Anderson argued that communities construct memories with a view to constructing identity (Megill, 2007, 47; Anderson, 1991).

## 3 Identities

### 3.1 Identification

'Your ID, please', the police officer asks. He or she wants to confirm your identity, by asking for your driving licence, passport or other legal identity card. People identify themselves with documents. If they belong to the *sans papiers*, the undocumented people, life is very difficult indeed. The documents often have an image of the person, mostly literally with a photo or a fingerprint. Identification leads to confirmation of identity that is resemblance to a particular person, but not to confirmation of identity in the sense of individuality, character and personal characteristics (Groebner, 2007; Lyon, 2009).

Who are we? As Franco Ferrarotti wrote, 'We are nothing in an absolute sense. We are only what we have been – more exactly, what we *remember* we were. We are memories personified' (Ferrarotti, 1994, 1; Ferrarotti, 1997, 4; see also Lyman, 1996). This answer shows that he chooses a constructivist approach to the connection between memories and identities. In this approach identities are constructed culturally, and are fluid and multiple. Another view (the essentialist approach) sees identity as intrinsic and fixed (Brubaker and Cooper, 2000; Kaplan 2000; Schwartz and Cook, 2002; Lyon 2009). Both positions view identity as 'real', either as a social construct or as intrinsic to individuals and communities. In both approaches 'identity' risks being reified, making identity some sort of objective entity, whereas

> Both 'collective memory' and 'collective identity' are rather the effects of intersubjective practices of signification, neither given nor fixed but constantly re-created within the framework of marginally contestable rules for discourse.
>
> (Boyarin, 1994, 23)

Brubaker and Cooper (2000) have tried to 'unbundle the thick tangle of meanings that have accumulated around the term "identity"' by proposing three *clusters* of terms: identification and categorization; self-understanding and social location; and commonality, connectedness and groupness. None of these covers the whole spectrum of 'identity', but together they provide an analytical framework for dealing with sameness among members of a group or category, (individual or collective) 'selfhood' and 'groupness' as a product of social or political action.

## 3.2 Social frameworks of identity

'Identities always involve others' (Lyon, 2009, 12). I am a Dutchman, I am one-quarter Frisian, I am grandfather, archivist and educator – and, for the greater part, all these identities have been constructed by memories. These memories function within social frameworks, the first being the family. The stories often repeated in the family enable us to fit into our own experience in a meaningful way. In this way we begin to understand who we understand ourselves to be. Out of the same need, people who were abandoned or adopted in childhood – and others who were victims of ill-treatment or abuse in boarding schools or homes – go in search of records of the institutions that replaced the family as keeper of personal histories. In these places they hope to find the stories and memories that can construct their social identity. There are many other situations that incite people to look for other sources to either affirm or redefine their identity.

Psychologist Nico Frijda suggests that appropriating the past is an element in the construction of an individual's identity. It does so in a dual way, by 'shaping or affirming the identity of one's group, and by accepting or redefining membership within that group' (Frijda, 1997, 109). This argument is shared by James Booth, who argues that 'gathering in' the past, appropriating it, 'gives us identity and a moral narrative of pride, shame, and indebtedness, that ties us across time to *our* past and the burdens this past imposes simply by virtue of being ours' (Booth, 1999, 254).

## 3.3 Collective identity

> What we are faced with – what we are living – is the constitution of both group 'membership' and individual 'identity' out of a dynamically chosen selection of memories, and the constant reshaping, reinvention, and reinforcement of those memories as members contest and create the boundaries and links among themselves.
>
> (Boyarin, 1994, 26)

As with individual identity, collective identity is based on memories, but collective memory also needs collective will and collective interests. 'The cohesion of collective identity must be sustained *through time*, through a collective memory, through lived and shared traditions, through the sense of a common past and heritage,' Morley and Robins (1995) write in their book *Spaces of Identity*.

Whether one is Australian, French, American, British or Canadian, it is impossible to divest oneself from the past, neither on the day of a memorial event like Anzac Day (25 April) or 11 November (Armistice Day in France and Belgium, Veterans Day in the United States and Remembrance Day in the British Commonwealth), nor all the year round, day and night. 'We are in the land of the perpetrators' means for Habermas and other Germans that their 'community of memory' cannot be freed from its Nazi past (Booth, 1999, 258). This presence of our past – as members of different, overlapping communities – is not merely genealogical or traditional: it is not something that you leave behind; the past as 'a foreign country' (Lowenthal, 1985) which you may or may not visit, as you like. The past is a moral imperative for our belonging to a community. The common past, sustained through time into the present, is what gives continuity, cohesion and coherence to a community (Morley and Robins, 1995). To be a family, a community (religious or otherwise) involves an embeddedness in its past. And this past is a living moral presence. A *community of memory* (a term proposed by Peter Burke as early as 1989) is also a community which shares shame and pride in the deeds of its fellow members, and shares its past, for better and for worse (Burke, 1989). The present generation cannot be held responsible for what their fathers and mothers, grandfathers and grandmothers did or did not do. But because they are members of a community of memory, the present generation share pride and shame. They may celebrate or they may apologize and make reparations for what was done by their community (Thompson, 2002).

For many groups the basis for their collective identity is the 'founding trauma', as Dominick LaCapra (2004, 56–7) has called it. This is an event in the past or even in the mythical past that is the centripetal force binding the members of the group. Examples are slavery, the Holocaust, the discrimination of homosexuals, the internment of Japanese Americans and Canadians, and also the death on the Cross, the Resurrection and other traumatic occurrences which are central to religions. Many communities cherish and cultivate their 'founding trauma' by storytelling, not only in the Bible and in the Koran, but also through many other means of memory work. This helps the transmission to future generations and the perpetuation of the community of memory. What is the role of archives in this process?

## 4 Archives

### 4.1 Touchstones of memory

Most studies conflate archives and collective memory (Hedstrom, 2010). However, archives are not *the* cultural or social memory of a community (Taylor, 1995, 11). They are 'among countless different devices used in the process of transforming individual memories into collective remembering' (Millar, 2006, 119). They are, in Verne Harris' words, a sliver of social memory (Harris, 2002). Laura Millar views archives as touchstones upon which memories may be retrieved, preserved and articulated. As Angelika Menne-Haritz (2001, 59) argued, archives do not store memory, but they offer the *possibility* to create memory. Margaret Hedstrom proposes

> Further understanding of the role of archives in collective memory formation depends on placing archival documents in relation to an array of other memory devices and singling out the unique contribution of archives to this process.
>
> (Hedstrom, 2010, 176)

### 4.2 Canon and archive

In Aleida Assmann's schema, cultural memory (see section 2.4) consists of what she formerly used to call functional and storage memory (Ketelaar, 2002), but recently termed the 'canon' and the 'archive' (her quotation marks). Any memory text – artefact, ritual, document or monument – can be part of the archive or of the canon. Assmann writes:

> The active memory of the canon perpetuates what a society has consciously selected and maintains as salient and vital for a common orientation and a shared remembering; its institutions are the literary and visual canon, the school curricula, the museum, and the stage, along with holidays, shared customs, and remembrance days.
>
> (Assmann, 2006, 221; 2010, 43)

The archival memory, on the contrary, lingers in a state of latency – Sam Wineburg (2001, 242–3) uses the term occlusion. It is accessible only to specialists; it is not 'transformed into a living memory supported by public awareness and validation by cultural institutions and the public media' (Assmann, 2006, 221; 2010, 44; see also Robin, 2003, 407–8). Not transformed into a living memory, or not yet, or no longer. The archive's and the canon's memories interact in both directions. And thereby 'cultural memory has an inbuilt capacity for ongoing changes, innovations, transformations, and reconfigurations' (Assmann, 2006, 221; 2010, 44). One is reminded of Pierre Nora's distinction between living memory and archival memory (Nora, 1996).

Although Assmann's 'archive' may be different from the archive as defined in section 1, and although I challenge Assmann's assumption that archival memory can be made dynamic only through permeating the borderline with functional memory, her schema has more merit than I formerly thought (Ketelaar, 2002). In the first place, the archive is neither conflated with cultural memory (Hedstrom, 2010), nor is it seen as something outside cultural memory, because it is conceptualized as one of the components of cultural memory. Also, I now see in her distinction between canon and archive a solution to the problem of how to define the unique qualities of archives as 'touchstones' for memory (Millar, 2006). I will return to this issue in section 4.7, after having discussed four conditions for the archive as a component of cultural memory. These are: inscription and spatiality; meaning making; appropriation; and invention and mediation.

## 4.3 Inscription and spatiality

Assmann's archive is storage memory, controlled by

> systems of recording that function as external means of storage, the most prominent being the technique of writing, which takes memory out of mental storage and fixes it independently of living bearers.
>
> (Assmann, 2011, 328; Ricoeur, 2004, 167)

As Derrida wrote, 'There is no archive without consignation in an external place which assures the possibility of memorization, of repetition, of reproduction, or of reimpression' (Derrida, 1996, 11). On the other hand, in the digital age memory is no longer seen as 'a single measurable capacity' stored away for later retrieval, because (as Laura Millar borrows from psychologist Endel Tulving) the tendency to link memory with storage in a randomly accessible and ever-present electronic 'place' has altered our understanding of the nature of remembering (Millar, 2006, 108). Nevertheless, place or space and inscription are essential: 'you need the space for storage and the mechanism for placing memories in the store correctly and for getting these back clearly and in a useable form' (Craig, 2002, 285).[7]

## 4.4 Meaning making

Identity formation is based on meaning making, as the title of a book by psychologist Urs Fuhrer indicates: *Cultivating Minds: identity as meaning making practice* (Fuhrer, 2004; Craven, 2008; Ketelaar, 2012). Fuhrer views forming an identity as a process that takes place in four mutually constitutive systems: the subject, objects, social partners and the world. Social partners communicate the social context for identity formation. Objects or artefacts interact between the self and her cultural context. This interaction through a medium is called mediation (Verbeek, 2005). These artefacts can be archival documents; social partners can be family members, colleagues or peers. An example is the making of a photo album, either physical, or virtual on Flickr; or arranging one's personal archives, keeping a blog or contributing to Flickr or YouTube or a community such as the one created by the National Archives of the United States with 'Our Archives' (www.ourarchives.wikispaces.net). In all these cases the meanings of information objects are co-created both in the framework of personal experience and in the interaction (of what Van Dijck calls mediated memories) with social partners who surround the blogger or wiki-contributor, with the networks and communities of which archive creator and archive user form a part (Van Dijck, 2007; Johnson, 2008).

## 4.5 Appropriation

Rituals celebrating a national holiday, religious rituals, etc. are living memory, whether celebrated or contested. 'Memory sites … only stay alive as long as people consider it worthwhile to argue about their meaning' (Rigney, 2010, 346; see also Spillman, 2003 and Zerubavel, 2003). To stay (or become) living, memory texts have to be taken possession of for one's own (appropriated), just as heritage exists only through appropriation: a patrimony needs not only a testator and (usually) a will, but also an heir who accepts the conditions and is prepared to cultivate the heritage (Leniaud, 2002). As living signs, memory texts 'must be cultivated to retain their significance; as cultivated objects, things can grow in significance over time and take on new layers of meaning' (Rochberg-Halton, 1986, 170). The rituals in the Netherlands on 4 May, the eve of the Liberation in 1945, today commemorate all people who have died in war or during peacekeeping operations from 1940 to the present day. One sees a comparable extension of meanings on Anzac Day in Australia and New Zealand. In Quebec, Victoria Day (the birthday of Queen Victoria (14 May), now celebrated on the first Monday before 25 May) has been National Patriot's Day since 2003, while elsewhere in Canada the long weekend of Victoria Day marks the end of the skiing season, the beginning of spring.

Archival documents do not constitute memory (Jimerson, 2009, 213). Only when the archive is actually used and activated does it cross the boundary with the canon (see section 4.2) and become part of the *living* and *lived* cultural memory (Steedman, 2001, 68). The archive is a living archive only when it is appropriated by a particular user or a community for a certain purpose. This appropriation is implicit, for example when a historian talks about 'my sources', or explicit when people talk about 'my file', when they mean the file created by a care provider or the immigration services. Ann Rigney writes:

> Meaning as such is never fixed once and for all, but is something that happens in the way events, texts, and other cultural products are appropriated (over and over again, always with a difference).
>
> (Rigney, 2010, 348)

## 4.6 Invention and mediation

Louise Craven notes that 'identity as meaning making is perpetually constructed and reconstructed through the experience of archival documents' (Craven, 2008, 17).

Experiencing archives entails, in Jacques Derrida's words, 'invention': on the one hand, discovering what is already there, and on the other hand, inventing, constituting someone or something (Derrida, 2010, 43). The Latin *invenio* has this double meaning: finding, discovering and inventing, realizing. In that invention the record acquires new meanings that help in structuring and restructuring the relationship between the self and the world.

Archival documents, as so many other artefacts, 'survive in ways unintended by makers and owners to become evidence on which other interpretations of the past can be reconstructed' (Radley, 1990, 58). They are recontextualized in different contexts and activated in a dynamic, open-ended process (Ketelaar, 2008). Invention does not just happen, it involves mediation. Mediation is not only (see section 4.4) experiencing archives through media (or technologies), nowadays, especially, digital technologies. Mediation is also interaction with and intervention by actors involved in definition, selection, organization, interpretation and presentation of meaning (Altheide, 1995; Blouin, 1999).

As to the former mediation: the custodians of both the canon and the archive (see section 4.2) play an active and significant role (Blouin, 1999; Bastian, 2009a, 121): 'their daily imprint on the archival record is inescapable' (Jimerson, 2009, 213). Archives are 'very active sites of constant and multiple possibilities: acquisition and destruction, cultural determinism and challenge, social conformity and opposition, opportunities gained and lost for discovery and repression' (Blouin and Rosenberg, 2011, 160). And the same is true for the canon. One may recall the fight about who should be listed as 'Great Britons' (BBC, 2002).

Technologies of mediation condition not only the form or the structure, but also the content of the record and thereby the memories and identities sustained by the record. As Derrida wrote, 'the mutation in technology changes not simply the archiving process, but what is archivable – that is, the content of what has to be archived is changed by the technology' (Derrida, 1996, 17; 2002, 46). With a mobile phone one creates a text message or picture which both in form and in content will be different from a message sent by e-mail or a message conveyed in a handwritten letter. Memory and media are shaping each other in a complex interplay with social and cultural norms, as José Van Dijck (echoing McLuhan) asserts in her book *Mediated memories* (Van Dijck, 2007). Blogs and social media connect private and public memories and identities, and allow for new experiences and representations of the self and others.

## 4.7 Archives and other memory texts

How to distinguish archives from other 'memory texts' like artefacts, songs, rituals, traditions and a myriad of other non-documentary touchstones (Ketelaar, 2005; Bastian 2009b)? I propose to answer that question by taking as a guide 'The Idea of Uniqueness', a classic essay by historian and archivist James O'Toole (1994). He reviewed four aspects of the uniqueness of an archival document: the physical document itself is unique, or the information it contains is unique, or the process which the record produced is unique, or, fourthly, the uniqueness is derived from the way individual items have been assembled into files, that is, the document in the context of other documents. O'Toole writes:

> If we are to identify uniqueness in some archival records, we must be precise about which of the four distinct characteristics we mean and why, in any particular case, one particular kind of uniqueness is important.
>
> (O'Toole, 1994, 658)

I would argue that of the four parameters the last two are the most important to define the unique qualities of archives as distinct from other memory tools. Archives are unique because of their 'contextual envelope' (Craig, 2002, 287), constituted by the uniqueness of the processes and functions that produced records and by the context of other documents created by the same activity over time. Archives are not unique because the information they contain is unique, and only rarely because the document as artefact has an intrinsic uniqueness. The latter is close to the symbolic significance of a document. O'Toole, in another essay, explored the symbolic nature of archival documents (O'Toole, 1993). His primary question was: 'When does the true significance and meaning of a record derive less from what appears in its surface text and more from its symbolic standing-in for something else?' (O'Toole, 1993, 238). Most archival documents which are venerated as artefacts – from the Magna Carta to the American Declaration of Independence – are not or no longer kept as unique sources of information, but because of their symbolic significance.

Stressing the uniqueness of archives in these contextual terms doesn't necessarily dismiss the archival practice of accepting a different view of 'archival memory texts'. For example, for Andrew Flinn 'the value of an archival document is not best understood as something innate to it, but by the significance invested in it by those who, including the archivist, have created, selected, shaped and used it *as an archive*' (Flinn, 2011, 161; my italics).

I agree that documents – as other cultural artefacts – do not possess an inherent value discernible within the documents themselves (Booms, 1987, 82; McRanor, 1996; Ketelaar, 2001). The value of a record or archive is 'in the eye of the beholder' (Digital Preservation Testbed, 2003). The creator, the user and the archivist alike construct stories which establish for them who they are and who they are not, where they fit in and where they do not, who belongs to them and who does not (Ketelaar, 2012). They find meaning and make meaning in an archive or a record and those meanings help, as I argued (section 4.6), in structuring and restructuring the relationship between the self and the world and thereby in the formation of their identities. However, the constructivist view of the value and meaning of archives should not lead to a blurring of the line between viewing something 'as archive' and an archive(s) 'as it is'.[8] The former is metaphoric, the latter has the unique qualities discussed by O'Toole. Some people think that there is a danger in lumping archives (archival documents) and other memory texts together (see sections 5.1 and 5.3). Kate Eichhorn warns:

> Since the archival turn in the early 1990s, researchers have reconfigured everything from collections of graffiti under highway overpasses to the human genome as types of archives. The plasticity of the concept has opened up new avenues through which to question the authority of the archive while simultaneously legitimizing non-institutional collections as important sites of research and inquiry. However, there is also a danger in the term's over-application. If any collection can be an archive, we risk losing sight of an important distinction between carefully constructed and highly regulated collections that produce 'official' narratives about the past and shape people's lives in the present and random collections of objects and documents that bring pleasure to the collector but have little or no impact on the larger order of things.
>
> (Eichhorn, 2008)

I see this differently. Let anything be 'as archives' and let everyone be an archivist (Ketelaar, 2006b). The question 'What is an archive?' is important for archival theory and methodology, but in practice it is more important to ask 'How does this particular individual or group perceive and understand an archive?' This allows 'locating cultural expressions beneath a wide and all-encompassing umbrella of records and archives' (Bastian, 2013). Whether these have little or no impact on what Eichorn calls 'the larger order of things' is not an essential characteristic of archive(s) 'as it is': created, received and maintained as evidence and/or as an asset by an organization or person, in pursuance of legal obligations or in the transaction of business or for its purposes (ISO 30300, 2011, 3.1.7).

## 5 Archival policies and practices

This section will explore how theories and concepts reviewed in the preceding sections could impact on policies and practices in the formation and keeping of records and archives. I will limit myself to giving some advice and providing some examples of approaches which may enhance the role of archives and archivists (understood in the broad definitions given in section 1) in the construction and transmission of individual and collective memories and identities.

### 5.1 Remembrance

Cultural practices of historical remembrance (to use Jay Winter's term) are not a substitute for archival memory but, rather, a complement to the archive (Winter, 2009; see also Corney, 2010). Americans celebrate Independence Day, on 4 July, to remember the day that the Declaration of Independence was accepted. The document is the basis for the American Dream, 'Life, Liberty and the Pursuit of Happiness'. It is not only America's national treasure; for many Americans it also determines a great part of their identity as American. It is a citizen's duty to make the trip to the National Archives in Washington to take a look at this document. A few years ago tens of thousands of Americans participated in the selection of the hundred most important documents in American history (www.ourdocuments.gov). More than three-quarters of those interviewed called the Declaration of Independence the most influential document in American history. In the USA they honour the Declaration of Independence; in New Zealand they take pride in their founding document, the Treaty of Waitangi between the British Crown and the Maori chiefs from 1840: Waitangi day, 6 February, is to them what 4 July is to the Americans. Even though people may not have seen the document for themselves, its symbolic meaning is of paramount importance: it affirms their identity. Archival policies and practices may capitalize on these ideas and feelings by prominently displaying the documents which their constituencies consider to be founding documents. Those documents could form the core of (face-to-face or virtual) educational programmes, publications, etc. These could be developed in collaboration with communities (see section 5.3).

Furthermore, archives could demonstrate on the web or in displays on the premises how identities are constructed and contested outside the archives but not without the archives. This is because it is in the archives that the documents are kept that form an essential basis for our collective memory, documents that are a touchstone for our self-image. However, it can be risky to consider the archive as a benchmark for identity (Paschild, 2012). It may be better to conceptualize the contribution of archives to processes of identification and categorization; self-understanding and social location; and commonality, connectedness and groupness (see section 3.1). This could entail taking the event inscribed in collective memory as a starting point for remembrance. The Middelburg Commerce Company (MCC) in the Netherlands, between 1732 and 1807, purchased 31,095 enslaved Africans in order to sell them in the West Indies. The Dutch engagement in the slave trade is a painful and shameful heritage. So are the archives of the MCC kept by the Zeeuws Archief (Zeeland Archives) in Middelburg. Only quite recently, the archives received recognition as a 'heritage of belonging' for descendants of the enslaved, and as essential for their identity – but also for Dutch society at large (see also section 5.4). The Zeeuws Archief is engaged in discovering the slaves' 'whispers' in the records and in presenting them to the descendants and to the general public (Kool-Blokland, 2012). In 2011 the MCC archives were recognized by UNESCO as a Memory of the World. The MCC archives will be on centre stage in 2014 at the national commemoration of the abolition of the slave trade in the Netherlands.

In this approach – as in the documentation strategy (see Chapter 2) – the question is how the event is represented in different memory texts (see section 2.4) and to what extent archives have or may have a specific role. Jeannette Bastian (2009a, 119–20) recommends this practice as a way to augment, enhance and contextualize the available records and to fill in undocumented and under-documented spaces. I share her proposition, because it allows us to continue regarding archives/records 'as evidence and/or as an asset by an organization or person, in pursuance of legal obligations or in the transaction of business or for its purposes, regardless of medium, form or format' (ISO 30300, 2011, 3.1.7). Bastian's approach also allows for the embedding of archives/records in a broader ecology of memory texts in whatever form or format. I use the term 'ecology' to stress the interdependence, mutuality and coexistence of archives/records and other memory texts in a societal context (Altheide, 1995). In my view, one should maintain the uniqueness of archives (see section 4.7), rather than name as archives anything which 'is put in an archive or is designated as an archive' (Flinn, 2011, 160). This, however, does not preclude assigning a broadly conceptualized 'archival value' to materials collected by community archives and lacking archival uniqueness (Greene, 2002).

## 5.2 Social frameworks of archives

Archival policies and practices may adopt Halbwachs' theory of the social frameworks of memory by focusing on the social frameworks of archives (see section 2.1). Blogs, social media and even traditional documentary genres question not so much the definition of records (as cited in 5.1 from ISO 30300) but, rather, the demarcation between personal and corporate, or private and public records (Bailey, 2008). A company CEO's blog and a civil servant's tweets may be records, but are they personal or corporate records? The histories recorded in one's personal records – is there still a clear line to draw in a Web 2.0 environment? – belong to 'those public narratives of community, religion, ethnicity and nation which make private identity possible' (Holland and Spence, 1991, 3, 91). Australians have discovered, in the memory work involved in *Bringing Them Home*, that there is no clear division between personal and collective stories, between private and public (Hamilton, 2003). Life stories of Aboriginals are about *we*, rather than *I* and the life stories of the 'stolen generation' have constituted an Australian *lieu de mémoire*, for both Aboriginals and non-Aboriginal Australians (Attwood, 2001; see also McKemmish et al., 2012; Murphy, 2011).

Archival policies and practices through the whole records continuum (Brothman, 2006) should take this nexus between the individual and the group, between public and the private, into account. The website of the National Archives of Australia claims 'Your story, our history'. Indeed, the living histories of individuals and families form part of a larger framework of communities' histories, contributing to local, regional and national identities and those of political, religious and other social groups. Quite natural, therefore, is the National Archives of Australia's contribution to the process following the formal national apology, delivered on 21 March 2013 by the Australian Government, to those affected by forced adoption practices (National Archives of Australia, n.d.). As part of this formal apology the National Archives is developing a website and exhibition to record the experiences of those affected by forced adoption and to increase awareness and understanding of these experiences in the community. Both projects are providing people the opportunity to tell their stories and to help the Australian community to understand and learn from these experiences.

Annette Kuhn reported on her 'memory work', using photographs from her family album and linking them with other public and private memory texts, discovering that an individual's memories

> spread into an extended network of meanings that bring together the personal with the familial, the cultural, the economic, the social, and the historical. Memory work makes it possible to explore connections between 'public' historical events, structures of feeling, family dramas, relations of class, national identity and gender and 'personal' memory.
>
> (Kuhn, 1995, 4)

Kuhn's findings are corroborated by Susanne Tucker's study of album makers and family historians. Scrapbooks and albums contain recontextualized (public and private) records, to be transmitted through time and space. For family history keepers,

> both public and private spaces will keep the records needed for their work, and both will serve as places where their own records can be deposited or willed. Important for archivists are considerations of where and under what circumstances these spaces are located. Clearly all personal archives will not come to repositories, yet they will have a public presence in other ways, and thus when showing family history, will tell a recontextualized history.
>
> (Tucker, 2009, 50–1)

And Tucker proposes various strategies for archivists and archival institutions to (re)claim a voice 'at the table of dynamic memory, in assisting in the development of circumstances that aid more actively in the transmission and pluralization of records' (Tucker, 2009, 265). One of the policies which she advocates is creating electronic spaces shared between family historians and archival institutions. Indeed, archival institutions are challenged to stimulate

> people to upload their documents, comments, stories – texts with meanings – to the memory institution's server, as an addition to the institutional holdings. Not just an addition: an enrichment because by establishing a relationship between private and public documents they become nodes in a network, whose value increases with each addition.
>
> (Ketelaar, 2003, 16)

How this works in an archival setting can be seen, for example, on the *Polar Bear Expedition Digital Collections* site of the Bentley Historical Library in Ann Arbor, conceived by Elizabeth Yakel and her team from the University of Michigan (Krause and Yakel, 2007; Bentley Historical Library, n.d.). Another example is *The People's Collection Wales*, a website which not only draws together the digital collections of heritage institutions in Wales, but is also a place where groups and individuals can share their memory texts. As the Terms and Conditions of Service on the website explain:

> Using virtual scrapbooks, users assemble items that they have found through search or uploaded themselves; these items can be text, images, videos or web links, about anything from paintings through to family history. The items can be assembled in the form of a story, collections, themes and or features. The People's Collection users can make connections with people of similar interests and form online community groups around specific topics with museums, archives and libraries as a continuing space of creativity and communication.
>
> (*People's Collection Wales*)

There are many other ways to connect private and public memories and texts (Yakel, 2011), especially on Facebook, Flickr, YouTube, with wikis and other Web 2.0 applications (Theimer, 2011a; 2011b). The *Archives 2.0* wiki (*Archives 2.0*) provides links to existing projects. Archival institutions could build upon the success of TV programmes such as *Who Do You Think You Are?* which retell the relationships between the familial, private and unique, and the public and universal in new ways (Little, 2011).

Public archives contain memory texts of relevance to private people. Adopted children, patients, clients, prisoners and other record subjects are co-creators involved in the record formation systems of governmental and care institutions (Ketelaar, 2012). This should lead archival institutions 'to adopt a participant model that involves repositioning record subjects as records agents' (*Oxford English Dictionary*: a person who acts upon someone or something; one who or that which exerts power; the doer of an action), as the *Position Statement on Archives and Indigenous Human Rights in Australia* proposes (McKemmish, Faulkhead and Russell, 2011, 109).[9]

Such a participatory archive, as Isto Huvila argued, focuses on participation in the archive not limited to a conversation about a record, but instead using the record 'as a conversation and an arena for participation' (Huvila, 2008, 27).

## 5.3 Communities

The conversation and participation in a participatory archive may well develop into a *community of records*. As proposed by Jeannette Bastian, a community of records may be 'imagined as the aggregate of records in all forms generated by multiple layers of actions and interactions between and among the people and institutions within a community' (Bastian, 2003, 5). Archivists should strive to grow from enablers of, into participants in, these communities of records (Yakel and Torres, 2007, 111). This requires building mutual trust and recognition of mutual rights and interests, as the Australian *Trust & Technology Project* proved (*Trust & Technology Project*, n.d.). A major outcome of the project is the Koorie Archiving System, which 'brings together, integrates, preserves and makes accessible existing records relating to Koorie communities, families and individuals from government, community and personal sources' (McKemmish, Faulkhead, and Russell, 2011, 233).

People identify themselves with social frameworks and are categorized by others as belonging to particular social groupings, to communities of memory which may also be imagined as communities of records. These communities seek inscription and spatiality in archival spaces established and managed either by the community or by mainstream collecting archival institutions (Bastian and Alexander, 2009).

Often a group establishes and uses an archive as a means to confirm its collective identity from its founding trauma (see section 3.3) and to maintain and even defend it to the outside. Flinn, Stevens and Shepherd

> argue that the defining characteristic of community archives is the active participation of a community in documenting and making accessible the history of their particular group and/or locality on their own terms.
>
> (Flinn, Stevens and Shepherd, 2009, 75)

Other characteristics of a community archive are subordinate to the active participation of the community. This also holds good for the sort of material collected by the community archive (see sections 4.7 and 5.1); this is determined by what the community thinks of value for forming, re-creating and transmitting the sense of shared experience and therefore of shared identity.

Apart from independent community archives, mainstream archives are endeavouring to connect communities to their collections (see the many examples provided by the UK Community Archives and Heritage Group[10]). A further strategy (rather than connecting communities to mainstream collections) would be, as Beth Yakel suggests, to focus on building and participating in communities (Yakel, 2011).[11] One could envisage models where mainstream archives and communities assume distributed custody of the communities' memory texts. An example is *Archif Menywod Cymru/Women's Archive of Wales*, which rescues material evidence of women's lives and experiences in Wales and places this in existing repositories (archives, museums, libraries) where it will be documented and preserved to professional standards, and made accessible to the public.[12] In the ecology I suggested (section 5.1), communities may use archives, museums and other memory institutions – be they mainstream or independent – as their spaces of inscription (section 4.3). This might lead to a rethinking of the archival process by involving the communities as equal partners, as suggested by Shilton and Srinivasan (2007). In their model the discussion of appraisal, arrangement, description and provenance is taken to a community level. I consider the archivists' primary contribution to such a holistic endeavour to be in effecting the uniqueness of archives/records (section 4.7) within the larger framework of memory texts.

## 5.4 Changing identities

The canon (see section 4.2) is kept alive by what Nora calls 'commemorative vigilance' (Nora, 1996, 7). If that vigilance fails, for example when the ritual of remembrance is no longer understood and no longer performed, the text goes from the canon into the archive (section 4.2). Migration may go in the opposite direction as well. An archival document can be cultivated as living memory, in many cases as a symbol or a fetish (O'Toole, 1993; Wood, 2000; Lloyd, 2007). Some documents are transferred from the archive, invented as living memory, sometimes to be returned to their latent status at a later stage. For a very long time the Treaty of Waitangi was generally ignored by Pakeha (non-Maori) in New Zealand, but since the 1970s it is recognized as the nation's founding document (www.nzhistory.net.nz). The founding acts of the Netherlands (the *Unie van Utrecht* of 1579, the Peace of Westphalia, the constitution of 1798) were awakened from their archival occlusion only when a centennial was to be celebrated. The acts were 'invented', so to say, and appropriated for the occasion.

Such invention and appropriation happen because of (and are caused by) changing memories and identities. Self-image and self-understanding of a group – identity therefore – are not unchangeable. They change when a community changes and, particularly, when its relation with other communities changes. It is therefore important that mainstream archives venture on the documentation of immigrants and minorities, not only for the benefit of these communities, but also for the mainstream community (Thomson, 2003).

The self-image of a community also changes when the attics of the cultural memory are being cleaned out. Slavery had gone from the cultural memory of most Dutchmen and was hidden in the archival memory – only accessible to specialists. It was only recently that it obtained a place in the official canon of the Netherlands and even in the Memory of the World, because of the registration by UNESCO of the archives of the slave-trading West Indian Company and Middelburg Commerce Company (see section 5.1). But the searchlight is shining on particular aspects of slavery and the slave trade, and these are looked upon in different ways by different groups and generations (see section 2.4). It is the same with the searchlight of archivalization that has to sweep the world for something to light up in the archival sense (Ketelaar, 2001). Archivists should realize that publicizing particular documents (and thus transferring them into the canon) will have effects on the living memories and identities of individuals and groups.

They should be vigilant and ensure that appropriation of archives by a particular group or for a particular cause does not endanger the integrity of the archives and the rights of other users, now and in the future (Cox, 2009; Ketelaar, 2009).

Because a record means various things to different people, across time-space (Nesmith, 2005), the identities which are claimed from and based on a particular archival heritage will be different. Communities are imagined (or constructed) (Anderson, 1991) and determined by a different choice for inclusion in the canon and the archive because of differences in time and place. The present choice of their memory texts will differ from that in the future. What may be relevant to one generation may be obnoxious to the next, and vice versa.

In 2011, together with a group of students of the University of Toronto, I did a research project on the transmission of memories between generations. Case studies showed the differences. The Canadian Lesbian and Gay Archive (CLGA) in Toronto – the largest but one LGBT archive in the world – finds its *raison d'être* in transmitting to younger people stories and texts from the struggle of homosexuals (Hall, 2011; see also Wakimoto, 2012). The Columbus Centre in Toronto obtained a grant of nearly a million dollars from the federal government to found a national archive that documents the internment of Italian Canadians between 1940 and 1943. The student researching this subject wrote:

> As a child of postwar Italian immigrants, I have never felt compelled to seek out the history of Italian Canadians in heritage institutions or repositories. The collective memories of my family's immigrant experience are more vibrant and relevant to me.
>
> (D'Angelo, 2011)

But when future generations lose this contact with those family memories, they will turn to the cultural memory of the community to strengthen their sense of sharing an Italian-Canadian culture:

> Years from now, when descendants of both pre- and postwar Italian immigrants are rediscovering their Italian roots, the Columbus Centre internment archives will provide records for a reinterpreted collective memory.
>
> (D'Angelo, 2011)

## 5.5 Politics of memory

The agency of the archivist in the construction and transmission of cultural memories is frequently overlooked in memory studies that do not take into account (probably do not know) the growing number of studies by scholars of archivistics (Schwartz and Cook, 2002; Jimerson, 2009; Tucker, 2009; Cook, 2011; Harris, 2011). Archival mediation entails appraisal, or assigning value to records, at every stage in the records continuum (Blouin, 1999; Brothman, 2006). Archivists mediate 'competitive and shifting cultural notions of value' (Blouin and Rosenberg, 2011, 153). Archivists – just like museum curators and historians – are always trying to bring documents across the border between dormant and active memory. Although the actors are not politicians, this is identity politics using or misusing cultural memory and cultural heritage (Thomassen, 2011). Archivists hold 'enormous power and discretion over societal memory, deeply masked behind a public image of denial and self-effacement' (Nesmith, 2002, 32).

Like memory, an archive is not just a place for storage, but a process, a mediated social and cultural practice (Ketelaar, 2006a). That process develops in a space. Any archive is a site of trauma and of contestation (Harris, 2000; 2007; Murphy, 2011) where battles about the politics of memory are fought. Because it will continue to be challenged, contested and expanded, the archive will be a living archive that, as I have advocated

> may help members of a community not only to come to grips with their own past but also to acknowledge that the past they share with neighbouring ethnic and political communities is not a monolithic truth, history, or memory, but allows, even requires, questioning and contestation. For this, the archive provides a space.
>
> (Ketelaar, 2009, 123–4)

But the archive is not only a space of contestation, but also, as Michael Moss writes,

> a place of 'dreams', of re-enactment for both the user and the archivist (curator), who together always are engaged either passively or actively in the process of refiguration that is never ending.
>
> (Moss, 2008, 83)

Constructing and reconstructing archival memory and social memory alike is a political act, an act of memory politics (Brown and Davis-Brown, 1998; Thomassen, 2011). The archivist cannot pretend to be outside these politics of memory: he or she is one of the actors who, in the words of Jacques Derrida,

> must practice a politics of memory and, simultaneously, in the same movement, a critique of the politics of memory.
>
> (Derrida and Stiegler, 2002, 63).

## 6 Conclusion

It is critical that archivists comprehend the connections between archives and the construction of individual and collective memories and identities. Such understanding is necessary to interject into *all* dimensions of the records continuum

> a larger social mission into archives and to align archives not only with the preservation of the past and production of history, but with the social causes of accountability, justice, identity formation, and reconciliation.
>
> (Hedstrom, 2010, 173)

Archives are unique because of their provenance, but they are constructs. So are memories and identities, which are imagined, constructed, maintained and transferred within social frameworks. In those processes archives may play a critical role, as touchstones and mostly in conjunction with other artefacts which are considered to be 'as archives'. Nevertheless, archive(s) 'as it is' have a unique quality and it is the archivist's calling to advocate that uniqueness benefiting many if not most processes of 'meaning making' leading to identification and categorization; self-understanding and social location; and commonality, connectedness and groupness. These identities are rooted in memories, and these memories need inscription and space. Both inscription and space will increasingly be 'located' 'in the cloud' and maintained (in distributed custody) by individuals, groups and memory institutions. Together they are actors in an ecology which comprises archives/records and other memory texts in a societal context. For archivists, this means a lot: partnerships with communities and professionals in other memory institutions; endeavouring to contribute to new forms of Web 2.0

and participatory archiving; and embracing a paradigm shift on the horizon, which Terry Cook labels *Community*, enriching 'our own identity as archivists, transformed to be relevant actors out in our society's communities more than proficient professionals behind the walls of our own institutions' (Cook, 2013, 116).

## Notes

1 I refrain from distinguishing between records and archives. Sir Hilary Jenkinson – that paragon of English archival methodology – warned in 1958 against 'flirting ... with Dr. Schellenberg and his arbitrary distinction between Records and Archives' (Jenkinson, 1980, 352).
2 From the website of *Identity: An International Journal of Theory and Research*, www.tandfonline.com/action/journalInformation?show=aimsScope&journalCode=hidn20#.UlgejoZJNzg.
3 From the website of the journal *Memory Studies*, http://mss.sagepub.com/.
4 Jacobsen, Punzalan and Hedstrom (2013, p. 228) mention five non-archivists, but they have accidentally classed Foote as an archivist.
5 In the English translation (Halbwachs, 1980, 48) the word 'individual' is missing.
6 Kuhn uses 'memory texts' in a narrower sense than I do in this chapter.
7 The Amsterdam city archives used as an inscription medium a computer installed in a travelling trunk that travelled among migrant organizations in Amsterdam. This facilitated migrant organizations in creating an archive of their memories that can be shared among community members; secondly, it acquired memories to be stored in the municipal archives (Vos and Ketelaar, 2007).
8 I borrow this distinction from Diana Taylor, *The Archive and the Repertoire. Performing cultural memory in the Americas*, Duke University Press, 2003, 3.
9 Archives could do more: see the special issues Archives and the Ethics of Memory Construction, *Archival Science*, **11** (2011) 1–168, and Archives, Identity, and Survivors of Out-of-home Care, *Archives and Manuscripts*, **40** (2012), 1–67.
10 Community Archives and Heritage Group, www.communityarchives.org.uk/index.aspx.
11 See for example the 'Archive Ambassadors' who were trained to act as important links between the local communities of Hampshire and the Isle of

Wight and the local record offices: www3.hants.gov.uk/archives/community-archives/archives-ambassador.htm.

12 The Women's Archive of Wales (www.womensarchivewales.org) is linked to the *People's Collection Wales* (see section 5.2). Another example is the Dutch Jewish Monument Community: by uploading pictures, information and stories about persons and families, people build this monument, together with the Jewish Historical Museum in Amsterdam: www.communityjoodsmonument.nl/?lang=en.

## References and further reading

Altheide, D. L. (1995) *An Ecology of Communication: cultural formats of control*, Aldine de Gruyter.

Anderson, B. (1991) *Imagined Communities: reflections on the origin and spread of nationalism*, 2nd edn, Verso.

*Archives 2.0*, http://archives2point0.wetpaint.com.

Assmann, A. (2006) Memory, Individual and Collective. In Goodin, R. E. and Tilly, C. (eds), *The Oxford Handbook of Contextual Political Analysis*, Oxford University Press, 210–24.

Assmann, A. (2010) Re-framing Memory: between individual and collective forms of constructing the past. In Tilmans, K., Van Vree, F. and Winter, J. (eds), *Performing the Past: memory, history and identity in modern Europe*, Amsterdam University Press, 35–50.

Assmann, A. (2011) *Cultural Memory and Western Civilization: functions, media, archives*, Cambridge University Press.

Attwood, B. (2001) Learning about the Truth: the stolen generations narrative. In Attwood, B. and Magowan, F. (eds), *Telling Stories: indigenous history and memory in Australia and New Zealand*, Bridget Williams Books, 183–212.

Bailey, S. (2008) *Managing the Crowd: rethinking records management for the Web 2.0 world*, Facet Publishing.

Bastian, J. (2003) *Owning Memory: how a Caribbean community lost its archives and found its history*, Libraries Unlimited.

Bastian, J. (2009a) Flowers for Homestead: a case study in archives and collective memory, *American Archivist*, **72**, 113–32.

Bastian, J. (2009b) 'Play Mas': carnival in the archives and the archives in carnival: records and community identity in the US Virgin Islands, *Archival Science*, **9**, 113–25.

Bastian, J. (2013) The Records of Memory, the Archives of Identity: celebrations, texts and archival sensibilities, *Archival Science*, **13**, 121–31.

Bastian, J. and Alexander, B. (eds) (2009) *Community Archives: the shaping of memory*, Facet Publishing.

BBC (2002) *BBC TWO Reveals the Nation's Top 100 Greatest Britons of All Time*, www.bbc.co.uk/pressoffice/pressreleases/stories/2002/08_august/21/100_britons.shtml.

Bentley Historical Library (n.d.) *Polar Bear Expedition Digital Collections*, http://quod.lib.umich.edu/p/polaread/about.html.

Blouin, F. (1999) Archivists, Mediation, and Constructs of Social Memory, *Archival Issues*, **24**, 101–12.

Blouin, F. X. and Rosenberg, W. (2011) *Processing the Past: contesting authority in history and the archives*, Oxford University Press.

Booms, H. (1972[1987]) Society and the Formation of a Documentary Heritage: issues in the appraisal of archival sources, *Archivaria*, **24**, 69–107. Trans. H. Joldersma and R. Klumpenhouwer. Originally published as: Gesellschafsordnung und Überlieferungsbildung: Zur Problematik archivarischer Quellenbewertung, *Archivalische Zeitschrift*, **68** (1972), 3–40.

Booth, W. J. (1999) Communities of Memory: on identity, memory, and debt, *American Political Science Review*, **93**, 249–63.

Boyarin, J. (1994) Space, Time and the Politics of Memory. In Boyarin, J. (ed.), *Remapping Memory: the politics of timespace*, University of Minnesota Press, 1–38.

Brothman, B. (2002) The Past that Archives Keep: memory, history, and the preservation of archival records, *Archivaria*, **51**, 48–80.

Brothman, B. (2006) Archives, Life Cycles, and Death Wishes: a helical model of record formation, *Archivaria*, **61**, 235–69.

Brothman, B. (2010) Perfect Present, Perfect Gift: finding a place for archival consciousness in social theory, *Archival Science*, **10**, 141–89.

Brown, R. H. and Davis-Brown, B. (1998) The Making of Memory: the politics of archives, libraries and museums in the construction of national consciousness, *History of the Human Sciences*, **11** (4), 17–32.

Brubaker, R. and Cooper, F. (2000) Beyond 'Identity', *Theory and Society*, **29**, 1–47.

Burke, P. (1989) History as Social Memory. In Butler, T. (ed.), *Memory: history, culture, and the mind*, Basil Blackwell, 97–113.

Caswell, M. (2010) Khmer Rouge Archives: accountability, truth, and memory in Cambodia, *Archival Science*, **10**, 25–44.

Confino, A. (1997) Collective Memory and Cultural History: problems of method,

*American Historical Review*, **102**, 1386–403.

Connerton, P. (1989) *How Societies Remember*, Cambridge University Press.

Cook, T. (2011) The Archive(s) Is a Foreign Country: historians, archivists, and the changing archival landscape, *American Archivist*, **74**, 600–32.

Cook, T. (2013) Evidence, Memory, Identity, and Community: four shifting archival paradigms, *Archival Science*, **13**, 95–120.

Corney, F. C. (2010) Remembering Communism in Modern Russia: archives, memoirs, and lived experience. In Todorova, M. (ed.), *Remembering Communism: genres of representation*, Social Science Research Council, 237–52.

Cox, R. J. (2009) The Archivist and Community. In Bastian, J. A. and Alexander, B. (eds), *Community Archives: the shaping of memory*, Facet Publishing, 251–64.

Craig, B. L. (2002) Selected Themes on the Literature on Memory and Their Pertinence to Archives, *American Archivist*, **65**, 276–89.

Craven, L. (2008) From the Archivist's Cardigan to the Very Dead Sheep: what are archives? What are archivists? What do they do? In Craven, L. (ed.), *What Are Archives? Cultural and theoretical perspectives: a reader*, Ashgate, 7–30.

Curthoys, A. (1994) 'Vietnam': public memory of an anti-war movement. In Darian-Smith, K. and Hamilton, P. (eds), *Memory and History in Twentieth-century Australia*, Oxford University Press.

Damasio, A. and Mulder, A. (2003) The Memory as Living Archive. Interview with Antonio Damasio. In Brouwer, J., Mulder, A. and Charlton, S. (eds), *Information Is Alive: art and theory on archiving and retrieving data*, V2_Publishing/NAI Publishers.

D'Angelo, A. (2011) Community Archives Case Study: Italian Canadians as enemy aliens: memories of WWII. Unpublished paper, School of Information, University of Toronto.

Daniel, D. (2010) Documenting the Immigrant and Ethnic Experience in American Archives, *American Archivist*, **73**, 82–104.

Derrida, J. (1996) *Archive Fever*, trans. E. Prenowitz, University of Chicago Press.

Derrida, J. (2002) Archive Fever: a seminar . . . In Hamilton, C. et al. (eds), *Refiguring the Archive*, Kluwer Academic Publishers, 38–80.

Derrida, J. (2010) *Copy, Archive, Signature: a conversation on photography*, ed. G. Richter, trans. H. Fort, Stanford University Press.

Derrida, J. and Stiegler, B. (2002) *Echographies of Television. Filmed interviews*, Polity Press.

Digital Preservation Testbed (2003) *White Paper Emulation: context and current status.*

Eichhorn, K. (2008) Archival Genres: gathering texts and reading spaces, *Invisible*

*Culture*, http://ivc.lib.rochester.edu/.

Elliott, A. (ed.) (2011) *Routledge Handbook of Identity Studies*, Routledge.

Erll, A., Nünning, A. and Young, S. B. (eds) (2008) *Cultural Memory Studies: an international and interdisciplinary handbook*, Walter de Gruyter.

Fentress, J. and Wickham, C. (1992) *Social Memory: new perspectives on the past*, Blackwell.

Ferrarotti, F. (1994) *The Temptation to Forget: racism, anti-Semitism, neo-Nazism*, Greenwood Press.

Ferrarotti, F. (1997) *L'Italia tra storia e memoria: appartenenza e identità*, 2nd edn, Donzelli.

Flinn, A. (2010) 'An Attack on Professionalism and Scholarship'? Democratising archives and the production of knowledge, *Ariadne*, **62**, www.ariadne.ac.uk/issue62/flinn/.

Flinn, A. (2011) The Impact of Independent and Community Archives on Professional Archival Thinking and Practice. In Hill, J. (ed.), *The Future of Archives and Recordkeeping: a reader*, Facet Publishing, 145–69.

Flinn, A., Stevens, M. and Shepherd, E. (2009) Whose Memories, Whose Archives? Independent community archives, autonomy and the mainstream, *Archival Science*, **9**, 71–86.

Foote, K. E. (1990) To Remember and Forget: archives, memory, and culture, *American Archivist*, **53**, 378–92.

Fortier, A. M. (2000) *Migrant Belongings: memory, space, identity*, Berg.

Frijda, N. H. (1997) Commemorating. In Pennebaker, J. W., Paez, D. and Rimé, B. (eds), *Collective Memory of Political Events: social psychological perspectives*, Lawrence Erlbaum, 103–27.

Fuhrer, U. (2004) *Cultivating Minds: identity as meaning making practice*, Routledge.

Greene, M. (2002) The Power of Meaning: the archival mission in the postmodern age, *American Archivist*, **65**, 42–55.

Groebner, V. (2007) *Who Are You? Identification, deception and surveillance in early modern Europe*, Zone Books.

Halbwachs, M. (1980) *The Collective Memory*, trans. F. J. Ditter and V. Y. Ditter, Harper & Row. Orig. edn *La Mémoire Collective*, Presses Universitaires de France, 1950. The newest critical edition is: *La Mémoire Collective*, ed. G. Namer, Albin Michel, 1997.

Halbwachs, M. (1992) *On Collective Memory*, ed. L. A. Coser, University of Chicago Press (translated abstracts from: M. Halbwachs (1925) *Les Cadres Sociaux de la Mémoire*, Librairie Alcan). The newest critical edition is: *Les Cadres Sociaux de la*

*Mémoire*, ed. G. Namer, Albin Michel, 1994.

Hall, R. (2011) Selected Issues in the Transfer of Collective Memory at the Canadian Lesbian and Gay Archive (CLGA). Unpublished paper, School of Information, University of Toronto.

Hamilton, P. (2003) Memory Studies and Cultural History. In Teo, H. M. and White, R. (eds), *Cultural History in Australia*, New South Wales University Press.

Harris, V. (2000) *Exploring Archives: an introduction to archival ideas and practice in South Africa*, 2nd edn, National Archives of South Africa.

Harris, V. (2002) The Archival Sliver: power, memory, and archives in South Africa, *Archival Science*, **2**, 63–86.

Harris, V. (2007) *Archives and Justice: a South African perspective*, Society of American Archivists.

Harris, V. (2011) Ethics and the Archive: 'an incessant movement of recontextualisation'. In Cook, T. (ed.), *Controlling the Past: documenting society and institutions. Essays in honor of Helen Willa Samuels*, Society of American Archivists, 345–62.

Hedstrom, M. (2002) Archives, Memory, and Interfaces with the Past, *Archival Science*, **2**, 21–43.

Hedstrom, M. (2010) Archives and Collective Memory: more than a metaphor, less than an analogy. In Eastwood, T. and MacNeil, H. (eds), *Currents of Archival Thinking*, Libraries Unlimited, 163–79.

Holland, P. and Spence, J. (1991) *Family Snaps: the meanings of domestic photography*, Virago.

Huvila, I. (2008) Participatory Archive: towards decentralised curation, radical user orientation, and broader contextualisation of records management, *Archival Science*, **8**, 15–36.

ICA (1996) *Code of Ethics*, International Council on Archives, www.ica.org/download.php?id=574.

ISO 30300 (2011) *Information and Documentation: Records Management. Part 2: Guidelines*, International Organization for Standardization.

Jacobsen, T., Punzalan, R. and Hedstrom, M. (2013) Invoking Collective Memory: mapping the emergence of a concept in archival studies, *Archival Science*, **13**, 217–51.

Jenkinson, H. (1980) The Problems of Nomenclature in Archives. In Ellis, R. H. and Walne, P. (eds), *Selected Writings of Sir Hilary Jenkinson*, Alan Sutton, 349–60 (first published in *Journal of the Society of Archivists*, **1** (1958), 233–9).

Jimerson, R. C. (2009) *Archives Power: memory, accountability, and social justice*, Society of American Archivists.

Johnson, A. (2008) Users, Use and Context: supporting interaction between users and digital archive. In Craven, L. (ed.), *What Are Archives? Cultural and theoretical perspectives: a reader*, Ashgate, 154–5.

Josias, A. (2011) Toward an Understanding of Archives as a Feature of Collective Memory, *Archival Science*, **11**, 95–112.

Jump, M. (2012) The Role of Archives in the Movement for the Recovery of Historical Memory in Spain. La Rioja: a regional case study, *Journal of the Society of Archivists*, **33**, 149–66.

Kaplan, E. (2000) We Are What We Collect, We Collect What We Are: archives and the construction of identity, *American Archivist*, **63** (1), 126–51.

Ketelaar, E. (2001) Tacit Narratives: the meanings of archives, *Archival Science*, **1**, 143–55.

Ketelaar, E. (2002) The Archive as a Time Machine. In *Proceedings of the DLM-Forum 2002: access and preservation of electronic information: best practices and solutions, Barcelona, 6–8 May 2002, INSAR European Archives News*, Supplement VII, 576–81.

Ketelaar, E. (2003) Being Digital in People's Archives, *Archives and Manuscripts*, **31**, 8–22.

Ketelaar, E. (2004) The Future Contained in Time Past: archival science in the 21st century, *Journal of the Japan Society for Archival Science*, **1**, 20–35.

Ketelaar, E. (2005) Sharing: collected memories in communities of records, *Archives and Manuscripts*, **33**, 44–61.

Ketelaar, E. (2006a) Writing on Archiving Machines. In Neef, S., Van Dijck, J. and Ketelaar, E. (eds), *Sign Here! Handwriting in the age of new media*, Amsterdam University Press, 183–95.

Ketelaar, E. (2006b) Everyone an Archivist. In Bütikofer, N., Hofman, H. and Ross, S. (eds), *Managing and Archiving Records in the Digital Era: changing professional orientations*, hier + jetzt, Verlag für Kultur und Geschichte, 9–14.

Ketelaar, E. (2008) Archives as Spaces of Memory, *Journal of the Society of Archivists*, **29**, 9–27.

Ketelaar, E. (2009) A Living Archive, Shared by Communities of Records. In Bastian, J. A. and Alexander, B. (eds), *Community Archives: the shaping of memory*, Facet Publishing, 109–32. A slightly different version is Ketelaar, E. (2012) Truths, Memories, and Histories in the Archives of the International Criminal Tribunal for the Former Yugoslavia. In van der Wilt, H. G., Vervliet, J., Sluiter, G. K. and Houwink ten Cate, J. Th. M. (eds), *The Genocide Convention: the legacy of 60 years*, Brill, 201–21.

Ketelaar, E. (2012) Cultivating Archives, *Archival Science*, **11**, 19–33.

King, J. L. and Star, J. L. (1990) Conceptual Foundations for the Development of Organizational Decision Support Systems, *Proceedings of the Hawaii International Conference on Systems Science*, 143–51.

Kool-Blokland, H. (2012) Silent Witnesses, *Het archief van de Middelburgse Commercie Compagnie als werelderfgoed*, Master in Archivistics thesis, University of Amsterdam, www.scriptiesonline.uba.uva.nl.

Krause, M. G. and Yakel, E. (2007) Interaction in Virtual Archives: The Polar Bear Expedition Digital Collections Next Generation Finding Aid, *American Archivist*, **70**, 282–314.

Kuhn, A. (1995) *Family Secrets: acts of memory and imagination*, Verso.

LaCapra, D. (2004) *History in Transit: experience, identity, critical theory*, Cornell University Press.

Landsberg, A. (2004) *Prosthetic Memory: the transformation of American remembrance in the age of mass culture*, Columbia University Press.

Leniaud, J. M. (2002) *Les Archipels du Passé: le patrimoine et son histoire*, Fayard.

Little, H. (2011) Identifying the Genealogical Self, *Archival Science*, **11**, 241–52.

Lloyd, A. (2007) Guarding against Collective Amnesia? Making significance problematic: an exploration of issues, *Library Trends*, **56**, 53–65.

Lowenthal, D. (1985) *The Past Is a Foreign Country*, Cambridge University Press.

Lyman, S. M. (1996) Some Dilemmas of History and Memory, *International Journal of Politics, Culture and Society*, **9**, 623–35.

Lyon, D. (2009) *Identifying Citizens: ID cards as surveillance*, Polity Press.

McIntosh, R. (1998) The Great War, Archives, and Modern Memory, *Archivaria*, **46**, 1–31.

McKemmish, S., Faulkhead, S. and Russell, L. (2011) (eds) Distrust in the Archive: reconciling records, *Archival Science*, **11**, 211–39.

McKemmish, S., Russell, L., Castan, M. and Iacovino, L. (2012) Editor's Introduction to Keeping Cultures Alive: archives and indigenous human rights, *Archival Science*, **12**, 93–111.

McRanor, S. (1996) A Critical Analysis of Intrinsic Value, *American Archivist*, **59**, 400–11.

Megill, A. (2007) *Historical Knowledge, Historical Error: a contemporary guide to practice*, University of Chicago Press.

Menne-Haritz, A. (2001) Access – the Reformulation of an Archival Paradigm, *Archival Science*, **1**, 57–82.

Millar, L. (2006) Touchstones: considering the relationship between memory and archives, *Archivaria*, **61**, 105–26.

Misztal, B. A. (2003) *Theories of Social Remembering*, Open University Press.

Moore, S. and Pell, S. (2010) Autonomous Archives, *International Journal of Heritage Studies*, **16** (4–5), 255–68.

Morley, D. and Robins, K. (1995) *Spaces of Identity: global media, electronic landscapes, and cultural boundaries*, Routledge.

Moss, M. (2008) Opening Pandora's Box: what is an archive in the digital environment? In Craven, L. (ed.), *What Are Archives? Cultural and theoretical perspectives: a reader*, Ashgate, 71–87.

Murphy, F. (2011) Archives of Sorrow: an exploration of Australia's stolen generations and their journey into the past, *History and Anthropology*, **22**, 481–95.

Nannelli, E. (2009) Memory, Records, History: the records of the Commission for Reception, Truth, and Reconciliation in Timor-Leste, *Archival Science*, **9**, 29–41.

National Archives of Australia (n.d.) *Forced Adoptions History Project*, www.naa.gov.au/about-us/partnerships/forced-adoptions.aspx.

Nesmith, T. (2002) Seeing Archives: postmodernism and the changing intellectual place of archives, *American Archivist*, **65**, 24–41.

Nesmith, T. (2005) Reopening Archives: bringing new contextualities into archival theory and practice, *Archivaria*, **60**, 259–74.

Newman, J. (2011–12) Sustaining Community Archives, *Archifacts*, October 2011–April 2012, 11–24.

Nora, P. (1996) General Introduction: between memory and history. In Nora, P. (ed.), *Realms of Memory: rethinking the French past* [on the jacket: *The construction of the French past*], I. Conflicts and divisions, trans. A. Goldhammer, Columbia University Press.

O'Toole, J. M. (1993) The Symbolic Significance of Archives, *American Archivist*, **56**, 234–55. Reprinted in Jimerson, R. C. (ed.), (2000) *American Archival Studies. Readings in theory and practice*, Society of American Archivists, 47–72.

O'Toole, J. M. (1994) On the Idea of Uniqueness, *American Archivist*, **57**, 632–58. Reprinted in Jimerson, R. C. (ed.), (2000) *American Archival Studies. Readings in theory and practice*, Society of American Archivists, 245–77.

Paschild, C. N. (2012) Community Archives and the Limitations of Identity: considering discursive impact on material needs, *American Archivist*, **75**, 125–42.

*People's Collection Wales*, www.peoplescollectionwales.co.uk.

Piggott, M. (2003) The Diary: social phenomenon, professional challenge, *Archives and Manuscripts*, **31**, 83–90.

Piggott, M. (2005) Archives and Memory. In McKemmish, S., Piggott, M., Reed, B.

and Upward, F. (eds), *Archives: recordkeeping in society*, Charles Sturt University, 299–328.

Piggott, M. (2012) *Archives and Societal Provenance: Australian essays*, Chandos Publishing.

Quintana, A. G. (2009) *Archival Policies in the Protection of Human Rights*, International Council on Archives, www.ica.org/download.php?id=971.

Radley, A. (1990) Artefacts, Memory and a Sense of the Past. In Middleton, D. and Edwards, D. (eds), *Collective Remembering*, Sage, 46–59.

Rapaport, L. (1997) *Jews in Germany after the Holocaust: memory, identity, and Jewish-German relations*, Cambridge University Press.

Ricoeur, P. (2004) *Memory, History, Forgetting*, trans. K. Blamey and D. Pellauer, University of Chicago Press.

Rigney, A. (2010) The Dynamics of Remembrance: texts between monumentality and morphing. In Erll, A. and Nünning, A. (eds), *A Companion of Cultural Memory Studies*, Walter de Gruyter, 345–53.

Robin, R. (2003) *La Mémoire Saturée*, Stock.

Rochberg-Halton, E. (1986) *Meaning and Modernity: social theory in the pragmatic attitude*, University of Chicago Press.

Schama, S. (1995) *Landscape and Memory*, Harper Collins.

Schwartz, J. and Cook, T. (2002) Archives, Records, and Power: the making of modern memory, *Archival Science*, **2**, 1–19.

Shilton, K. and Srinivasan, R. (2007) Participatory Appraisal and Arrangement for Multicultural Archival Collections, *Archivaria*, **63**, 87–101.

Spillman, L. (2003) When Do Collective Memories Last? Founding moments in the United States and Australia. In Olick, J. (ed.), *States of Memory: continuities, conflicts, and transformations in national retrospection*, Duke University Press, 161–92.

Steedman, C. (2001) *Dust*, Manchester University Press.

Taylor, H. (1995) Heritage Revisited: documents as artifacts in the context of museums and material culture, *Archivaria*, **40**, 8–20.

Theimer, K. (2011a) Interactivity, Flexibility and Transparency: social media and Archives 2.0. In Hill, J. (ed.), *The Future of Archives and Recordkeeping: a reader*, Facet Publishing, 123–43.

Theimer, K. (ed.) (2011b) *A Different Kind of Web: new connections between archives and our users*, Society of American Archivists.

Thomassen, T. (2001) A First Introduction to Archival Science, *Archival Science*, **1**, 373–85.

Thomassen, T. (2011) *Archiefwetenschap, erfgoed en politisering*, Amsterdam

University Press, http://dare.uva.nl/aup/en/record/374809.

Thompson, J. (2002) *Taking Responsibility for the Past: reparation and historical justice*, Polity Press.

Thomson, A. (2003) 'The Empire Was a Bar of Soap': life stories and race identity among British emigrants travelling to Australia, 1945–71. In Teo, H. M. and White, R. (eds), *Cultural History in Australia*, New South Wales University Press, 201–13.

*Trust & Technology Project* (n.d.), http://infotech.monash.edu/research/about/centres/cosi/projects/trust/.

Tucker, S. (2009) The Most Public of All History: family history and heritage albums in the transmission of records. PhD thesis, University of Amsterdam. http://dare.uva.nl/record/325290.

UNESCO (2002) *Memory of the World General Guidelines to Safeguard Documentary Heritage*, http://unesdoc.unesco.org/images/0012/001256/125637e.pdf.

Van Dijck, J. (2007) *Mediated Memories in the Digital Age*, Stanford University Press.

Van Engen, H., Janssens, G., Kwanten, G. and Pompe, K. M. (eds) (2012) *Archives without Borders/Archivos sin Fronteras. Proceedings of the International Congress in The Hague, August 30–31, 2010/Actas del Congreso Internacional en La Haya, 30–31 de agosto, 2010*, Vlaamse Vereniging voor bibliotheek, archief & documentatie.

Verbeek, P. P. (2005) *What Things Do: philosophical reflections on technology, agency, and design*, Pennsylvania State University Press.

Vos, V. J. and Ketelaar, E. (2007) Amsterdam Communities' Memories: research into how modern media can be applied to archive community. In Stillman, L. and Johanson, G. (eds), *Memory Constructing and Sharing Memory: Community Informatics, Identity and Empowerment: Selected papers from the 3rd Prato International Community Informatics Conference; Community Informatics Research Network 9–11 October 2006*, Cambridge Scholars Publishing, 330–42.

Wakimoto, D. K. (2012) Queer Community Archives in California since 1950. PhD thesis, Queensland University of Technology, http://eprints.qut.edu.au/53189/1/Diana_Wakimoto_Thesis.pdf.

Wineburg, S. (2001) *Historical Thinking and Other Unnatural Acts: charting the future of teaching the past*, Temple University Press.

Winter, J. (2009) Historians and Sites of Memory. In Boyer, P. and Wertsch, J. V. (eds), *Memory in Mind and Culture*, Cambridge University Press, 252–68.

Wood, H. (2000) The Fetish of the Document: an exploration of attitudes towards archives. In Procter, M. and Lewis, C. P. (eds), *New Directions in Archival Research*, Liverpool University Centre for Archive Studies, 20–48.

Yakel, E. (2011) Who Represents the Past? Archives, records, and the social web. In Cook, T. (ed.), *Controlling the Past: documenting society and institutions. Essays in honor of Helen Willa Samuels*, Society of American Archivists, 257–78.

Yakel, E. and Torres, D. A. (2007) Genealogists as a 'Community of Records', *American Archivist*, **70**, 93–113.

Zerubavel, E. (2003) Calendars and History: a comparative study of the social organization of national memory. In Olick, J. (ed.), *States of Memory: continuities, conflicts, and transformations in national retrospection*, Duke University Press, 315–37.

CHAPTER 6

# Under the influence: the impact of philosophy on archives and records management

Rachel Hardiman

## 1 Introduction: scope and emphasis

The other chapters of this book have examined some of the rich and evolving body of theory developed within the recordkeeping disciplines and professions. The purpose of this chapter is to outline the ways in which philosophies and theories from beyond the bounds of recordkeeping have influenced 'our' discourses and practices. It aims to consider the lineage of ideas that have had an impact on our thinking in the context of the broader streams of Western thought from which they have been adopted.

To cover the vast potential area of this topic is clearly impossible in the scope of a single chapter. What is presented here will be cursory, highly selective and greatly simplified; it is pitched at the level of 'big-picture' philosophy rather than models and techniques, which necessarily serves to de-emphasize the considerable influence of the more technocratic borrowings from business and information science. Its treatment of historiography, a fundamental external influence, is minimalist. It suffers from various severe parochialisms – for instance, it is based primarily on academic and professional journal literature and refers almost exclusively to English-language publications.

While, in one sense, philosophy applies to all aspects of records and archives, just as it applies to all aspects of life in general, it has been brought to bear more specifically on a number of issues, many of long standing but some more directly linked to recent social, cultural and technological developments. The most basic aspects of recordkeeping depend on a number of concepts and assumptions about how we interact with the world – whether there is an external reality to which we can gain direct or even indirect access; whether our modes of expression and communication (including records) can adequately represent the acts and thoughts of which they are traces, whether the record is as much a means of structuring or even of creating 'reality' as it is of representing it.

This chapter starts its journey with Immanuel Kant (section 2), whose inauguration of modern philosophy brings all of these things to the fore, along with other perennial questions relating to the way that human beings live or should live within society and the need to balance or reconcile competing social and individual needs and desires. The limits of freedom; the formation and recognition of individual and collective identities; the conflicting drives of reason and instinct, altruism and self-interest; the complex roots of and desire for memory and forgetting; the workings, use and misuse of power – all of these have been explored in great depth and subtlety within a wide variety of philosophical frameworks. A number of these have already been mentioned in earlier chapters: perhaps the most familiar to our disciplines in recent times are figures such as Jacques Derrida and Michel Foucault, with their postmodernist perspectives on meaning, justice and power and on the prominent literal and metaphorical role of recording and archiving within this context. However, our literature bears witness to many instances where the philosophical and theoretical traditions have been explored for the light they can throw on theory and practice: sometimes, philosophy has entered into the company of more familiar visitors such as historiography or organizational studies; sometimes it has been admitted in its own right, in the person perhaps of Jeremy Bentham and his concepts of evidence, or of Paul Ricoeur and his investigation of time and memory. Despite the stereotype of philosophy as remote and cerebral, it is also at the heart of the activist traditions relating to social justice, recognition and inclusiveness that increasingly motivate our disciplinary discourse.

Some brief notes on terminology: firstly, to avoid unwieldy and repetitive phraseology, I shall from now on use the acronym ARK (Archives and Recordkeeping) as a stand-in for 'archives and records discipline(s), profession(s) and practice(s)'. Secondly, the terms 'philosophy' and 'theory' are used interchangeably, as is common practice in the humanistic disciplines. Thirdly, when referring to history and historiography, I will use 'history' to mean narratives or analyses about the past and 'historiography' to mean the theory and principles of 'history'. Finally, the term 'postmodernism' is so ill-defined that it is often used to refer to a very wide range of theoretical positions – in section 7.3.2 I use the term more narrowly (excluding poststructuralism, for instance).

I have made a conscious decision to minimize references and footnotes but have included suggestions for further reading throughout. Since the purpose of this chapter is to introduce a topic of which no prior knowledge on the part of the reader is assumed, the sources used are general rather than detailed, technical or academic. There are many examples available of the adoption of theory for use within ARK, but only a handful can be reflected here. I have tried to ensure that the works cited give a sense of the possibilities and the way they have been integrated into ARK theory and practice, and of the authors in our disciplines dealing with such topics.

A note on important resources: the *Internet Encyclopedia of Philosophy* (IEP), *Routledge Encyclopedia of Philosophy* (REP) and *Stanford Encyclopedia of Philosophy* (SEP) are peer-reviewed academic online projects. The website of Luke Mastin (2008), a non-academic with an interest in philosophy, offers clear and concise overviews of many of the major traditions and thinkers. Kenny (2010) provides a book-length history of Western philosophy. In the ARK world also useful are *Archival Science* (2009) Special issue: The Philosophy of the Archive; *Archivaria* (2001) Themed section: The Postmodern Archive; and *Journal of Documentation* (2005) Special issue: Library and Information Science and the Philosophy of Science. In addition, Budd (2001) and Leckie et al. (2010) offer Library and Information Science perspectives on philosophy and theory. Throughout this chapter further reading is suggested, but for all definitions and major figures it is recommended to consult the relevant entry in IEP, REP, SEP or Mastin.

The greatest direct external disciplinary influences on ARK have come from the fields of history and the social sciences. Research in the social sciences (including our sibling discipline of Library and Information Science) is conducted within underlying theoretical 'paradigms' or philosophical orientations, and this chapter is loosely organized around these paradigms.

The differences between the paradigms lie in their stances towards:

- Metaphysics: inquiry and speculation about the nature of being and existence
- Ontology: the nature of existent entities
- Epistemology: the nature of knowledge
- Politics/ideology.

To follow, are brief explorations of paradigms most relevant to our discipline. Further perspectives can be found in Gilliland and McKemmish (2004, 163–71), where the authors examine the different theoretical paradigms and their implications for ARK research.

## 2 The Kantian context of modern philosophy

The schools of thought represented within the paradigms reached their current state in a philosophical landscape largely created and still influenced by **Immanuel Kant** (1724–1804).

Before we continue, these (simplified) definitions may be helpful:

- **Causality:** the relationship between cause and effect.
- **Empiricism:** philosophical stance arguing that knowledge can arise only from sensory perception and experience (Greek *empeiria*).
- **Rationalism:** philosophical stance arguing that knowledge can arise only from reason.

Responding to the extreme empiricist and sceptic **David Hume** (1711–76), who denied even the principle of causality, Kant's achievement was to effect a synthesis of those apparent irreconcilables, empiricism and rationalism.

To do this, Kant carried out what he described as his philosophic 'Copernican revolution'. Yes, knowledge could be derived from concepts and reason as well as from experience, but only at the price of accepting that the real objects of the world were beyond our direct cognitive grasp. Our knowledge can derive only from the 'phenomenal' realm of perception, not the 'noumenal' realm of reality which, if it were accessible, would be so only through *nous* (Greek for mind or thought). However, though our minds play an active role in constructing what we think of as 'reality', they are innately receptive to the unknowable real. Thus the operations and discoveries of science retain their validity, since they are derived from a phenomenal realm that is a reasonably trustworthy representation of the hidden realm of the 'thing in itself'. We are now so accustomed to the idea that reality is wholly or partly constructed through our minds that we have to remind ourselves of the revolutionary force of Kant's system. Thus, for instance, the now common understanding within ARK that our taxonomic or descriptive frameworks do not simply distort 'objective reality', but actually help to constitute it, has its roots firmly planted in Kantian soil.

Kant presented his enquiry into the possibilities of knowledge through reason and experience in *Critique of Pure Reason* (1781); he elaborated his moral and ethical philosophy in the *Critique of Practical Reason* (1788) and his philosophy of aesthetics and imagination in *Critique of Judgement* (1790). The Kantian inheritance later gave rise to the important distinction, which became for a long time a gulf, between analytic and continental philosophy:

- **Analytic philosophy:** originated in the anti-idealist, anti-Kantian thought of Frege and was initially based on a rigidly logical and empiricist version of positivism that became predominant in the Anglophone world.
- **Continental philosophy:** a catch-all term for more speculative, less empirically and scientifically oriented strands of philosophy, which fully or partly includes most non-positivist approaches.

## 3 The research paradigms and their early development

### 3.1 Scientism

The paradigm of **scientism** is most often invoked in terms of its subset **positivism**:

- **Positivism:** aims at the acquisition of objective knowledge, with a complete separation of observing subject and observed object or fact. It assumes that the objects of our perception can be unproblematically apprehended through the senses and described through language.
- **Scientism:** the idea that the methods of the natural – in particular, the physical – sciences are applicable to all fields of enquiry.

Positivism is derived from the philosophy of **Auguste Comte** (1798–1857), who insisted that society should be studied in the same scientific, objective modes as the natural – especially the physical – sciences. Comte's six-volume *Course on Positive Philosophy* (1830–42) was the first systematic programme for the 'scientific' study of society. Science, he claimed, deals only with 'positive' facts, empirically determined; society, being part of nature, should be studied using the same scientific methods that had so successfully revealed the workings of the physical world.

Comte's philosophy was part scientific, part utopian. If the over-reliance of Enlightenment philosophies on reason alone could lead to the violence and social dissolution of the French Revolution, a focus on scientific empiricism and non-metaphysical theory could be a progressive step towards the systematic acquisition of true knowledge that would lead to a better ordering of society. Neither metaphysics nor theology had any place in this system of knowledge. Comte's idea of a science of society had considerable influence, and his anti-clericalism made positivism a particularly powerful philosophy for progress in Latin America.

Modern sociology was effectively initiated as a positivistic field by Comte, building on work by **Saint-Simon** (1760–1825), elaborated in very different ways by **Karl Marx** (1818–83) and established securely as an academic discipline by **Émile Durkheim** (1858–1917). A loosely positivist orientation was to remain dominant, though by no means universal, in the social sciences for well over a century after Comte. Post-positivism is used either as a blanket term to describe all later reactions to positivism, or as denoting an approach that retains a scientific orientation and remains largely committed to ontological realism, but accepts greater doubt at the epistemic level.

## 3.2 Interpretive/critical

What primarily differentiates non-positivist from positivist positions is the role allowed to interpretation and subjective experience:

- **Interpretivism:** can be used to cover virtually all anti-positivist theoretical positions, with its strongest form found in constructivism, according to which we actually construct rather than simply interpret objects of thought and experience.
- **The critical approach:** a foundation of Kant's philosophy, is central to streams of thought that have a political and emancipatory element: drawing to a significant extent on Marxism, they argue that an emphasis on knowledge as scientific, objective and neutral serves to naturalize and therefore conceal oppressive and unjust social relations that are historical and contingent rather than natural. The purpose of studying society is not simply to understand it but to offer a well-founded critique of existing social relations as a starting point for a movement towards greater freedom and social justice.

And another definition to help with what follows:

- **Hermeneutics**: The theory of interpretation, initially applied to complex texts and their contexts and later to the entire field of human culture and communication.

### 3.2.1 Vico: a humanist in the Enlightenment; the philosophy of history

Interpretivism is frequently presented as an anti-positivist mode, but interpretation-based philosophical traditions long antedate positivism. Classical and scriptural hermeneutics, enriched by the humanist philological methods of the Renaissance, had a significant impact on historiography through the ideas of **Giambattista Vico** (1668–1774). Against the rationalist Descartes, he held that the human mind could have secure knowledge only of its own products, of the cultural and social rather than the natural realm, acquired through historical study rather than the methods of the natural sciences. He was the first to argue in a sustained way that societies in different ages have very different cultural and intellectual frameworks. Little regarded in his own age, his work has since had a steadily increasing influence and resonance.

### 3.2.2 Hegel and Marx: dialectic idealism, dialectic materialism, alienation and the 'other'

Some of the most significant and influential post-Kantian thinkers emerged in the traditions of German idealism and romanticism, important aspects of which stand behind the interpretive and critical paradigms. **G. W. F. Hegel** (1770–1831) strove to create a unitary philosophical framework where the apparent contradictory plurality of existence could finally be resolved and the essential unity of the world, a world conceived as 'spirit' (*Geist*), achieved. The individual human subject was a sliver of this universal spirit, and as such not standing outside reality, as in Kant's system, but within it (albeit in a currently alienated way that precluded true knowledge and integration).

To understand Hegel and Marx, consider the following definitions:

- **Dialectic:** in modern philosophy, a form of critique whereby contradictory positions are exposed (Kant) or through which they are examined and developed dynamically to show that they are ultimately reconcilable (Hegel).

- **Materialism**: the stance that only matter has real existence and that apparently immaterial phenomena (such as thought or mental states) have purely material causes.
- **Teleology**: the idea that an object or process can be explained wholly or partly in terms of its (supposed) final state or purpose (Greek *telos*, end).

Hegel had a highly teleological view of history as the dialectical unfolding of spirit through different stages, though he insisted on the particular character of each society and period, and on the impossibility of considering individual subjectivity apart from the historical and social context. Many of his ideas – such as his dialectic of thesis, antithesis and synthesis; the concepts of alienation and the 'other' – have become fundamental to the way in which philosophy, politics and culture have been articulated since.

➔ The concept of the 'other' has entered both ARK and the wider body of cultural discourse on 'the archive': both literal and more metaphorical archival cultures have played a significant role in constituting various marginal or subordinate groups as 'other' – as the subjects of case files for official control, for instance, or through pejorative and demeaning descriptive terms. Aspects of recent ARK theory and practice have sought to counter this, to offer instead a 'hospitality to "otherness"' (Harris, 2001).

Among Hegel's more politically radical successors was **Karl Marx**, until he broke decisively with Hegelian idealism to build his own philosophy of historical materialism, where the dialectical and teleological motors adopted from Hegel were worked out in the material world rather than the realm of ideas. The Industrial Revolution transformed the landscape of ideas along with those of city and country. For Marx, the fulfilment of the dialectical process would lie not in the unity of the world–spirit but in the emancipation of humanity through the development and perfection of the forces and relations of production in a succession of class struggles. He conceived his philosophy in a scientistic (though anti-positivist) mode, uncovering the laws through which history would work itself out; now largely discredited as science, it retains considerable power as critique.

### 3.2.3 The flowering of hermeneutics: interpretation and understanding

Romantic and idealist influences saw hermeneutics metamorphose from a primarily methodological technique into a fully fledged philosophical orientation. The validity of positivistic science as a model for history was contested by **Johann Gustav Droysen** (1808–84), who called for a history based on understanding (*Verstehen*) rather than explanation. Droysen's concerns were more systematically articulated by **Wilhelm Dilthey** (1833–1911), who insisted on the epistemological and methodological distinction between the natural sciences and the hermeneutically based cultural sciences. Dilthey also elaborated the idea of the 'hermeneutic circle', the constant movement between the content, form and context of a text, and between the text and its tradition.

➔ The hermeneutic concern with texts, contexts and their interrelation has obvious relevance to ARK, and has found a place in our literature (e.g. Lovblad, 2003; see also section 7.2.1).

## 4 An introduction to ARK and philosophy: some significant debates

Two separate but not unrelated sites of debate over theory arose in ARK over the last three decades. The 1980s and 1990s saw a debate over the nature and future direction of archival theory, an early shot being fired by Frank Burke in his 1981 article 'The Future Course of Archival Theory in the United States'. (See Cook, 1984, 29 n.2 and Trace, 2002, 158 n.55 for a list of some significant contributions to this debate.) This engagement brought into relief a number of features and divisions. Firstly, there is the question of whether theory in an overarching sense has any validity at all in ARK: is it really nothing more than 'much ado about shelving' (Roberts, 1987)? Secondly, if it is accepted that there is a place for ARK theory, what should its nature be? And should (or could) it be largely independent or must it be derived from other fields, most notably historiography and the social sciences?

A number of contributions, notably Stielow (1991) and Mortensen (1999), drew widely on the post-positivist philosophies that are the subject of sections 6.2 and 7.2 below to suggest possible models for ARK. Stielow adduces, among other topics, the validity of non-scientistic theory; the changing nature of historiography (see section 6.4); and the value of critical theory (sections 6.2.3 and 7.2) to the ethical dimension of ARK. Mortensen includes issues such as the retreat of science itself from more hard-core scientistic assumptions about theory and knowledge (section 7.1); the already significant dependence of ARK theory on Weber's ideas about bureaucratization (section 6.2.1); and the potential of Actor-Network Theory (section 7.2.4) as a tool for understanding practice. Also of note was the 1987 publication in English of Hans Booms' important article (1972) on the need for ARK to tackle the crucial questions of archival value and appraisal in the context of wider social and historiographical trends, ranging from the deeper problems raised by an unmanageable quantity of documentation through the nature of the documentary heritage in a pluralistic and democratic rather than a bureaucratic or authoritarian society. Others, such as Cappon (1982) and Eastwood (1993), were considerably less receptive to the use of external theory, particularly the sort that could be characterized as belonging to the tradition of Continental philosophy.

The 'pro-theorists' having largely won this debate, the nature of much of the theory actually developed or adopted was attacked under the banner of postmodernism in a second debate of the 1990s and 2000s. (Prominent 'postmodern' ARK theorists include Brien Brothman, Terry Cook, Bernadine Dodge, Verne Harris, Tom Nesmith and Joan Schwartz; see also section 7.3.3 and the lists provided in Cook, 2001a, 10 n.13 and Nesmith, 2002, 25 n.2). A significant target of this assault was what critics saw as the strong positivist tendencies in ARK theory, not to mention practice. Some of the theory thus criticized drew on long-standing ARK traditions (such as the development and extension of diplomatics associated most closely with Luciana Duranti); some of it lay in new developments intended to address the radically altered digital documentary landscape (such as the 'transactional' concept of recordkeeping associated with David Bearman and the Pittsburgh Project). The 'postmodernists' viewed both as adhering in different ways to a confidence in objective knowledge and judgement that had been comprehensively undermined by the epistemological and ethical challenges raised by non-positivist philosophy.

## *Bibliography/further reading – general*

**On ARK:** In addition to the ARK papers of Booms (1987), Mortensen (1999) and Stielow (1991), also relevant are Alvesson and Sköldberg (2009) and Strydom (2008).

**On philosophy:** Cascardi (1999); Critchley (2001); Norris (2000); Rockmore (2003).

**On social science:** Alvesson and Sköldberg (2009); Gilliland and McKemmish (2004); Lincoln et al. (2011); Myers (1997/2012); Pickard (2013); Ritzer and Goodman (2003, Ch.1, 2 and 6); Strydom (2008); J. H. Turner (2001).

## 5 Historiography: interpreting the text of the past

The radical rupture of the French Revolution brought about Romantic and conservative reactions that, for different reasons, treasured the past in its own right. In this context, the rather austere Romantic and deep-dyed conservative **Leopold von Ranke** (1785–1886) transferred to history the full rigour of the techniques of source criticism of his previous philological studies.

- **Rankean history:** the still-influential tradition of history associated with von Ranke, characterized methodologically by the critical study of primary sources and a narrow focus on political and state history, and institutionally by the professionalization of history.

Ranke insisted on the priority of primary sources and the need to engage in rigorous criticism and evaluation of all available sources, with a particular focus on unpublished archival documents. This approach has its roots in the antiquarian application of humanist critical textual scholarship to the documents of the past. One of the crowning achievements of such scholarship had been the development of the science of diplomatics by the Benedictine **Jean Mabillon** (1632–1707), where the authenticity of monastic charters (and, by extension, any record) was proved or disproved through careful examination of the textual, paratextual, material, formal and custodial aspects of the document and its transmission.

➔ Diplomatics, one of the foundations of ARK theory and practice, has remained an important element and has in recent decades been revitalized and renewed for the digital age, most notably by Duranti (e.g. 1998, 2010).

In significant points, it is not so much the novelty of Ranke's ideas that made them so influential as his contribution towards the institutionalization of history. History was conceived by Ranke as an independent discipline, conducted by professional historians. Past eras had to be judged in terms of their own specificity: in this, he was resolutely opposed to Hegel's idealist, teleological historiography. His history was the history of states and politics rather than of society or culture, let alone the lives of ordinary people, and the university seminar was to be the crucible in which the skills of new generations of historians were forged. This served to restrict legitimacy and authority in the writing of history even further, excluding or marginalizing various groups (most notably women) in the field of professional history.

Rankean history is often misleadingly described as positivist: indeed, Ranke can as easily be placed within the hermeneutic tradition of Vico, conceptualizing the past itself as a metaphorical text to be subjected to a hermeneutic reading. The methodological turn to archival research and the careful sifting of evidence in history was definitive and lasting, but it did not in itself betoken a 'scientific history' in the positivist sense adopted by figures such as Fustel de Coulanges in France and Lamprecht in Germany. Ranke's liberal, anti-clerical French contemporary **Jules Michelet** (1798–1874) spent many hours in the archives, but his was history in a Romantic rather than a positivist vein. Droysen and Dilthey's hermeneutic approaches also serve to undermine any notion of a modernist historiography shaped exclusively by Rankean, let alone positivist, ideals.

One of the most striking departures from Rankean history (broadly conceived) was that of the Swiss historian **Jacob Burckhardt** (1818–97), who effectively established modern art and cultural history. His 1860 *The Civilization of the Renaissance in Italy* crystallized the Renaissance as a separate and coherent period; in its cultivated yet amoral, Machiavellian ethos, he saw the birth of modernity and the individual. In this and in his writings on ancient Greece, he was a notable influence on the early Nietzsche, though he had little sympathy with the younger thinker's doctrines of power and will.

## *Bibliography/further reading*

**General:** Burrow (2007)

**Historiography**: Evans (2000, Ch.1); Hughes-Warrington (2008).

## 6 High modernity to the 1960s

Sections 2 to 5 have outlined the first stages in the development of the philosophical and disciplinary terrains which still form part of our twenty-first-century intellectual landscape. By the time we come to figures such as Weber and Nietzsche, we have entered a world that is recognizably our own in many respects: the scientistic and interpretive paradigms must now adapt to the promises and threats offered by a world of mass production and consumption (not to mention mass slaughter), scientific and technological innovation on an unprecedented scale, social upheaval and individual angst.

### 6.1 Scientistic

#### 6.1.1 Positivism and analytic philosophy

Later positivists sought to address perceived shortcomings in the Comtean model. As a philosophy of science, positivism was diverted by **Ernst Mach** (1838–1916) into a radical empiricist channel. As a science of society, sociology was consolidated as an academic discipline by **Émile Durkheim** (1858–1917), whose legacy has also had a profound influence on anthropology and the cultural study of religion. Like Comte, he insisted on a scientific approach that dealt only with observed facts; however, these included 'social facts', phenomena at the collective or abstract or structural level, that had an objective existence partly independent of individuals. Durkheim rejected any role for individual motivation and psychology in explaining social facts. This insistence was a major weakness in his concern to understand the socially stressful and alienating effect of modernity, leaving later figures such as Weber to attempt to remedy his neglect of the 'micro' elements of society in favour of the 'macro'.

- **Logical positivism**: philosophical stance that saw meaning as lying only in mathematics and logic, or derived from a thoroughgoing empiricism coupled with the 'principle of verifiability', whereby all empirical observation must be capable of verification.

In the aftermath of World War 1, Mach's radical empiricism was supplemented by a 'linguistic turn' derived from **Gottlob Frege** (1848–1925), focused on language and logic and the construction of true statements: this resulted in the 'logical positivism' that was to become a central feature of analytic philosophy, based on observation of sensory data which enabled the building of theory through the verification of hypotheses. The logical positivism of the **Vienna Circle** of thinkers, who included Wittgenstein, Carnap and Neurath and (initially) **Karl Popper** (1902–94), was brought to the Anglophone world when many members of the Circle emigrated under the threat of Nazism. Popper, however, broke with the positivist tradition, finding the naive (in the sense of simple) empiricism of logical positivism and its model of verification philosophically untenable.

Philosophy of language became a cornerstone of the analytic tradition, cemented into place by the 1921 *Tractatus Logico-Philosophicus* of **Ludwig Wittgenstein** (1889–1951), which argued that language represented reality through forming a sort of mental picture of the world. So central was Wittgenstein's contribution, however, that when he radically changed his mind in his later work it threw much of the analytic tradition into disarray. The *Philosophical Investigations*, published in 1953, argued that meaning depends not on reference or representation, but on the use of language in various contexts. In using language, we engage in various 'language games' appropriate to the context; these 'games' have rules which can be simple or complex.

Among other important developments in the philosophy of language was J. L. Austin and John Searle's speech act theory, whereby language was seen as not merely indexical or referential but as performative.

➔ Within ARK, Geoffrey Yeo (who has explored the broader philosophical and interdisciplinary realm on several occasions) linked ideas on record as representation to an exploration of speech act theory (Yeo, 2010) and the performative and conventional dimension in the notion of record. Seeing records as representing actions or events rather than providing information about them, Yeo notes that the sort of discrete 'elementary' record at the level of transactions is often of a performative rather than merely informational nature, effectively constituting a speech act. This serves to undercut views of the record, on the one hand, as an objective fact (e.g. a record embodying a declaration or promise does not guarantee that this was carried out) and, on the other, as having at best a problematic connexion with events and 'author' (the record irreducibly represents an action in the world, regardless of further interpretation and re-contextualization).

### 6.1.2 Pragmatism

This period also witnessed the flowering of the pragmatist philosophy of **William James** (1842–1910) and **Charles S. Peirce** (1839–1914) in the social sciences, to which it was applied by John Dewey and Herbert Mead. Pragmatism originated in the non-positivist scientific tradition derived by Peirce partly from left-Hegelianism and influenced by the hermeneutic approaches of Dilthey and Simmel. It focused on the usefulness rather than the 'truth' of theories – scientific theories were tools for solving problems. In contrast to positivism and the analytic tradition, pragmatism rejected both the correspondence theory of truth and the possibility of separating 'facts' from 'values'. Peirce also developed a pragmatically inflected semiotic theory independent of Saussure's structuralist semiotics (section 6.2.2).

### 6.1.3 Information science: document theory

Although this chapter does not cover information science in general, space must be made for document theory, still strongly associated with the two major figures of the twentieth-century 'documentalist' movement, **Paul Otlet** (1868–1944) and **Suzanne Briet** (1894–1989). Briet's semiotically based approach, in particular, has considerable relevance for current ARK contexts and ideas. Otlet was a visionary who worked towards a global bibliographic index, in the belief that the availability of knowledge and information would foster world peace. Funding from the Belgian government enabled him to set up the 'Mundaneum', a vast set of cross-referenced and linked cards intended to collate all documented knowledge. Otlet's definition of 'document' was broad; though he placed particular emphasis on the book, he also included material objects and artefacts, images and the new media of the day (e.g. sound recordings).

In her 1951 paper 'What Is Documentation?' Briet allows not only inert material objects but living creatures to assume the status of document, defined as 'a proof in support of a fact'. Her most arresting example of this is a live antelope: as an animal in the wild, it is just an animal, but if kept in a zoo as an object of study, it becomes a document in support of scientific theories and observations. While Otlet's vision was in a somewhat positivist mode, Briet's was informed by broader humanistic, philosophical and scientific ideas: her prescient ideas of knowledge and information as produced through and embedded in social and cultural practices foreshadowed later theorists such as Latour.

➔ Tourney (2003) discusses the relevance of the Documentation movement to ARK, suggesting in particular that Briet's understanding of a document is better suited to the digital age than more traditional models. She suggests that some of the difficulties that have arisen within ARK over the meaning and definition of a 'record' (at times with very concrete legal rather than merely theoretical implications) could have been addressed far more effectively had Briet's work been more widely known. (Indeed, discussion of the nature of the record is a perennial topic on ARK practitioner discussion lists; Briet's definition not only offers an arguably better 'fit' for the sort of recorded information that gives rise to such discussion in the first place, it also creates an analytic as well as an intertextual connection between the record of the ARK professional and the term as used in phrases such as 'the geological record'.) Lund (2009) provides an overview and literature review of document theory to date.

*Bibliography/further reading*

**Information science:** Briet (1951); Buckland (1997); Day (2001); Lund (2009); Lund and Buckland (2008).

**Philosophy and social sciences:** Fuller (2001); Lukes (2001); Ritzer and Goodman (2003, Ch.3).

**Semiotics:** Chandler (1994).

## 6.2 Interpretive/critical

### 6.2.1 Neo-Kantian social theory: Weber and Simmel

**Max Weber** (1864–1920) attempted to reconcile the interpretive/critical and scientistic strands in theories of social and economic organization that were at once scientific and hermeneutic. Weber is probably best known (certainly in ARK circles) for his work on rationalization and bureaucracy. Rationalization refers to the change in the nature of society from a more traditional stage characterized by authority or 'charismatic' rule to one characterized by reason and law. The cost of rationalist progress was the 'disenchantment' of the world, the elimination of a role for the irrational, spiritual and mystical and the marginalization of the individual in a complex, efficient impersonal system. This had profound and alienating negative effects. Weber saw the social sciences as needing both scientific (empirical, systematic) and interpretive research, and agreed with Dilthey in seeing understanding as the mode appropriate to the social and human sciences.

**Georg Simmel** (1858–1918) focused on the 'micro' level of social interactions. He was one of the earliest theorists to engage in a sustained way with the fragmented, disengaged and frenetic life of the modern metropolis and the psychological and social tactics adopted by individuals to cope with its stresses. Less well considered at the time than other 'classical' social theorists, he is now seen, with his prescient theories of modernity, consumption and consumerism, as a seminal and still relevant figure in cultural studies (section 7.3.6).

### 6.2.2 Phenomenology and structuralism

Firstly some brief definitions:

- **Phenomenology**: philosophical approach or method that focuses on the subjective mental experience of phenomena, without considering matters such as their ontological status or their causes.
- **Structuralism**: philosophical stance that assigns a determining role to structured interrelationships between the elements of systems of signification, whether linguistic, cultural or social.

These two extremely influential approaches emerged in the first two decades of the twentieth century. The phenomenology of **Edmund Husserl** (1859–1938) considers interaction with the world and the objects of experience (imaginary as well as real) to be the fundamental concern of philosophy. It is an approach opposed both to language-based speculation that ignores the experiential realm and to positivistic reductionism. We interact with phenomena through the richly articulated and structured social, cultural, psychological, linguistic and embodied experiences of our 'lifeworld'. Phenomenology developed along a number of distinct paths, both in the evolving thought of Husserl and in that of other, later thinkers, the most influential among whom was Husserl's student **Martin Heidegger** (1889–1976) (see also section 6.2.3), who inaugurated existential and hermeneutic phenomenology.

Structuralism, first elaborated by **Ferdinand de Saussure** (1857–1913) as a linguistic theory, had an enormous influence on subsequent Continental philosophy. Its central premise is that social and cultural phenomena must be studied in terms of their structures and the interrelationship of their parts. Saussure conceived language as having two dimensions: the deep structural layer of *langue* and the surface layer of utterance or speech, *parole*; his linguistics is focused on the former. Saussure's is a semiotic model, whereby meaning is constructed and communicated through signs: in language, signs take the form of words. Meaning is created through the relationships and differences between signs, which are wholly arbitrary in themselves, in the context of the overall structural system. This is therefore a radically constructivist perspective, and Saussure saw not only meaning and 'external' objects but subjectivity itself as being constructed through language.

This framework spread to other disciplines, including literary theory, the anthropology of Claude Lévi-Strauss, and the structuralist Marxism of Louis Althusser.

➔ Within ARK, Wake (2008) draws on structuralist narratological theory and the poststructuralist thought of Derrida in exploring the way in which the archive itself has a narrativizing force in the history of reading and re-reading of a collection of historical letters. The letters speak not simply for or through themselves but also through the narrative framework of their literal and metaphorical misdirections, the motives and practices of those through whose hands they passed, and the intent and preconceptions of their intended and unintended readers. The journal *Archival Science* (2012) has devoted an issue to exploring the application of genre theory (a structuralist form of criticism and analysis) to ARK. The concept of genre is shown to be of value in terms of enhancing understanding both of documentary collections (from the types of document used by private individuals to structure their everyday life to those characteristic of the holdings of a community archives) and of the tools (such as description or finding aids) used within ARK practice itself.

### 6.2.3 Hermeneutics and critical theory

The hermeneutic tradition was given a transformational existential and phenomenological turn by **Martin Heidegger**, whose *Being and Time* (1927) posits hermeneutics as not simply an interpretative method or an epistemological orientation, but the human 'way of being' in the world, interpretation as an existential rather than a cognitive faculty.

The 1920s saw the founding of the Institute of Social Research in Frankfurt, where the **Frankfurt School** of critical theory was elaborated by figures such as **Theodor W. Adorno** (1903–69) and **Max Horkheimer** (1895–1973) and drew within its ambit further influential thinkers such as **Walter Benjamin** (1892–1940). The critical theorists sought to correct what they saw as mechanistic, quasi-positivistic applications of Marxist philosophy, partly through a theoretical elaboration of the cultural, 'superstructural' aspects of Marx's model. Taking an eclectic approach and influenced by recent sociologists such as Weber, they emphasized psychological and cultural factors, producing the first sustained analyses and theorization of the role of popular culture. They consciously adopted a Kantian notion of 'critique' of both society and, reflexively, their own theoretical activity. The Frankfurt School was criticized both contemporaneously and subsequently for pessimism (particularly after the Nazi era) and for a simplistic view of mass culture as a mechanism for duping the masses rather than an arena in which dominated classes and groups could subversively create some space for agency and resistance.

### 6.2.4 Structural functionalism, ethnomethodology and ethnography

- **Ethnography**: anthropological/sociological fieldwork-based study of particular societies or groups and sub-groups.
- **Ethnomethodology**: a sociological theory and practice that focuses on practice and meaning-making in everyday life, particularly in organizational contexts.
- **Structural functionalism**: a sociological theory that examines society at the 'macro' level of structures and the way in which social elements (e.g. norms, institutions) function to create society as an organic whole.

The functionalist strands of Durkheim's sociology were developed along more constructivist lines. The structural functionalism of **Talcott Parsons** (1902–79) and **Robert Merton** (1910–2003) enjoyed considerable influence and popularity in the post-World War 2 years. It subsequently underwent a steep decline in significance but has seen some renewed interest in recent years. Functionalism draws on Durkheim, Weber and systems theory and sees society in terms of interrelated functions and systems, with individuals occupying various (and multiple) functional roles.

A not insignificant role in the eclipse of structural functionalism was played by the success of ethnomethodology, developed by **Harold Garfinkel** (1917–2011) partly in response to the shortcomings of Parsons' theory. Deriving from the phenomenological tradition, ethnomethodology was a significant factor in the increasing sophistication and influence of constructivist theory and practice. Unlike functionalist approaches, it focused on the internal ways in which social actors acquire and deploy common-sense reason and knowledge to make sense of the world and absorb the structural, normalizing elements through which they were supposed to construct and reproduce the social. As a phenomenological research method, it is highly empirical.

All this has made ethnomethodology a very important tool of organizational analysis, where it reveals that actual practice is far more flexible and complex than that prescribed by the formal systems and rules under which institutions supposedly operate. It has been used extensively in the social study of science and technology; Actor-Network Theory (section 7.2.4) derives its practice to a significant extent from ethnomethodology.

➔ Ethnomethodology has been put to use in a number of ARK studies, including Trace (2002) and Nycyk (2008). Trace argues for a post-positivist perspective, focusing in particular on ethnomethodology and ethnography; she discusses a number of sociological studies dealing with the role of recordkeeping in law enforcement settings in order to demonstrate that the record is part of a complex nexus of institutional procedures, everyday practices, tacit knowledge and negotiation between actors. Nycyk uses ethnography in a case study on records management in the construction industry to reveal and explore small-scale everyday resistance to change.

## *Bibliography/further reading*

**Critical theory:** Simons (2002).
**Ethnomethodology:** Clayman (2001); Ritzer and Goodman (2003, Ch.11).
**Structural functionalism:** Lucas (2007); Ritzer and Goodman (2003, Ch.7).

**Structuralism:** Ritzer and Goodman (2003, Ch.17).
**Weber and Simmel:** Ritzer and Goodman (2003, Ch.3 and 4), and S. P. Turner (2001).

## 6.3 Philosophies of modernity

A significant aspect of this period was the emergence of the concept of modernity as a social and historical condition, in the thought of figures such as **Friedrich Nietzsche** (1844–1900), Durkheim, Weber and Simmel. Some of their ideas derived from previous generations: the core concept of alienation, for instance, derives from the thought of Hegel and Marx, and from Marx too came the idea of commodification which underlay future theories of consumption and consumerism. Angst and alienation, and the experience of life in a modernity of ceaseless movement, change and dislocation (physical, social and psychological), were treated in various different ways by these theorists.

Nietzsche and **Sigmund Freud** (1856–1939) are crucial figures in any account of modernity. Both dealt, in very different ways, with the crisis of the individual in an age of modernity where the rational framework of the Enlightenment seemed to be unravelling in the technological and psycho-social complexities of the new age. Nietzsche saw all attempts at securing metaphysical or transcendental foundations for epistemology or ethics as doomed to failure. His famous aphorism that 'God is dead, and we have killed him' expresses his view that in our vaunting of reason and science, we have ourselves removed the grounds for all belief in external meaning and values of any sort. Our much-prized rationalism has led only to nihilism (corrosive or liberating, depending on one's perspective), with no external prop for our selves.

Freud, too, saw the self as distorted by our rational and social frameworks, but for him the distortion was carried out largely through unconscious mechanisms of repression at the level of the psyche. His psychoanalytical approach was effectively a form of hermeneutic and semiotic analysis, through which the underlying unconscious layers of the 'text' of the human mind could be reached through careful reading and interpretation of its obscure and riddling surface.

These philosophies of modernity flowed into – indeed, are to a significant extent constitutive of – the postmodernism of the late twentieth century, and lend weight to a perspective that either dismisses or significantly blurs the distinction between modernity and postmodernity.

### *Bibliography/further reading*

**Modernity:** Delanty (2007); Malpas (2005, 33–55); Ritzer and Goodman (2003, Ch.16); Scott (2006).

## 6.4 Historiography

Although the promise of Comtean scientific history proved elusive, history was increasingly influenced by both positivist and non-positivist sociology in its concern for investigating society at large and in its growing use of statistics and quantitative methods. Social and cultural history based on demographic data became increasingly common, as did histories (often written from a critical perspective) dealing with particular social groups such as the working class or women. History also became more receptive to cross-fertilization from other disciplines such as anthropology, from which it made both Durkheimian and structuralist borrowings. While Marxist history and historiography exerted a considerable influence, other historiographical traditions from the previous century were also developed by figures such as **Benedetto Croce** (1866–1952) and **R. G. Collingwood** (1889–1943), who both drew on Vico and on the Idealist tradition.

The French **Annales School** built on the cultural and social history pioneered by figures such as Michelet and Burckhardt. Founded by **Marc Bloch** (1866–1944) and **Lucien Febvre** (1878–1956) in the 1920s as a purposefully interdisciplinary endeavour, the Annales School drew deeply on Durkheim's concept of *mentalités* and also later, in the work of **Fernand Braudel** (1902–85), on structuralism. Braudel conceived of a 'total history' in which geographical and environmental factors played a significant role; underlying the more evanescent history of human events was the *longue durée* of structural processes. Though it greatly enriched the historical discipline, Braudel's history suffered from the general problem of structuralist theory: its inability to adequately account for or explain change over time. Other *Annalistes,* such as **Emmanuel Le Roy Ladurie** (b.1929), concentrated on reconstructing the lives of individuals and communities; his *Montaillou* of 1975 is one of the first examples of 'microhistory'.

➔ ARK theorist Tom Nesmith, who has written on the links between ARK and history on several occasions, has examined the relevance of Le Roy Ladurie's 'total history' to the concept of 'total archives' (Nesmith, 1981). While noting the particular type of record amenable to the 'total history' approach – longitudinal serial data such as parish registers and the implication that this might have for archives – Nesmith also draws attention to the unexamined presupposition underlying the concept of 'total archives', namely, that there is a 'total past' that can in some sense be preserved and represented through the records.

The impact of quantitative sociological and economic thinking on history is evidenced in the development of 'cliometrics', whereby data from the past is subjected to statistical analysis. While this can be illuminating and has the capacity to overturn supposed historical 'facts' that are little more than assumptions (such as, for instance, standards of living, or age at marriage), it is fraught with difficulty, not least because the data is generally inadequate and opaque.

➔ Nesmith (1982) has explored the tensions between the requirements of social historians seeking to base their work on large sets of quantitative data and the nature of existing archival records; he raises the continuing need for historical knowledge and skills within ARK. The Old Weather project, a collaborative public initiative of many archival and research institutes, shows what is possible when archival data – in this case, weather observations made on US ships for the past 150 years – is available in the full, comprehensive and consistent form that is genuinely amenable to meaningful quantitative analysis.

### *Bibliography/further reading*

Hughes-Warrington (2008).

## 7 Towards the twenty-first century: pluralization, fragmentation and (post)modernism(s)

### 7.1 Scientistic

Over the last four decades of the twentieth century, naturalistic philosophy in the analytic tradition finally lost its hegemonic position in the social sciences. Significant disruptive factors internal to the scientistic tradition included the destabilization of the referential view of language. External factors included an increasing suspicion of remote, expert-driven science in the 'atomic age'.

Pragmatism, after a long dormant period in the shade, has revived since the 1970s to such an extent that the analytic tradition has been partly fused with it. This interpretive–pragmatic turn in analytic philosophy included the post-positivist work of **Thomas Kuhn** (1922–96), whose idea of science as developing through a revolutionary series of substitutions between incommensurable paradigms has proved influential well beyond its original application. However, pragmatism also split into a number of strands differing in their orientation towards the analytic tradition: these ranged from a 'neoclassical' pragmatism that retained the non-positivist but scientistic approach of Peirce and James to the 'neo-pragmatism' of Richard Rorty (section 7.3.2), which has as much in common with postmodernism as with the pragmatist tradition.

Though the natural sciences did not by any means abandon their claims to seek objective truth, they now accepted that the positivistic model was inadequate even for matters of natural science, and simply inappropriate in many other areas. This left greater space for non- and anti-positivist 'scientific' theories, such as the 'critical realism' elaborated by **Roy Bhaskar** (b. 1944) from the late 1970s.

### *Bibliography/further reading*

**Critical realism:** Alvesson and Sköldberg (2009, 39–49); Budd (2010).
**Kuhn:** Hughes-Warrington (2008, 210–19).

## 7.2 Interpretive/critical

- **Constructionism/constructivism**: the view that our knowledge of the world is a shared mental and social construct rather than gained through unmediated access to any external reality.

The increasing influence of the non-positivistic traditions has brought social constructivism (or constructionism) to prominence in many recent approaches. Its fundamental premise is that reality itself, or at least our perceptions and understanding of the world, is not something 'out there' but is constructed through social and linguistic mechanisms, interactions and norms. A seminal text is Peter Berger and Thomas Luckmann's *The Social Construction of Reality* (1966); **Berger** (b.1929) and **Luckmann** (b.1927) found their main influence in phenomenology, but also in other figures such as Marx, Nietzsche, Durkheim and Weber. They wished to resolve the 'social facts' of Durkheim and the subjective meaning approach of Weber.

Weak constructivism allows that social 'objects' have an agreed epistemological reality and no ontological reality, but that they are underpinned by and dependent on objective 'brute facts'.

Strong constructivism claims that 'reality' is constructed through and through. A wide range of current philosophical approaches incorporate constructivism in one way or another. Its strongest opponents are naive/empiricist realists, though it has also been criticized (especially in its strong version) for ignoring the biological component of thought and culture and for moral and intellectual relativism.

### 7.2.1 Hermeneutics

Hermeneutics continued to be extended and enriched by **Hans-Georg Gadamer** (1900–2002), influenced by phenomenology but also harking back, in his seminal work *Truth and Method* (1960), to earlier humanistic concepts. Unlike many earlier hermeneuticians, Gadamer denied that interpretation could recover the original meaning of texts or of the author's intent; rather, what we are faced with are rich, ever-shifting layers of pre-interpretation and re-interpretation, so that text is a sort of living artefact with which, along with the entire textual tradition, we have an inter-subjective and reciprocal relationship. **Paul Ricoeur** (1913–2005) proposed a reconciliation between critical theory and Gadamer's tradition-oriented hermeneutics, since the ambiguities of text and context create openings for critical or ideological developments and interventions.

➔ Given its focus on interpretation and reconstruction, it is not surprising that hermeneutics has appealed to a number of ARK theorists. Ricci (2008) advocates the adoption of a hermeneutic framework for dealing with the complex issues involved in the restoration of moving images – the impossibility of reconstructing a fixed archival 'original'; different ways of conceptualizing moving images as object or event; the role of ARK practitioners as historical agents. He outlines two case studies to illustrate his arguments and, drawing on literary criticism and hermeneutics, sets out five questions that should be addressed to ARK theory and practice.

### 7.2.2 Critical theory

During the 1960s, a new generation of critical theorists, represented by **Jürgen Habermas** (b.1929) and **Karl-Otto Apel** (b.1922), came to prominence. They sought to accommodate all three of the analytical, interpretative and critical traditions; Apel in particular developed the concept of a 'transcendental pragmatics', influenced by Peirce. The left-Hegelian heritage of critical theory is central to Habermas' complex and syncretic approach, as is the Marxist insistence on change as well as interpretation, though Habermas rejected Marx's determinism. His acceptance of aspects of Peircean pragmatism caused him to re-articulate his core theory around 'communicative action', arguing that the possibility of emancipation resided in pragmatically oriented reflexive social relations of rational communication.

Another central aspect of Habermas' thought is the relationship between 'lifeworld' and 'system'. The Husserl-derived concept of lifeworld refers to the range of assumptions and presuppositions shared by actors in their various spheres of activity. It is within the lifeworld that knowledge and culture are shared and passed on; it is held together through communication and consensus. The perspective of the system, on the other hand, is that of structures – most notably the systems of money and power, including the economy and various state and social institutions (e.g. the family). Increasingly, the system has come to 'colonize' the lifeworld, forcing upon it its values and instrumental rationality, distorting communication and manipulating the mechanisms of consensus.

Habermas' ideas have been criticized on a number of grounds: that rational communication makes unrealistic demands on individual actors in terms of self-reflexivity and breadth of knowledge; that the lifeworld itself is home to non-rational and dysfunctional values and discourses even without the intervention of the system; and that he has watered down the more radical emancipatory heritage of critical theory by an over-emphasis on communication and consensus.

Habermas focused on the public sphere to the neglect of private social relations, a deficiency addressed by **Axel Honneth** (b.1949). Honneth's move to correct this involves replacing language with the Hegelian concept of 'recognition' as the central element of communication. Critique is therefore based on a struggle for recognition against various modes of social disrespect, to lead to a happier society with self-confident, self-respecting subjects.

### 7.2.3 Feminism and standpoint theory

While the central focus of earlier feminism (the 'first wave' of the nineteenth and early twentieth centuries) had been to secure the vote for women, the 'second-wave' feminism that emerged in the 1960s extended the focus to broader legal, social and cultural inequalities. Other philosophical traditions had, of course, engaged with feminist concerns, and many feminist thinkers worked (and still work) from within these traditions – **Simone de Beauvoir** (1908–86), for instance, within existentialism and Marxism. A wide and often antipathetic range of feminist positions developed during the second wave, ranging from liberal and individualistic to radical and collective feminism. By the 1980s, certain feminists were raising questions about gender-neutrality in epistemology and science, and feminist theories of knowledge and ethics and feminist philosophies of science emerged.

One influential strand was 'standpoint theory'; central figures include **Sandra Harding** (b.1935), **Dorothy Smith** (b.1926) and **Patricia Hill Collins** (b.1948). Strong standpoint epistemology holds that all dimensions of traditional knowledge are 'masculine' and that the disempowering effect of this requires a new mode of knowledge production based on women's experience. The less essentialist weak position adopted by thinkers such as Smith is more reflexive, diminishing the emphasis on differences between genders, though also assuming that knowledge is 'gendered'. Hill Collins has coined the term 'intersectionality' to describe the multiple overlapping and mutually reinforcing forms that oppression can take, and argues that people experience inequality differently, depending on the particular conjunctions of status, race, class, gender, etc. that affect them.

Standpoint theory has its roots in Hegel's *Phenomenology of the Spirit*, with its famous 'lordship and bondage' parable. This complex account of the achievement of self-consciousness through mutual recognition provides two central elements of standpoint theory. Firstly, it shows the subordinated achieving self-consciousness and the capacity for overcoming their condition through a dialectical process of engagement with the dominant. Secondly, it raises the idea of double or dual consciousness whereby the marginalized are obliged to survive by adopting the perspectives not only of their own situation but of the dominant groups as well.

Standpoint theory has a resonance for marginalized and oppressed groups other than women; in Australia an indigenous standpoint theory is being elaborated by thinkers such as Martin Nakata and Dennis Foley. Nakata (2007, 214) stresses that this does not involve the privileging of marginalized experience as an unassailable source of authority: such qualifications of standpoint theory seek to defuse criticism that it is effectively a form of identity politics and an essentialist philosophy that in fact reinforces the matrix of value-laden binary oppositions such as male/female, reason/emotion that it claims to combat.

➔ Dunbar (2006) explores the use of Critical Race Theory (CRT) as a means of creating a reflexive approach within ARK to bring to light implicit racial bias. CRT has its roots in US legal scholarship but also draws heavily on critical theory, postcolonialism and standpoint theory. Dunbar considers three aspects of CRT of relevance to ARK: the preservation of 'counterstories', or narratives from marginalized groups; the identification within ARK discourse and practice of 'microaggressions', pervasive acts of often unarticulated or unconscious forms of discrimination; and the furtherance of 'social justice' by incorporating within ARK the means of representing the identities and voices of the under-represented.

### *Bibliography/further reading*

**Feminism:** Ritzer and Goodman (2003, Ch.13).
**Lifeworld:** Fincher (2007); Ritzer and Goodman (2003, Ch.15).
**Ricoeur:** Hughes-Warrington (2008, 300–8).
**Social constructivism:** Alvesson and Sköldberg (2009, 23–39).
**Standpoint theory:** Nakata (2007).

## 7.2.4 Structural functionalism and Actor-Network Theory

Structural functionalism was revived by **Niklas Luhmann** (1927–98), who drew on developments in cognitive biology as well as systems theory. He stressed the contingency of systems, including society, and took from biology the idea of autopoiesis, referring to systems (such as cells and other organisms) that create their own basic elements. Luhmann conceived of society as an autopoietic, closed, self-organizing system whose most basic element is communication.

➔ Lemieux (1998) sees the functional structuralist tradition as underpinning much ARK macro-appraisal theory and offers a detailed and thorough exploration of the value of Henry Mintzberg's models of organizational typology as an extension of such theory; she uses two existing case studies as 'controls' on the validity of her hypotheses. Mintzberg's seven types of organization, conceptualized as structured along functional lines, are seen as offering a more flexible model for the actual context of and sites of responsibility for records creation than the Weberian model.

One of the most influential developments of social constructivism is **Actor-Network Theory** (ANT), associated primarily with **Bruno Latour** (b.1947), **Michel Callon** (b.1945) and **John Law**. It is partly derived from the semiotic theory of **Algirdas Greimas** (1917–92), from whom it derives its insistence on the role of non-human actors: things and constructs such as organizational units, IT systems, machinery, infrastructure elements all influence human action. Materiality is central to ANT: not only the actors but the knowledge produced by them is material, in the form of 'inscriptions' such as records, reports, data, books and research papers. Socio-technical networks are created through the circulation of inscriptions, the network consisting of all the human and non-human actors involved or invoked.

ANT stresses the way in which social and cultural factors are pervasive, though its constructivism is tempered by the non-human elements in the networks and actors and by its rejection of the idea of 'society' as a pre-existing phenomenon. Its research mode is determinedly empirical, an ethnography of actors and network nodes: it eschews explanation or theorizing in favour of 'following the actors'.

➔ Within ARK, Frohmann (2008) describes two sets of case studies undertaken within an interdisciplinary framework that draws on aspects of poststructuralism and postmodernism, but primarily uses Latour and

Callon's ANT to investigate the complex social and organizational operations of a 'documentary politics'. One of these studies, conducted by the anthropologist Marilyn Strathern, showed the way in which audit documentation becomes a self-referential agent that constitutes the very thing it is meant to serve, i.e. the audit.

### 7.2.5 Agency/structure: Giddens and Bourdieu

- **Structuration theory**: sociological theory, most closely associated with Anthony Giddens, examines society in terms of both social structure and individual agency.

The structuration theory of **Anthony Giddens** (b.1938) regards structure and agency as inseparable, working dialectically through the reflexive activity of social actors. Structures do not exist independently of actors, and enable as well as constrain individual action: thus, agency is made possible by structure. Giddens sees actors as having a wide range of competencies and knowledge that enable them to continuously and recursively embody, instantiate, work with and alter social structures and interrelationships: this knowledge is to a significant degree tacit. The constant process of structuration, effected through flows between the three dimensions of signification, domination and legitimation and their associated modalities of interpretative schemes, facility and norms, forms routines. Structuration theory has been criticized on a number of grounds; for example, as operating at too high a level of abstraction and as ignoring much of the material context of actors' environments.

➔ Structuration theory underlies the records continuum theory developed by Upward, McKemmish and others: Upward, in a two-part article (1996, 1997), sets out the details of the records continuum model and its basis in structuration theory and postmodernist thinking. Characterizing 'classical' recordkeeping theory as partly based on a concern with objective structures, he sees Giddens' theory as focused instead on how systems are articulated. Structuration theory's reflexive, process-based interaction between structures and actors offers a dynamic model far more suited to the complexities of the continuum model with its movements out from (and back to) the initial event of record creation.

→ An offshoot of Giddens' work, De Sanctis and Poole's adaptive structuration theory (AST), has been explored within ARK by Foscarini (2010). She advocates its use along with other 'soft' systems frameworks in preference to more rigid systems-engineering schemata, to enable an adequate understanding of the complex interactions of actors, systems and artefacts in the setting of organizational records creation and management. AST focuses on the structurating role of information technology; Foscarini sees its concern with the mutual interactions between actors and technology and the contingency of the outcomes of this interaction as offering a more fruitful model for understanding the introduction of, e.g. an ERMS (electronic records management system), than viewing it in terms of 'impact'.

**Pierre Bourdieu** (1930–2002), like Giddens, had an interest in the agency–structure question and in the tension between the subjective experience of the individual and the objective structures of society. With a strong phenomenological focus on the everyday experience of the individual, he elaborated a number of highly influential concepts, such as field and habitus, distinction and cultural capital.

### *Bibliography/further reading*

**Actor-Network Theory:** Bowker (2007); Callon (2001); Law (1992–2011).
**Bourdieu, cultural capital and habitus:** Field (2006); Ritzer and Goodman (2003, Ch.15); Stones (2006).
**Luhmann:** Ritzer and Goodman (2003, Ch.9); Rogowski (2007).
**Structuration theory:** Giddens (1984); Ritzer and Goodman (2003, Ch.15); Stones (2007).

## 7.3 Hybridity and 'the epoch of post-everything'

The final quarter of the twentieth century saw the proliferation within Continental philosophy of a variety of disparate but nonetheless recognizably related philosophical stances. Despite the suggestion in the 'post-' prefix of novelty and the supersession of previous modes of thought, the 'post-' philosophies have deep roots in (and arguably belong to) the Kantian and post-Kantian traditions that they aim to challenge: some theorists, for instance, use the term 'late modernity' rather than 'postmodernity'. The acknowledged centrality of modernist figures such as Nietzsche, Saussure and Heidegger also implies significant continuity. In general, it is more fruitful to think in terms of a pervasive condition of postmodernity characterizing the contemporary globalized era, in which the philosophical and scientific inheritance of the Enlightenment has been put under stress and partly diverted into strange and unforeseen channels, but not superseded.

### 7.3.1 Poststructuralism

- **Deconstruction**: a mode of textual analysis that looks for hidden contradictions and ambiguities within texts that, when revealed, subvert or call into question the surface meaning of the text.
- **Poststructuralism**: a reaction against and extension of structuralism (section 6.2.2) that problematizes structuralist assumptions that systems can be self-contained and that the dichotomies on which they depend can be stated unambiguously.

Poststructuralism both reacts against and develops structuralism, taking issue with those aspects that posited real or external bases for both structural frameworks/elements and their interactions. In contrast, poststructuralism sees 'reality' as constructed through the differential play of signification in systems lacking any foundational anchor-points. It also allows for non-structural causal mechanisms within systems, such as power or desire. Among the most prominent poststructuralist philosophers are the two 'post-' theorists perhaps best known in ARK circles: **Jacques Derrida** (1930–2004) and **Michel Foucault** (1926–84).

Derrida saw structuralism as retaining, albeit in attenuated form, the 'myth of presence': that is, the notion that true understanding comes from unmediated access to the object of enquiry. The process of 'deconstruction' is a fundamental tool of poststructuralist critique: developed by Derrida as a philosophical–critical method from his reception of phenomenology and structural linguistics, it is most fully set out in his *Of Grammatology* (1967). Deconstruction denies the capacity of language or any other sign-system to break free from the indeterminacy of its web of signification. It operates by exploring and highlighting contradictions, tensions and slippages within textual signification, in order to demonstrate that language is not straightforward or straightforwardly descriptive of an external 'reality'.

A central aspect of deconstruction is its ability to pick apart the sets of binary oppositions that underpin structuralist accounts (e.g. nature/culture, inside/outside, masculine/feminine). The seemingly unproblematic meanings generated by such dichotomies are inherently unstable and ambiguous; each of the terms depends for its own meaning and force on its opposite or 'other' term, which it seeks to repress but never entirely succeeds in so doing. This applies to ideological and normative as well as literary discourse: theorists on culture, gender and race have also found deconstruction a powerful tool – Edward Saïd's critique of 'orientalism', for example (section 7.3.4), involves the deconstruction of various binary characterizations of 'west' and 'orient'.

The concepts or metaphors of 'trace' and 'archive' were highly significant for Derrida; his *Archive Fever* (1995) is perhaps best known in this context. In a style typical of his writings, Derrida plays with the term 'archive' to unpack its various denotations and connotations – as a place (the 'house of the archon', or magistrate); as a beginning or a command (both translating the Greek *arkhē*); as an externalization, a mark on a substrate either material or psychic. As a function of the psyche, the archive is threatened by Freud's 'death drive', the drive of radical destruction and erasure; the desire to prevent such loss of trace and memory finds its expression in 'archive fever'. For Derrida, the archive signifies and (at times literally) embodies our impossible desire for the originary, for that which is not already merely a trace or mark: the events that left their archival trace (whether as documentary records or as marks on the body, such as that of circumcision) are lost to us at the very point that the trace is created – the origin of the archive is forever inaccessible.

Foucault's thought, like Derrida's, is partly derived from the philosophy of Nietzsche; he employs Nietzschean 'genealogy' and a textual/conceptual 'archaeology' to highlight the ways in which our social practices are constituted and constrained through discourse and 'discursive formations'. As with Derrida, 'the archive' is a significant element of Foucault's ideas: it is not a place or a collection of records but, rather, among other things, the sum total of legitimate 'statements' under a given discursive formation. For Foucault, the 'statement' is the smallest unit of discourse, which, in conjunction with other statements, embodies the culturally specific rules that make a discursive expression meaningful. What is meaningful in one context may not be meaningful in another: the expression 'the earth is a sphere', for instance, is not based on meaningful statements within a flat-earth perspective.

Central to Foucault's thought is the idea of power, which flows through and activates, but can also disrupt and divert, the normative structures of discursive formations. It is enacted through and on bodies as well as discursively. Foucault's genealogies of crime and punishment, sexuality and other social constructs aim at examining relations between knowledge and power, which are inextricably linked. Power in the Foucauldian sense does not reside in fixed points or agents of a system but flows through it and can be temporarily appropriated by any agent or institution: it is erroneous to mechanistically equate power with status, position or formal authority. Nonetheless, institutionalized power is central to the control and constitution of people within society.

**Roland Barthes** (1915–80) initially worked largely within the structuralist tradition, analysing the semiotics of texts and images, as in his famous article 'Myth Today' (1957). By the publication of 'The Death of the Author' (1967), he had moved from the free-playing but anchored linguistic systems of structuralism to a position that denied any non-discursive points of origin: the 'author' is not an external individual subject who creates a text but is, rather, a sort of fiction of the discourse itself. Similarly, the text creates the role of 'reader'. Like Derrida, Barthes sees discourse and language as a never-ending and self-contained process of difference, deferral of meaning and signification, where meaning, though not arbitrary, is not constituted through reference to an extra-linguistic world.

➔ In relation to ARK, such a perspective acts to subvert any confidence that the individual or aggregate record – including the record of its passage through the recordkeeping and archival process – can claim to unambiguously reflect either the events it represents or the intentions of its notional authors.

The literary theory of **Julia Kristeva** (b.1941), who is also a significant figure in poststructuralist feminist and psychoanalytic thought, overlaps with that of Barthes. One of her major contributions is the concept of intertextuality, derived partly from the ideas of **Mikhail Bakhtin** (1895–1975). No text or other signifying activity exists as a discrete entity or act: every specific textual object exists within and is partly constituted by (and itself partly constitutes) the totality of texts and sign systems of the culture that produces it.

### 7.3.2 Postmodernism

- **Postmodernism**: An eclectic body of philosophical positions that deny the possibility of objective and universal foundations for knowledge and ethics, overlapping to a considerable extent with poststructuralism; can also be seen in terms of an existential 'condition of postmodernity' rather than a philosophical stance as such.

Postmodernism was initially a movement in the sphere of architecture and art. It replaced the rationalist aims of modernist architecture and the formalism that characterized modernist art (and literature) with an ironic eclecticism that reused and juxtaposed elements from earlier styles, subverting the order and coherence of the modernist ethos through pastiche, self-referentiality, fragmentation and ambiguity. Postmodernist philosophy adopts the same ironic, eclectic and anti-foundationalist stance in relation to modernist philosophy. Nietzsche, with his sceptical and iconoclastic attitude towards fixed 'truths' and values, was a seminal influence.

While postmodernism is most closely associated with French philosophy, there are also distinctive approaches from Italian postmodernists such as Vattimo, drawing on thinkers such as Vico and Croce as well as the broader hermeneutic tradition. The postmodernist pragmatism of **Richard Rorty** (1931–2007) is grounded in analytic rather than Continental philosophy, though it is far removed from the original moderate anti-foundationalist aims of Peirce, James and Dewey. It, too, has been significantly influenced by hermeneutics.

In his 1979 book *The Postmodern Condition: a report on knowledge*, **Jean-François Lyotard** (1924–98) described postmodernity in terms of a breakdown of the universalizing frameworks inherited from Enlightenment thinking into a plurality of competing approaches – 'language games' in the sense posited by Wittgenstein – none of which could claim ascendancy or priority over the others. Postmodernity could be defined, he stated, as 'incredulity toward metanarratives': the conflicts and horrors of the twentieth century have shown the universalizing narratives of figures such as Kant, Hegel or Marx to be chimerical and false or, at worst, instrumental in causing such conflicts.

Lyotard explicitly grounds his position in Kant's *Critique of Judgement*, concerning judgement in aesthetic matters but also in all areas where imagination is called for. This emphasis on the third of Kant's three critiques while rejecting the preceding epistemological and ethical critiques means that postmodernism can and has been criticized as an aestheticizing response to epistemological, political and ethical issues and problems. For instance, the ironic postmodern destabilization of boundaries between high and low culture, fact and fiction, news and entertainment provides an intellectual backdrop to a 'spectator experience' where war takes on the aspect of a video game and Instagram images bring the aesthetic of a fashion magazine to mass social revolt.

**Jean Baudrillard** (1929–2007) pushes postmodernism's denial of the originary and its fascination with surface and pastiche to greater extremes. He argues that our contemporary world of hypertrophied virtual media imagery, where financial and libidinal economies alike are driven by consumption and revolutionized by new technologies, is a 'hyperreal' world of simulation and that the objects (real or conceptual) that we perceive are mere simulacra, 'copies without originals', free-floating signs.

Poststructuralist and postmodernist theories have had a significant impact on historiography, though considerably less so on the actual practices of history. Notable figures such as **Hayden White** (b.1928) and **Dominick LaCapra** (b.1934) have foregrounded the literary and narrative aspects of history writing, pointing out that works of history function in ways very similar to fictional texts, through plotting, narrative, metaphor and rhetoric. Barthes spoke of historical discourse as engaged in the creation of a 'reality effect', White in *Metahistory* (1973) stated that historical narrative could be 'emplotted' in any of the genres of tragedy, romance, comedy or satire. As with any other texts or intertexts, both the documentary 'evidence' of the past and the works of history based upon it are held to be ambiguous and indeterminate in meaning.

### 7.3.3 Influence of poststructuralism and postmodernism on ARK theory

'Postmodernist' thought has had a significant influence on recent ARK theory, leading to an increasing acceptance that records and archives provide a partial and ambiguous rather than objective and accurate view of the past. Both the records and the institutions and individuals that create, select and manage them exist within structures of power and ideology that influence what is kept and who has access to it. Grazley (2011), Hardiman (2009) and Heald (1996) examine this influence, Grazley particularly highlighting the difficulties in relating the demands of a postmodernist perspective to actual practice. She notes, for instance, that any postmodern scepticism towards the relationship between record and truth must be balanced by a regard for that relationship as seen by the legal codes of the ARK practitioner's society, and refers to the difficult task faced by professionals in new roles called for by a more activist orientation. Poststructuralist and postmodernist understandings of power are examined in a special issue of *Archival Science* (2002) on 'Archives, Records and Power'.

Many authors have engaged with postmodernism in specific ARK contexts. In a wide-ranging paper, Todd (2006) considers some of the issues surrounding privacy legislation, discussing the ideas of Derrida as well as of various ARK theorists. He notes the dilemma between safeguarding the individual's rights to privacy from state surveillance and retaining personal information to enable individuals and groups to claim rights and identities and to construct their own narratives. This dilemma is partly one contained within postmodernist perspectives themselves: on the one hand, there is the understanding of the archive as a site of domination and power, on the other, the desire for justice as a recognition of multiple micro-narratives.

The historian Andrew Prescott (2008) has explored the significance of poststructuralist and postmodernist thought for ARK, partly through the lens of historiography and museology; among other topics, he examines the textuality of records in the light of theorists such as Barthes. He notes, among other examples, the work of some historians who have approached mediaeval legal records using the techniques of literary criticism, enabling them not only to reach a deeper understanding but to reveal at times the literally fictive nature of some supposedly factual record types. Kaplan (2002) points, from a broadly poststructuralist perspective, to the value of adopting some of the rich theoretical insights developed by anthropologists, who, like archivists, are 'intermediaries between a subject and its later interpreter' (Kaplan, 2002, 211). She notes that the anthropologist Bronislaw Malinowski's ground-breaking arguments in favour of abandoning the pretence of the 'invisibility' of the ethnographer were contemporaneous with the publication of Jenkinson's *Manual*, with its reaffirmation of the invisibility of the archivist.

A number of ARK theorists have produced a substantial body of work over the years that takes up the postmodernist challenge. The sustained and evolving engagement of Brien Brothman includes a challenge to the antipathy of many in ARK to broader philosophical perspectives, in particular those of Derrida (Brothman, 1999). He sees recent orientations within ARK towards the fields of business and information management as exacerbating an already ingrained indifference to philosophy. Terry Cook's clarity of thought and expression has greatly facilitated the introduction of postmodernist complexities and their relevance to ARK (e.g. Cook, 2001a and 2001b). Bernadine Dodge (e.g. Dodge, 2002) takes a more Baudrillard- and McLuhan-influenced, late-modern perspective than most of the ARK postmodernists, highlighting the destabilizing and disorienting effects that a virtual, globalized consumer economy brings to ARK along with all other aspects of contemporary life and subjectivity.

A specifically Derridean approach is evident in the work of Verne Harris (e.g. Harris, 2001), who finds in postmodernism an approach to counter what he sees as the exclusionary and monophonic straitjacket of the cruder aspects of 'positivist' thinking and practice. In his activities to further archival and social justice, he has fiercely criticized the institutional role of government archives and of positivistic archival practice in buttressing and serving the apartheid regime in South Africa. He has, however, also come to reject the underlying oppositions that he initially looked to in this struggle: the metaphors of records and archives as light shone on the darkness, for instance, or as memory in place of forgetting. Instead, Derrida's deconstruction and problematization of dichotomies means that we must accept that any binary opposition serves to create some form of repression, injustice, the exclusion of the other: 'there is extreme danger in a reason that gives no space to mystery ... extreme danger in the mystery that gives no space to reason' (Harris, 1999, 14). Eric Ketelaar (2002) brings the perspectives of Foucault and Latour to bear on the working of power through archival institutions and through documentation in his distinctively relaxed yet incisive style. Like Brothman and Cook, Tom Nesmith has had an enduring concern with both the relationship of ARK with history/historiography and the relevance of postmodernist theory to ARK. He has explored how postmodernism has rendered problematic traditional views of the stability of the record and the neutrality of ARK professionals (Nesmith, 2002).

Photographs have been a fruitful focus of postmodernist approaches, perhaps inevitably, given their association with objectivity and truth and the fact that they have always occupied a very marginal place in an ARK theory and practice overwhelmingly focused on textual records. The most notable theorist in this context has been Joan Schwartz; she has drawn on aspects of visual studies that combine poststructuralist and postcolonial ideas to suggest ways in which ARK can become better equipped to understand the semiotic and ideological functions of photographic images (Schwartz, 2002).

### *Bibliography/further reading*

**General:** Agger (1991); Gordon (2002); Jameson (1991); Lemke (1994); Norris (2000); Ritzer and Goodman (2003, Ch.17); Visser (1993).

**Historiography**: Hughes-Warrington (2008, Chs. on Jenkins, White); Malpas (2005, 80–104).

**Intertextuality**: Chandler (1994, Ch.13).

**Postmodernity**: Lyon (2000).

## 7.3.4 Postcolonialism, hybridity and globalization

- **Orientalism**: a theoretical approach that critiques the way in which Western discourse has defined and constructed the East in terms that render it an effete and alien 'other' to Western epistemological and cultural modes.
- **Postcolonialism**: a poststructuralist and critical philosophical movement concerned with the profound cultural, political and economic issues that affect the former colonies of imperialist powers.
- **Subalternity**: a term used in postcolonialist theory to denote the multiply marginalized condition of the non-elite majority population of (former) colonies.

From the American Revolution onwards, struggles for freedom drew on the ideals and rhetoric of Enlightenment and post-Enlightenment philosophy; influential early postcolonialist thinkers, such as **Frantz Fanon** (1925–61), also drew heavily on this inheritance, particularly in its Hegelian and Marxist forms with their theorization of both revolutionary struggle and the constitution of the 'other'. Like Marx, Fanon saw violence as inevitable in the struggle against a hegemony itself maintained by violence. Fanon was also influenced by phenomenology and existentialism, and used his knowledge as a practising psychiatrist, alongside his own experiences and radicalization as a black subject of French colonial rule, to explore the pathology and psychological dimensions of colonization in *Black Skin, White Masks*.

The work of **Edward Saïd** (1935–2003), in particular his 1978 *Orientalism*, has been extremely influential across a range of disciplines. He draws on the structuralist and poststructuralist work of Foucault and Althusser to examine the constitution and disempowerment of the Orient (for Saïd, almost exclusively the Middle East) as an exotic and inferior 'other' by Western academic discourse of the modern era. The West exerted control through both the systematic collection of information as an act of power in itself and the subsequent casting of this information in terms of opposing binaries: West/East, familiar/strange, rational/irrational, masculine/effeminate.

The experience of colonial rule in the Indian subcontinent gave rise to a distinctive body of postcolonialist thought, of which the leading lights include **Gayatri Spivak** (b.1942) and **Homi K. Bhabha** (b.1949). Spivak elaborated the notion of subalternity, originally derived from the Marxist theoretician Antonio Gramsci, to refer to the experience of people and cultures subject to colonization; she particularly explored the double oppression of women, their marginalization within their own culture further exacerbated by that culture's subordinate position within colonial and neo-colonial relations. Drawing on various strands of poststructuralist and critical theory as well as on Marxism, she applied Foucault's notion of 'epistemic violence' to the discourse and knowledge systems of subordinated groups, silenced under the hegemony of Western modes of thought and expression. While opposed to essentialism and notions of the 'authenticity' of the subaltern or marginalized, Spivak advocates 'strategic essentialism' as a political stance to foster solidarity and collective responses to oppression.

➔ Within ARK, Jeannette Bastian has drawn in a nuanced way on postcolonial, poststructuralist and postmodernist theory. Among other work, she has examined (e.g. Bastian, 2013) postcolonialism's impact on theories of 'the archive' and archives, highlighting the complexities of creating, finding or reconstituting postcolonial archive(s) in a context not only of Western political and epistemological imperialism but also of 'internal' inequalities between local elites and subalterns. In seeking to develop a suitable framework for the capture, description and preservation of the written, oral and embodied record of Caribbean carnival, she has also turned to disciplines such as anthropology, history and historiography and, most notably, performance studies.

- ➔ Though often presented through the prism of practical challenges rather than theoretical exploration as such, the complex issues involved in serving the ARK needs of indigenous peoples and minority ethnic groups are inevitably strongly influenced by postcolonial and postmodernist insights. This emerges in works such as Christen's (2011), who considers the issues around shared management of and access to the records of a native American people. In the context of pluralizing ARK education, AERI-PACG (2011) draws partly on postcolonialist perspectives in acknowledging the need for ARK educators to take into account the non-Western intellectual and cultural backgrounds of an increasingly diverse student population.
- ➔ Kurtz (2006) offers an interesting exploration of a number of issues related to ARK and indigenous groups in the USA – the tensions arising in drawing on postcolonialist theory in this context, given the anomalous relation of the USA (and other 'breakaway settler colonies') to postcoloniality; the question of whether any institutional form of ARK in a postcolonial context can avoid replicating structures of domination; and the tensions between the 'de-centering' logic of postcolonialism and the localizing pull exerted by the materiality of an archival collection.

Bhabha emphasizes the hybrid identities and cultures fostered by colonialism, and their increasing global pervasiveness. For the colonized, their interactions with the representatives and institutions of the colonial power entailed a literal and cultural bilingualism and the adoption of multiple and shifting subject positions. This 'colonial mimicry' and the mobile and diasporic nature of the globalized world are factors in creating what Bhabha describes as a 'vernacular cosmopolitanism'.

The stunted or imperfectly developed nature of the nation-state model in many postcolonial contexts has resulted in fault-lines and conflicts around, for example, religion and ideology rather than along national lines. The integration of even the most 'underdeveloped' regions of the world into a globalized economy brings greater fluidity to postcolonial relations between nations, groups and individuals and gives a further impetus to the formation of hybrid cultures and identities. **Arjun Appadurai** (b.1949), a significant theorist of globalization, draws on Benedict Anderson's influential concept of 'imagined communities' to argue that such localized imaginings have been superseded by increasingly deterritorialized global 'imagined worlds'.

➔ Within ARK literature, Gutiérrez (1994) draws on aspects of postmodern, postcolonialist, globalization and critical philosophies to elaborate on the complex configurations, both intensely localized and fully globalized, of embodied gender and ethnic identities. He notes the way in which the body is so often the site on which identities of self and other are constructed. The physically larger crania of Westerners compared to Africans and native Americans adduced as 'scientific' evidence of intellectual superiority in the nineteenth century; privilege granted or withheld depending on gender; aberrant or transgressive sexuality subjected to censure and often overt repression in the service of maintaining 'normal', culturally dominant constructs. In turn, the 'othered' have sought to forge or 'reclaim' their own identity, resulting in an often fissiparous proliferation of at times mutually antagonistic identities. Gutiérrez sees two possible paths for the future: an inward focus on local identities or a globalized focus on broader unities above and beyond the local and the locally embodied.

### 7.3.5 Post-feminism? Essentialism vs performance

Feminism has had an ambivalent relationship to 'post-' theories. On the one hand, there is a great deal in deconstruction, 'genealogy', and the dethroning of dominant metanarratives that is very congenial to feminist concerns. On the other hand, there remains an awareness that a denial of subjectivity is at odds with the feminist need for at least a tactical concept of stable individual subjects and social collectivities for whom rights may be claimed. Women, too, are seen as in need of Spivak's 'strategic essentialism'.

Despite postmodernism's anti-essentialist logic, there is in fact a certain essentialist strand in poststructuralist and postmodernist feminism, particularly in French feminism, which is very much focused on the body as a site and system of signification and which takes a distinctly psychoanalytical approach. **Luce Irigaray** (b.1930) sees the need for establishing a separate feminine subject-position and language (language, psychology and philosophy alike allowing only a masculine subjectivity).

**Hélène Cixous** (b.1937) coined the term *écriture féminine* to describe a form of discourse intended to permit women to emancipate themselves from what she saw as the constricting patriarchal and masculine nature of existing modes of thought, linguistic genres and conventions.

One of the most prominent poststructuralist philosophers dealing with sexuality and gender is **Judith Butler** (b.1956). She questions all essentialist notions of gender, sex and sexuality including the category 'woman'. Drawing on Foucault and on Austin's speech act theory, she theorizes gender as a performance carried out in conformity with linguistic and cultural norms.

### *Bibliography/further reading*

**Bhabha:** Castle (2007, 202–3).
**Butler:** Castle (2007, 204–6).
**Feminism/postfeminism:** Barrett (2000).
**Globalization:** Axford (2000); Ritzer ed. (2007).
**Hybridity:** García-Canclini (2001).
**Postcolonialism:** Appiah (1991); Robotham (2000).
**Saïd and Orientalism:** Alatas (2007); Castle (2007, 241–2); Chua (2007).
**Spivak:** Olson and Fox (2010).
**Strategic essentialism:** Wolff (2007).

### 7.3.6 Cultural studies

Pressure of space forbids all but the briefest mention of the important field of cultural studies, so diffuse and interdisciplinary that it defeats even the rudimentary level of synopsis possible here. Though extremely eclectic, it draws mainly on various strands of structuralism (e.g. semiotics), critical theory and poststructuralism; media, popular culture and consumerism are important foci of study. Recent work in museology and heritage studies shows the influence of cultural studies perspectives, as do broader treatments of information.

➔ In ARK theory, Rekrut (2005) draws on museology and heritage studies to explore the material dimension of records and archives, arguing for the need of a greater awareness within ARK of the ways in which context and meaning is constructed through materiality as well as textuality. The physicality of records can not only give them a powerful emotional charge as artefacts from the past, it also provides both context and content: the material aspects can embody cultural choices or statements on the part of the creator or can illuminate the context of production and custody. Taylor (1988) draws on the media theory of **Marshall McLuhan** (1911–1980) to discuss the impact of technological mediation on the cultural practices of records creators and users and on ARK ideas and practice, and the need to consider the non-textual aspects of meaning that resides in the media themselves apart from the content and context of the records. Moving from pre-literate, oral societies through to the 'post-literate' digital age, he notes the ways in which changing needs have brought into being recording and communication technologies that in turn have affected the way in which recordkeeping has been administered.

#### *Bibliography/further reading*

Castle (2007, 72–8); Edgar and Sedgwick (2008); Fine (2002); Maxwell (2000).

### 7.3.7 Criticisms

Perhaps the most obvious weakness of postmodernism is that it can itself be critiqued as just another metanarrative, and thus by its own criteria is no more plausible than the positions it aims to dismiss. However, in rejecting the validity of much of the Western philosophical and scientific tradition it has inevitably provoked more specific resistance, and intense and often ill-tempered ideological and cultural battles have broken out over the truth-claims of both science and history, and over values and ethics.

While most postmodernist thinkers are committed to social change, justice and ethics, their rejection of Enlightenment thought has nonetheless been seen as 'ethically disastrous and politically retrograde' (Norris, 2000, 35). Lyotard's concept of justice as the refusal to judge between narratives, for instance, leaves us with no legitimate way of discriminating between science and pseudo-science, or of declaring cultural practices such as female genital mutilation to be illegitimate. Attacked from the political and cultural right (e.g. Hicks, 2004) as a left-wing nihilist and relativist assault on values, the 'post-' theories have also drawn considerable criticism from the liberal and more radical left, often for not dissimilar reasons. Sokal and Bricmont's debunking book *Intellectual Impostures* (1997) is motivated in part by a concern that social constructivist and postmodernist approaches have undermined and enervated the more activist and emancipatory critical philosophies of the left; Habermas, too, has engaged in an extended critique of (and dialogue with) postmodernism. Furthermore, critics like Jameson and Botting have argued that postmodernism is at heart a description rather than a critique of, or site of resistance to, capitalism (Jameson, 1991; Botting, 2004, 236–7).

Some thinkers from the postcolonial world are far from happy at postcolonialism's repudiation of Western epistemologies. Meera Nanda sees the demotion of Western rationality in favour of local 'ways of knowing' as a well-meaning but condescending gesture that effectively denies rationality and rational modes of thought to non-Western people. Instead, 'the postmodern elements of the constructivist science critique strengthen the premodern elements of postcolonial societies' (Nanda, 1998, 281).

In historiography, too, concerns about jettisoning all distinction between true(er) and false(r) accounts of the past go beyond the merely academic. The Holocaust is often taken as the litmus test: if all narratives and language games are equally valid, if all history is essentially fictive, on what grounds can we legitimately reject Holocaust-denying narratives? While Lyotard steered suspiciously close to maintaining that this, too, must be considered a valid option, Hayden White was moved to concede that the Holocaust could not be emplotted as comedy or romance; that it, in fact, was one of a class of 'modernist events' that resisted such treatment. A further criticism of postmodernist historiography is that it effectively erects a straw man of 'positivist history' which has never in fact existed: much of Richard Evans' *In Defence of History* (2000) is given to demonstrating this.

## *Bibliography/further reading*

Botting (2004); Evans (2000); Hicks (2004); Jameson (1991); Koertge (1998); Nanda (1998); Norris (2000).

## 8 Conclusion

It is hoped that this rapid tour has at least been successful in suggesting that ARK would benefit from more rather than less engagement with philosophical perspectives, and in offering some points of entry for further exploration. Aspects of the theoretical tradition have already been fruitfully applied to ARK theory and practice; extensions of this might see, for example, more exploration of Honneth's ideas on recognition in the growing literature on community recordkeeping and archives. The use of ANT and ethnomethodology in the study of organizational recordkeeping might usefully be supplemented by the application of Habermas' ideas on lifeworld and system to explore the tensions and contradictions between the aims and values of ARK and other stakeholders and the wider institutional and political contexts in which they operate. If this chapter causes its readers to think about and put into effect other possibilities of their own, it will have fulfilled much of its purpose.

## References and further reading

AERI and PACG (2011) Educating for the Archival Multiverse, *American Archivist*, **74** (1), 69–101. Collaboratively authored by members of the Archival Education and Research Institute (AERI) and the Pluralizing the Archival Curriculum Group (PACG).

Agger, B. (1991) Critical Theory, Poststructuralism, Postmodernism: their sociological relevance, *Annual Review of Sociology*, **17**, 105–31.

Alatas, S. F. (2007) Saïd, Edward W. In Ritzer, G. (ed.), *The Blackwell Encyclopedia of Sociology*, Blackwell, 3997–8.

Alvesson, M. and Sköldberg, K. (2009) (Post-)Positivism, Social Constructionism, Critical Realism: three reference points in the philosophy of science. In *Reflexive Methodology: new vistas for qualitative research*, 2nd edn, Sage, 15–52, www.sagepub.com/upm-data/28039_02_Alvesson_2e_Ch_02.pdf [Pre-print proof].

Appiah, K. A. (1991) Is the Post- in Postmodernism the Post- in Postcolonial? *Critical Inquiry*, **17** (2), 336–57, http://appiah.net/wp-content/uploads/2010/10/Is-the-post-in-postmodernism-the-Post-in-Postclonial-Critical-Inquiry-17.2.-1991.pdf.

*Archival Science* (2002) Special issue: Archives, Records and Power, *Archival Science*, **2** (3–4).

*Archival Science* (2009) Special issue: The Philosophy of the Archive, *Archival Science*,

**9** (3–4). Papers from the conference held in Edinburgh, 10–11 April 2008.

*Archival Science* (2012) Special issue: Genre Studies and Archives, *Archival Science,* **12** (4).

*Archivaria* (2001) Themed section: The Postmodern Archive, *Archivaria,* **51**.

Axford, B. (2000) Globalization. In Browning, G. et al. (eds), *Understanding Contemporary Society: theories of the present,* Sage, 238–51.

Barrett, M. (2000) Post-feminism. In Browning, G. et al. (eds), *Understanding Contemporary Society: theories of the present,* Sage, 46–56.

Bastian, J. A. (2013) The Records of Memory, the Archives of Identity: celebrations, texts and archival sensibilities, *Archival Science,* **13**, 121–31.

Booms, H. (1972[1987]) Society and the Formation of a Documentary Heritage: issues in the appraisal of archival sources, *Archivaria,* **24**, 69–107. Trans. H. Joldersma and R. Klumpenhouwer. Originally published as: Gesellschafsordnung und Überlieferungsbildung: Zur Problematik archivarischer Quellenbewertung, *Archivalische Zeitschrift,* **68** (1972), 3–40.

Botting, F. (2004) Culture, Literature, Information, *Critical Studies,* **23**, 215–49. Issue on Post-Theory, Culture, Criticism.

Bowker, G. (2007) Actor-Network Theory. In Ritzer, G. (ed.), *The Blackwell Encyclopedia of Sociology,* Blackwell, 20–1.

Briet, S. (1951 [2006]) *What is Documentation?* Scarecrow Press. Translated and edited by R. E. Day and L. Martinet with H. G. B. Anghelescu. Originally published in 1951 as *Qu'est-ce que la Documentation*? Éditions Documentaires Industrielles et Techniques, http://ella.slis.indiana.edu/~roday/what%20is%20documentation.pdf.

Brothman, B. (1999) Declining Derrida: integrity, tensegrity, and the preservation of archives from deconstruction, *Archivaria,* **48**, 64–88.

Buckland, M. (1997) What is a 'Document'? *Journal of the American Society for Information Science,* **48** (9), 804–9, www.columbia.edu/cu/libraries/inside/units/bibcontrol/osmc/bucklandwhat.pdf.

Budd, J. M. (2001) *Knowledge and Knowing in Library and Information Science: a philosophical framework,* Scarecrow Press.

Budd, J. M. (2010) Roy Bhaskar's Critical Realism. In Leckie, G. K. et al. (eds), *Critical Theory for Library and Information Science: exploring the social from across the disciplines,* Libraries Unlimited, 29–39.

Burke, F. W. (1981) The Future Course of Archival Theory in the United States, *American Archivist,* **44** (1), 40–6.

Burrow, J. (2007 [2009]) *A History of Histories: epics, chronicles, romances and inquiries from Herodotus and Thucydides to the twentieth century*, Penguin Books. First published by Allen Lane in 2007; published by Penguin Books, 2009.

Callon, M. (2001) Actor Network Theory. In *International Encyclopedia of the Social and Behavioral Sciences*, Pergamon Press, 62–6. Editors-in-Chief: Neil J. Smelser and Paul B. Baltes.

Cappon, L. J. (1982) What, then, Is there to Theorize About? *American Archivist*, **45** (1), 19–25.

Cascardi, A. J. (1999) *Consequences of Enlightenment*, Cambridge University Press.

Castle, G. (2007) *The Blackwell Guide to Literary Theory*, Blackwell.

Chandler, D. (1994–) *Semiotics for Beginners*, Aberystwyth University. Online book begun in 1994 and updated as needed, www.aber.ac.uk/media/Documents/S4B/semiotic.html. Subsequently also published in a print edition (*Semiotics: the basics*, Routledge 2007).

Christen, K. (2011) Opening Archives: respectful repatriation, *American Archivist*, **74** (1), 185–210.

Chua, P. (2007) Orientalism. In Ritzer, G. (ed.), *The Blackwell Encyclopedia of Sociology*, Blackwell, 3343–5.

Clayman, S. E. (2001) Ethnomethodology: general. In *International Encyclopedia of the Social and Behavioral Sciences*, Pergamon Press, 4865–70. Editors-in-Chief: Neil J. Smelser and Paul B. Baltes.

Cook, T. (1984) From Information to Knowledge: an intellectual paradigm for archives, *Archivaria*, **19**, 28–49.

Cook, T. (2001a) Archival Science and Postmodernism: new formulations for old concepts, *Archival Science*, **1** (1), 3–24.

Cook, T. (2001b) Fashionable Nonsense or Professional Rebirth: postmodernism and the practice of archives, *Archivaria*, **51**, 14–16.

Critchley, S. (2001) *Continental Philosophy: a very short introduction*, Oxford University Press.

Day, R. E. (2001) European Documentation: Paul Otlet and Suzanne Briet. In *The Modern Invention of Information: discourse, history, and power*, Southern Illinois University Press, 7–37.

Delanty, G. (2007) Modernity. In Ritzer, G. (ed.), *The Blackwell Encyclopedia of Sociology*, Blackwell, 3068–70.

Dodge, B. (2002) Across the Great Divide: archival discourse and the (re)presentations of the past in late-modern society, *Archivaria*, **53**, 16–30.

Dunbar, A. W. (2006) Introducing Critical Race Theory to Archival Discourse: getting the conversation started, *Archival Science*, **6** (1), 109–29.

Duranti, L. (1998) *Diplomatics: new uses for an old science*, SAA, ACA and Scarecrow Press.

Duranti, L. (2010) Structural and Formal Analysis: the contribution of diplomatics to archival appraisal in the digital environment. In Hill, J. (ed.), *The Future of Archives and Recordkeeping: a reader*, Facet Publlishing, 65–88.

Eastwood, T. (1993) Nailing a Little Jelly to the Wall of Archival Studies, *Archivaria*, **35**, 232–52.

Edgar, A. and Sedgwick, P. (eds) (2008) *Cultural Theory: the key concepts*, 2nd edn, Routledge.

*Encyclopædia Britannica Online*, Historiography, www.britannica.com/EBchecked/topic/267436/historiography [Paywall].

Evans, R. J. (2000) *In Defence of History*, 2nd edn, Granta. First published 1997; republished with Afterword by author 2000.

Field, J. (2006) Cultural Capital. In Scott, J. (ed.), *Sociology: the key concepts*, Routledge, 45–6.

Fincher, W. (2007) Lifeworld. In Ritzer, G. (ed.), *The Blackwell Encyclopedia of Sociology*, Blackwell, 2651–3.

Fine, B. (2002) *The World of Consumption: the material and cultural revisited*, 2nd edn, Routledge.

Foscarini, F. (2010) Understanding the Context of Records Creation and Use: 'hard' versus 'soft' approaches to records management, *Archival Science*, **10** (4), 389–407.

Frohmann, B. (2008) Documentary Ethics, Ontology, and Politics, *Archival Science*, **8** (3), 165–80.

Fuller, S. (2001) Positivism, History of. In *International Encyclopedia of the Social and Behavioral Sciences*, Pergamon Press, 11821–7. Editors-in-Chief: Neil J. Smelser and Paul B. Baltes.

Furner, J. (2004) Conceptual Analysis: a method for understanding information as evidence, and evidence as information, *Archival Science*, **4** (3–4), 233–65.

García-Canclini, N. (2001) Hybridity. In *International Encyclopedia of the Social and Behavioral Sciences*, Pergamon Press, 7095–8. Editors-in-Chief: Neil J. Smelser and Paul B. Baltes.

Giddens, A. (1984) *The Constitution of Society: outline of the theory of structuration*, Polity Press.

Gilliland, A. and McKemmish, S. (2004) Building an Infrastructure for Archival Research, *Archival Science*, **4** (3), 149–97.

Gordon, D. (2002) Post-structuralism and Post-modernism. In *Encyclopedia of the Enlightenment*, Oxford University Press – online publication.

Grazley, J. (2011) *Many Journeys, No Map: navigating the postmodern archival landscape with courage and care*, ARMA International Educational Foundation, www.armaedfoundation.org/pdfs/Paper_grazley_Jana_2011.pdf [accessed 23 March 2012; no longer available].

Gutiérrez, R. A. (1994) Decolonizing the Body: kinship and the nation, *American Archivist*, **57** (1), 86–99. Special Issue: 2020 Vision.

Hardiman, R. (2009) En Mal d'Archive: postmodernist theory and recordkeeping, *Journal of the Society of Archivists*, **30** (1), 27–44, www.academia.edu/910549/En_mal_darchive_Postmodernist_Theory_and_Recordkeeping [Preprint].

Harris, V. (1999) Law, Evidence and Electronic Records: strategic perspective from the global periphery, *South African Archives Journal*, **41**, 3–19.

Harris, V. (2001) Seeing (in) Blindness: South Africa, archives and passion for justice. Paper delivered at *Annual Conference of the Archives and Records Association of New Zealand (ARANZ), August 2001, Wellington*, http://scnc.ukzn.ac.za/doc/LibArchMus/Arch/Harris_V_Freedom_of_Information_in_SA_Archives_for_justice.pdf.

Heald, C. (1996) Is there Room for Archives in the Postmodern World? *American Archivist*, **59** (1), 88–101.

Hicks, S. R. C. (2004) *Explaining Postmodernism: skepticism and socialism from Rousseau to Foucault*, 1st edn, Scholargy Publishing.

Hughes-Warrington, M. (2008) *Fifty Key Thinkers on History*, 2nd edn, Routledge.

Ilerbaig, J. (2010) Specimens as Records: scientific practice and recordkeeping in natural history research, *American Archivist*, **73** (2), 463–82.

*Internet Encyclopedia of Philosophy*, www.iep.utm.edu, General editors: James Fieser and Bradley Dowden.

Jameson, F. (1991 [2003]) *Postmodernism, Or, The Cultural Logic of Late Capitalism*. Duke University Press, 10th reprinting in paperback.

Jenkins, K. and Munslow, A. (eds) (2004) *The Nature of History Reader*, Routledge.

*Journal of Documentation* (2005) Special issue: Library and Information Science and the Philosophy of Science, *Journal of Documentation*, **61** (1).

Kaplan, E. (2002) 'Many Paths to Partial Truths': archives, anthropology, and the power of representation, *Archival Science*, **2** (3), 209–20, www.nyu.edu/classes/bkg/methods/kaplan.pdf.

Kenny, A. (2010) *A New History of Western Philosophy*, Oxford University Press. Single-volume edition of four-volume series.

Ketelaar, E. (2002) Archival Temples, Archival Prisons: modes of power and protection, *Archival Science*, **2** (3), 221–38, http://home.hccnet.nl/e.ketelaar/ArchivalTemples.pdf.

Koertge, N. (ed.) (1998) *A House Built on Sand: exposing postmodernist myths about science*, Oxford University Press. Online version.

Kurtz, M. (2006) A Postcolonial Archive? On the paradox of practice in a Northwest Alaska project, *Archivaria*, **61**, 63–90.

Law, J. (1992–2011) *Notes on the Theory of the Actor Network: ordering, strategy and heterogeneity*, Centre for Science Studies, Lancaster University. Originally published in *Systems Practice*, **5** (1992), 379–93. This version published 25 September 2011 on the author's website, www.heterogeneities.net/publications/Law1992NotesOnTheTheoryOfTheActorNetwork.pdf.

Leckie, G. K. et al. (eds) (2010) *Critical Theory for Library and Information Science: exploring the social from across the disciplines*, Libraries Unlimited.

Lemieux, V. (1998) Applying Mintzberg's Theories on Organizational Configuration to Archival Appraisal, *Archivaria*, **46**, 32–85.

Lemke, J. L. (1994) *Semiotics and the Deconstruction of Conceptual Learning*, http://academic.brooklyn.cuny.edu/education/jlemke/papers/jsalt.htm. Author's online version of article originally published in *Journal of the Society for Accelerative Learning and Teaching*, **19** (1994), 67–110.

Lincoln, Y. S., Lynham, S. A. and Guba, E. G. (2011) Paradigmatic Controversies, Contradictions, and Emerging Confluences, Revisited. In Denzin, N. K. et al. (eds), *The Sage Handbook of Qualitative Research*, 4th edn, Sage, 97–128.

Lovblad, H. (2003) Monk, Knight or Artist? The archivist as a straddler of a paradigm, *Archival Science*, **3** (2), 131–55.

Lucas, J. W. (2007) Structural Functional Theory. In Ritzer, G. (ed.), *The Blackwell Encyclopedia of Sociology*, Blackwell, 4860–3.

Lukes, S. (2001) Durkheim, Émile (1858–1917). In *International Encyclopedia of the Social and Behavioral Sciences*, Pergamon Press, 3897–903. Editors-in-Chief: Neil J. Smelser and Paul B. Baltes.

Lund, N. W. (2009) Document Theory, *Annual Review of Information Science and Technology*, **43** (1), 1–55.

Lund, N. W. and Buckland, M. (2008) Document, Documentation, and the Document Academy: introduction, *Archival Science*, **8** (3), 161–4.

Lyon, D. (2000) Post-modernity. In Browning, G. et al. (eds), *Understanding Contemporary Society: theories of the present*, Sage, 221–37.

Malpas, S. (2005) *The Postmodern*, Routledge.

Mastin, L. (2008) *The Basics of Philosophy: a huge subject broken down into manageable chunks*, www.philosophybasics.com/index.html.

Maxwell, R. (2000) Cultural Studies. In Browning, G. et al. (eds), *Understanding Contemporary Society: theories of the present*, Sage, 281–95.

Mortensen, P. (1999) The Place of Theory in Archival Practice, *Archivaria*, **47**, 1–26.

Myers, M. D. (1997/2012) *Qualitative Research in Information Systems*, Association for Information Systems (AISWorld) (updated 21 March 2013), www.qual.auckland.ac.nz/. Originally published as Myers, M. D. (1997) Qualitative Research in Information Systems, *MIS Quarterly*, **21** (2), 241–2. AIS website version includes updates.

Nakata, M. N. (2007) An Indigenous Standpoint Theory. In *Disciplining the Savages: Savaging the Disciplines*, Aboriginal Studies Press, 213–25.

Nanda, M. (1998) The Epistemic Charity of the Social Constructivist Critics of Science and Why the Third World Should Refuse the Offer. In Koertge, N. (ed.), *A House Built on Sand: exposing postmodernist myths about science*, Oxford University Press, 286–311.

Nesmith, T. (1981) Le Roy Ladurie's 'Total History' and Archives, *Archivaria*, **12**, 127–33. Review article.

Nesmith, T. (1982) Archives from the Bottom Up: social history and archival scholarship, *Archivaria*, **14**, 5–26.

Nesmith, T. (2002) Seeing Archives: postmodernism and the changing intellectual place of archives, *American Archivist*, **65** (1), 24–41.

Norris, C. (2000) Post-modernism: a guide for the perplexed. In Browning, G. et al. (eds), *Understanding Contemporary Society: theories of the present*, Sage, 25–45.

Nycyk, M. (2008) Records management practices in construction industries: Australian perspectives, *Records Management Journal*, **18** (2), 140–9, http://espace.library.uq.edu.au/eserv/UQ:152020/UQ_AV_152020.pdf [Preprint].

Olson, H. A. and Fox, M. J. (2010) Gayatri Chakravorty Spivak: deconstructionist, Marxist, feminist, postcolonialist. In Leckie, G. K. et al. (eds), *Critical Theory for Library and Information Science: exploring the social from across the disciplines*, Libraries Unlimited, 295–9.

Pickard, A. J. (2013) *Research Methods in Information*, 2nd edn, Facet Publishing.

Prescott, A. (2008) The Textuality of the Archive. In Craven, L. (ed.), *What Are Archives? Cultural and theoretical perspectives: a reader*, Ashgate, 31–51.

Rekrut, A. (2005) Material Literacy: reading records as material culture, *Archivaria*, **60**, 11–37. Special Issue: First International Conference on the History of Records and Archives (I-CHORA I).

Ricci, S. (2008) Saving, Rebuilding, or Making: archival (re)constructions in moving image archives, *American Archivist*, **71** (2), 433–55.

Ritzer, G. (ed.) (2007) *The Blackwell Companion to Globalization*, Blackwell.

Ritzer, G. and Goodman, D. J. (2003) *Sociological Theory*, 6th edn, McGraw-Hill.

Roberts, J. W. (1987) Archival Theory: much ado about shelving, *American Archivist*, **50** (1), 66–74.

Robotham, D. (2000) Post-colonialism and Beyond. In Browning, G. et al. (eds), *Understanding Contemporary Society: theories of the present*, Sage, 84–96.

Rockmore, T. (2003) Remarks on the Structure of Twentieth Century Philosophy, *Ars Disputandi*, **3** [no pagination], www.arsdisputandi.org/publish/articles/000128/.

Rogowski, R. (2007) Luhmann, Niklas. In Ritzer, G. (ed.), *The Blackwell Encyclopedia of Sociology*, Blackwell, 2675–8.

*Routledge Encyclopedia of Philosophy Online*, www.rep.routledge.com/ [Paywall]. Lead editor: Edward Craig.

Schwartz, J. M. (2002) Coming to Terms with Photographs: descriptive standards, linguistic 'othering,' and the margins of archivy, *Archivaria*, **54**, 142–71.

Scott, J. (2006) Modernity. In Scott, J. (ed.), *Sociology: the key concepts*, Routledge, 110–13.

Simons, J. (ed.) (2002) *From Kant to Lévi-Strauss: the background to contemporary critical theory*, Edinburgh University Press.

Sokal, A. and Bricmont, J. (1997[1998]) *Intellectual Impostures: postmodern philosophers' abuse of science*, Profile Books. Originally published as *Impostures Intellectuelles* (Éditions Odile Jacob, 1997); translated by the authors.

*Stanford Encyclopedia of Philosophy*, http://plato.stanford.edu/. Principal editor: Edward N. Zalta.

Stielow, F. J. (1991) Archival Theory Redux and Redeemed: definition and context toward a general theory, *American Archivist*, **54** (1), 14–26.

Stones, R. (2006) Habitus. In Scott, J. (ed.), *Sociology: the key concepts*, Routledge, 79–82.

Stones, R. (2007) Structuration Theory. In Ritzer, G. (ed.), *The Blackwell Encyclopedia of Sociology*, Blackwell, 4867–9.

Strydom, P. (2008) Philosophies of the Social Sciences. In Crothers, C. (ed.), *Historical Developments and Theoretical Approaches in Sociology, in Encyclopedia of Life Support Systems (EOLSS)*, EOLSS Publishers for UNESCO. Developed under the auspices of UNESCO.

Taylor, H. (1988) 'My Very Act and Deed': some reflections on the role of textual records in the conduct of affairs, *American Archivist*, **51** (4), 456–69.

Todd, M. (2006) Power, Identity, Integrity, Authenticity, and the Archives: a comparative study of the application of archival methodologies to contemporary privacy, *Archivaria*, **61**, 181–214.

Tourney, M. M. (2003) Caging Virtual Antelopes: Suzanne Briet's definition of documents in the context of digital age, *Archival Science*, **3** (3), 291–311.

Trace, C. B. (2002) What Is Recorded Is Never Simply 'What Happened': record keeping in modern organizational culture, *Archival Science*, **2** (1), 137–59, www.ischool.utexas.edu/~cbtrace/pubs/CBT_ArchScience_2002.pdf.

Turner, J. H. (2001) Positivism: sociological. In *International Encyclopedia of the Social and Behavioral Sciences*, Pergamon Press, 11827–31. Editors-in-Chief: Neil J. Smelser and Paul B. Baltes.

Turner, S. P. (2001) Weber, Max (1864–1920). In *International Encyclopedia of the Social and Behavioral Sciences*, Pergamon Press, 16401–7. Editors-in-Chief: Neil J. Smelser and Paul B. Baltes.

Upward, F. (1996) Structuring the Records Continuum. Part one: Post-custodial principles and properties, *Archives and Manuscripts*, **24** (2), 268–85, www.infotech.monash.edu.au/research/groups/rcrg/publications/recordscontinuum-fupp1.html [Institutional online version].

Upward, F. (1997) Structuring the Records Continuum. Part two: Structuration theory and recordkeeping, *Archives and Manuscripts*, **25** (1), 10–35, www.infotech.monash.edu.au/research/groups/rcrg/publications/recordscontinuum-fupp2.html [Institutional online version].

Visser, N. (1993) The Epoch of Post-Everything, *Southern African Review of Books*, (September/October), 19–20.

Wake, P. (2008) Writing from the Archive: Henry Garnet's Powder-Plot Letters and archival communication, *Archival Science*, **8** (2), 69–84.

Wolff, K. (2007) Strategic Essentialism. In Ritzer, G. (ed.), *The Blackwell Encyclopedia of Sociology*, Blackwell, 4797–9.

Yakel, E. (1996) The Way Things Work: procedures, processes, and institutional records, *American Archivist*, **59** (4), 454–64. Special Section on Diplomatics and Modern Records.

Yeo, G. (2010) Representing the Act: records and speech act theory, *Journal of the Society of Archivists*, **31** (2), 95–117.

CHAPTER 7

# Participation vs principle: does technological change marginalize recordkeeping theory?

Alan R. Bell

## 1 Introduction

Recordkeeping is, essentially, a profession predicated upon control. Such control may be to ensure the 'moral defence' of the archive or to prevent a reversion 'to primitive habits' and the unreasonable destruction of archives and records (Jenkinson, 1965, 152), or it may be to encourage 'efficient management' and 'the minimum charge for space and maintenance' (Schellenberg, 2003, 37). Control may be exerted by different agents, including the records creator, originating organization, users, communities or recordkeepers; what Harris (2005, 115) might characterize collectively as 'recordmakers', recognizing the influence of those agents upon the record and the influence of the record upon them. However, regardless of the agency applying control and despite debate on the extent to which objective control is achievable or desirable, the necessity of establishing systems and processes designed to ensure fixity – 'the quality of being stable and resisting change' (Pearce-Moses, 2005) – and warrant the authenticity, reliability and integrity of records and archives (see, for example, ISO, 2001) is, arguably, at the core of professional practice. When it is distilled to absolute basics, recordkeepers decide what to preserve, for how long and the most suitable way to dispose of records; they apply measures to ensure the longevity of records for an appropriate period of time; and they organize, list and manage access to records (Jimerson, 2009, 10). Without some degree of consistency, these activities would be haphazard and largely meaningless, hence the standardized, codified and controlled nature of the recordkeeping profession.

In a volume dedicated to a re-examination and exploration of the theoretical foundations of aspects of the profession, it seems prudent, in this chapter, to reflect on the relevance of theoretical discourse in recordkeeping at a time when the role and purpose of the records professions is challenged continually by a rapidly evolving technical, informational and cultural landscape. In a world where 'technology [has] expanded the scale of human creativity and social interaction', where 'creative participatory culture [has become] global' (Stryker, 2012, 14) and where the internet has changed fundamentally personal and organizational relationships with information and the understanding of what it is to be part of a community, significant questions are raised concerning the fitness for purpose of recordkeeping. Are recordkeepers risking obsolescence by 'merely finding new ways of saying the same thing, based on the same well-worn concepts' (Bailey, 2008, 124)? Is there a danger of recordkeeping becoming an irrelevance, concerned only with 'official' records and marginalized as 'nothing more than the nomination of the visible' – a mere articulation of 'what is obviously imposed by things themselves' (Foucault, 2002, 144)?[1] Are the parameters offered by recordkeeping orthodoxies of decreasing consequence as a wider memetic[2] relationship (Dawkins, 1976, cited by Stryker, 2012, 15–33) with information in its broadest sense evolves, 'branch[ing] out in countless ways, shifting and merging' and defying attempts to impose control upon a connected 'nonlinear, nonhierarchical structure of ideas' (Stryker, 2012, 28 and 36)?

Despite such concerns, an argument for the enduring relevance of recordkeeping can be made, even at a time when the relationship between people and information is so fluid. That fluidity hints not at an importance for recordkeeping that is based upon the practical rationale for keeping records but one which, in a Derridian sense (Derrida, 1998, 1), casts the archive (and, for the purposes of this analysis, the record) as a source of influence and something influenced, transcending and embodying the 'irruptive violence of time' (Foucault, 2002, 144) and, by extension, the 'irruptive violence' of change. Put another way, modern recordkeeping theory and understanding provides a filter through which, either individually or, more likely, in combination with other social, cultural or philosophical constructs, the apparent dissonance created by changes in technology and online participatory culture can be considered, and multiple narratives and relationships can be articulated.

Clearly, to analyse fully the issues raised by the questions outlined above, factors other than technological change should be considered, and other chapters of this volume examine recordkeeping theory in many different contexts. Spatial and editorial considerations will necessarily limit the exploration in this chapter to a consideration of themes arising from the impact of technological change. The chapter will, therefore, consider the evolving tension between technological change and recordkeeping and consider the nature of recordkeeping and the record in the context provided by conceptual and theoretical debate within the profession. Acknowledging this limited scope, it will conclude with some thoughts and suggestions on the relevance of recordkeeping in changing times, which, when read in combination with the rest of the volume, may contribute to such ongoing debates. The aim is not to provide a comprehensive overview of technological change, to think about practical responses to such change or to analyse in depth the evolution of recordkeeping theory. Rather, the intention is to consider how the work of authors like Verne Harris, Frank Upward and Geoffrey Yeo might inform a discussion of the importance of recordkeeping at a time when it would be all too easy to dismiss it as an irrelevance, behind the times, superseded and belonging to a lost age of ledgers, hanging files and minute books.

## 2 How did we get here? The evolving tensions between technological change and recordkeeping

Technology has changed wholly the way that organizations conduct their activities and individuals conduct their lives. Computers have made the creation, interrogation and exchange of information much easier. The modern organization could not function without the systems that manage major line-of-business activities (such as sales, payroll or human resources) or the computers used by individuals at work for communication and productivity. At home, computers have fostered fundamental changes in areas such as healthcare, banking and travel, have altered patterns of leisure and communication with friends and family and are even changing the way people remember; '[a]lmost without noticing it, we've outsourced important peripheral brain functions to the silicon around us' (Thompson, 2007). Indeed, 'in a world of hyper-connectivity driven by technology that knows no bounds', where people establish meaningful relationships on messageboards or via social networks (insofar as such interactions have meaning to the individuals concerned), it is becoming reasonable to argue that, moment by moment, the use of computing platforms is 'redefining or transforming our modern-day notion of friendship' and changing what it means to be part of a community (Pattakos and Duncan, 2010). Projects such as Google Glass, Google's spectacles which allow the wearer to augment reality by having information overlaid directly in their eyeline or to capture images and records based on their line of sight, may take this phenomenon even further, making the construction of real-time personal or community-based digital 'life-logs' (or, indeed, real-time recordings of constructed narratives and memories) a reality, despite the many privacy concerns raised by 'wearable' computing (BBC News, Technology, 2013). Developments of this type have the potential to renew once again the collective understanding of what it means to 'record' or to 'participate' and the mechanisms by which that can be achieved.

The benefits realized from computers are based upon the ever-increasing capability to process ever more, and ever more types, of data and information. Gordon Moore, in a seminal article in 1965, recognized and codified this exponential growth in the power of computers. He noted that the 'number of transistors on integrated circuits [and, therefore, computing power] doubles approximately every two years'; a maxim that became known as 'Moore's Law'. 'His prediction has proven to be uncannily accurate, in part because the law is now used in the semiconductor industry to guide long-term planning and to set targets for research and development' (Wikipedia, *Moore's Law*).

Tracing the exponential development of computers is not difficult. Since the end of World War 2 computing technology has evolved from the mainframe computers of the 1950s through the invention and adoption of the personal computer during the 1970s and 1980s, to the internet and mobile computing, beginning in the 1990s and reaching remarkable levels of sophistication in the 2000s (for more on the development of computing and personal computing see, for example, Levy, 2000; Levy, 2001; Wozniak and Smith, 2006; or Isaacson, 2011). Bailey, in chapters 2 and 3 of his book *Managing the Crowd* (2008), characterizes the evolution of computing technology as undergoing three major paradigm shifts: from mainframe to personal computer; the growth of the internet following the invention of the world wide web; and the development of Web 2.0 and the use of the web itself as a platform.[3]

The shifts between computing paradigms, however characterized, are worthy of note here as they reveal how the Jenkinsonian construct of

'Archive-maker', creating, classifying and depositing his records in an orderly way (Jenkinson, 1965, 152), or a Grigg-like registry system based upon time-bound triggers and outcomes (see, for example, Appendix 3 of The National Archives, *Appraisal Policy*, 2004) are challenged by the randomness of user actions as their abilities, horizons and senses of self and community are changed by and expressed through technology. As Duranti notes (1995, 9), the empowerment of users with technology gives them an 'exhilarating sense of freedom from … bureaucratic structures, procedures and forms', moving them away from the controlled processes of traditional recordkeeping practice. This is something that cannot be undone, and attempts to turn back the clock, to contain the activities of recordmakers and remove their burgeoning sense of 'ownership and autonomy' (Bailey, 2008, 152), or to impose order on the messy and uniquely personal relationship that people have with technology and information, are, largely, futile. Both professionally and personally people have moved on as the metaphorical firewalls that compartmentalize different aspects of life and work are eroded and as that erosion is accelerated by technological change (see, for example, Semple, 2012).

The messy relationship identified above between people, technology, records and information can be illustrated in reference to the work of Harris (see for example Harris, 2005, 124–5 and Harris, 2007, 239–52). Although considering themes much wider than the impact of technological change upon the relevance of recordkeeping, his points are helpful in this context. Drawing on Derrida, he suggests that the terms 'information' and 'communication' express inadequately the notion that information is fashioned and interpreted in multiple contexts, through multiple cognitive filters (experiential learning, social mores and so on) and that all actions in respect of the record have a political dimension (insofar as they represent the power dynamics arising from and contained within records, and in respect of actions upon and informed by them). Ultimately, Harris (2005, 124–5) suggests that impressions of 'reality' or 'actuality' in information are not absolute. Instead, the relationship between information and reality arises via a prism of contexts and filters; a constructed Derridian 'fictional fashioning'. The agency and actions of recordmakers necessarily make 'the archive' and 'the record' contested constructions, 'not simply … hallowed shrine[s] of Truth' (Jimerson, 2009, 20).

Perhaps, then, technological change is doing something more vital to recordkeeping than forcing an evaluation of whether our tools and principles remain fit for purpose? Perhaps, instead, it is forcing the recordkeeping profession through the looking-glass, making it engage with some of the difficult and complex semantic and intellectual debate that has been taking place for years, but that, practically, it was possible to ignore and 'get on with things' and continue with the worthwhile and everyday work of processing and providing access to records. Tentatively, it does seem possible to suggest that the profession may be arriving at a confluence between the different agencies of recordmakers; between the messy and uncontrolled actions of users (in respect of their adoption of technology) and the sophistication of theoretical discourse in recordkeeping, with each agency, in turn, influencing, providing perspective and helping to articulate the role of the recordkeeper and recordkeeping in changing times.

## 3 Technological change and the record

When thinking about the relationship between recordmakers and technology, the evolution of computing platforms and interfaces is an interesting one. As computing moved out of the laboratory and away from the realm of instructions on punched cards and programming of mainframes by people in white coats, and towards modern personal computers, the conceptual idea of a 'record' arguably survived. Personal computing (i.e. the use of computing for desk-based administrative tasks rather than the processing of large amounts of data for analysis) was predicated, at least initially, upon people using machines for activities that had physical analogues. Word-processed 'documents' were recognizable as letters, memoranda, reports, agendas or minutes, entries in databases were a modern equivalent of card indexes, items were 'filed' in a directory structure and even e-mail, now seen as one of the great unsolvable recordkeeping problems, given the enormous expansion in its use and purpose (see, for example, Bailey, 2008, 83), began as a simple written communication channel: electronic 'mail' – simply a faster way of transmitting your written thoughts or instructions to an intended recipient (or recipients).

McDonald (see 2005, 1) famously described the unstructured use of computers in offices as the 'wild frontier'. Similarly, Duranti (1995, 9) when noting the 'exhilarating sense of freedom' mentioned above, did so in the context of user responses to personal computing's 'produc[ing] the sloppiest records creation ever in the history of record making'. However, a case could be made that things did not become truly 'wild' until the third of Bailey's (2008, 25–37) paradigm shifts in computing technology: the move away from the use of software installed on specific machines and towards the use of the web as a platform for the creation, storage, use, reuse and transmittal of information and for social interaction, community formation and reformation – 'Web 2.0'.

## 3.1 The survivial of 'records'

It is helpful to pause and reflect on the survival of the idea of 'records' for what, in computing terms, is a relatively long time. A major tipping-point was the development of the graphical user interface (GUI). This was a significant step forward in usability, as the user did not need to be able to program a system or remember complicated textual commands. The GUI introduced the era of WYSIWYG computing (what you see is what you get), the desktop metaphor and the paper paradigm (Wikipedia, *Desktop Metaphor*). The development of the first GUIs at Xerox's renowned Paolo Alto Research Centre (PARC) and their subsequent adoption by Apple for the Lisa and the Macintosh, in turn influencing Microsoft's development of the Windows operating system (see, for example, Levy, 2000), is fundamental to the exponential growth and acceptance of personal computing seen during the last 35 years.

From a recordkeeping perspective, the widespread acceptance and use of GUIs was incredibly important as it normalized the 'document metaphor' or 'paper paradigm' in computing. As noted above, people were not 'computing'; they were writing a document or completing an entry in a ledger in almost exactly the same way as they had been when holding a physical object in their hands. Similarly, those electronic objects could be saved inside folders in just the same way as a memo would be placed in the correct hanging file in a filing cabinet. The GUI also allowed a visual representation of how a particular folder structure had been set up, without the user needing to remember a directory hierarchy and navigate through it using text-based commands. The act of saving something to a particular folder helped to reinforce a perception that users were 'making records'. They may have been saving to a hierarchical folder structure of their own making and one which was uncontrolled in a recordkeeping sense (in terms of a lack of naming conventions or the central control afforded by a team of registry clerks), but, intellectually, the process was essentially the same as it had been with physical records.

The document metaphor also facilitated an attachment to traditional conceptions of the record for recordkeepers. If users were able to see their activities in terms of 'creating records' and 'filing', selecting the objects worthy of retention in a folder structure (or of being filed) and discarding the rest, recordkeepers, for their part, could continue to use the same language and description of process in the electronic realm as they had in the paper one. Clearly, it was possible to identify problems, issues and points of divergence (see, for example, McDonald, 2005, 1–17, Duranti, 1995 or Bantin, 2008, 1–22), and the above is necessarily an oversimplification to illustrate a point, but, arguably, the adoption of computing technology had not, at this point, challenged profoundly basic conceptions of 'records': 'information created, received and maintained as evidence and information by an organization or person, in pursuance of legal obligations or in the transaction of business' (ISO, 2001, 3.15). Indeed, writing in 1998, Morelli noted that 'in order to achieve its potential recordness, an entity must be instantiated by recognizing that it exists through indexing or some equivalent process' (Morelli, 1998, 173), cleaving to the notion of declaration or capture as fundamental to an object's achieving the status of 'record'.

The document metaphor helps, in part, to explain the rise of the Electronic and Document and Records Management System (EDRMS) in the early 2000s. EDRMS allowed the capture of electronic objects as records, grounded in existing and well-understood professional principles. Records were managed in a system based upon a controlled, policy-driven approach to classification, retention and disposition. Essentially, they facilitated the management of electronic records according to the structures designed for physical recordkeeping and implemented electronic processes and procedures familiar to recordkeepers.

## 3.2 The freedom of the web

Whilst this may be a useful model where electronic information and records exist in paradigms analogous with their physical counterparts, it breaks down when viewed from the perspective of the memetic development of ideas and information discussed above. Forcing users to adhere to policy when they have broken away from the structures and norms that such policy was designed to codify is difficult and may be counter-productive. The web as a platform empowers users and breaks both the relationship enshrined in the document metaphor between information, records and computing platform, and a user's inclination to conform. As Semple indicates (2012, 17–19), the use of Web 2.0 represents a shift in the control of information from centralized systems to individuals. In situations where they are compelled to conform, users are '[unlikely to give any thought] as to how a file is named, or where it should be stored, [because] all sense of enthusiasm, autonomy and ownership has been squeezed out of them' (Bailey, 2008, 152); that sense of 'enthusiasm, autonomy and ownership' arising from the ability to manipulate and respond to information in a personal way, using tools selected by them, not the organization (or the recordkeeper).

In the context of this chapter, it is this freedom to define and redefine the relationship with information that is the important aspect of Web 2.0, not the use of such tools for the promotion and advocacy of recordkeeping services (although for more on that see Theimer, 2010, 2011a and 2011b). Web 2.0 offers a clear expression of the Derridian assertion that 'the archiving trace, the archive, is not simply a recording, a reflection, an image of the event. It shapes the event. "The archivization produces as much as it records the event"' (Harris, 2007, 41). The web as platform provides an opportunity for the interaction with information that impacts upon the information (or record) itself as much as the record impacts upon the recordmaker. Indeed, the web as a platform is perhaps the most visible articulation yet of the concept of 'recordmakers' (Harris, 2005, 115), removing as it does the boundaries between agents interacting with, influencing and influenced by records and information.

If dialogues on information at its most fundamental level are included in this analysis, the blurring of boundaries between record and recordmaker are perhaps unsurprising. Gleick (2012, 10), drawing on the work of John Archibald Wheeler, notes that 'the bit [the smallest unit of data] is the irreducible kernel and … information forms the very core of existence'. In an echo of discourses on the archive and the record, Gleick suggests that reality arises at its most basic level from the posing of yes/no questions and the processing of the results (information). Outcome (or interpretation) is affected or even determined by observation – the 'paradox of the observer' (Gleick, 2012, 10) – thus the 'observer becomes a communication channel'

(Gleick, 2012, 261). Gleick's comments call to mind the assertion that any interpretation made by the recordmaker 'has no meta-textual authority', each interpretation being influenced by and the result of the cognitive filters of the individual (Harris, 2007, 42). As such, the memetic exchange and development of ideas and information online could be said to mirror life at some level; '[genes] encapsulate information and enable procedures for reading it in and writing it out. Life spreads by networking ... "what lies at the heart of every living thing ... is information, ... instructions"' (Gleick, 2012, 8 citing Dawkins, 2012). The exchange of information and the interaction between it in the form of instructions refined and evolved on the basis of each interaction suggests, according to Gleick (2012, 10), that information 'may be more primary: more fundamental than matter itself', noting Wheeler's pithy maxim on the nature of being – 'It from Bit'. If the relationship with information can be outlined in such a fundamental way, then the desire for interaction, informed by individual or community senses of self, should be unsurprising. Engagement with information, records and recordmakers forms an aspect of what psychologists might characterize as interactionist identity negotiation; a process through which 'people [obtain] a steady supply of nourishment for their identities' (Swann and Bosson, 2008, 448).

## 3.3 Fixity, fluidity and records

The focus on the exchange of 'information' in Web 2.0, irrespective of the container of that information, is also interesting. It recasts familiar computing metaphors as useful only in certain circumstances and too inflexible to cope with the real-time nature of conversations and the exchange of information online; conversations and exchanges refined and influenced (or evolved) by each new interaction and the agency of the user (or recordmaker). For example, 'opening' and 'closing' documents makes 'little sense for the live, constantly evolving web "page." For a rapidly changing page, the pause, play and rewind metaphor borrowed from [the user interface of a] music player [may be] more appropriate'. Similarly, the 'conceptual metaphor of a party, with many overlapping public conversations, works much better than the document metaphor' when thinking about how people interact online using social platforms (Rao, 2010). This logic asserts the primacy of content over structure, the informational component being identified as the most important part of any object. Such understanding of the lack of fixity, the fluidity and the need to represent information in a continually evolving sense rather than as something static is moving from the web back into software and systems. The redesign of the Microsoft user interface in Windows 8 is based upon clean access to information; a fundamental rejection of hierarchical organization, folder structures and the skeuomorphism[4] inherent in the paper paradigm and document metaphor. Microsoft has attempted to reconceptualize or redefine the way that computing platforms operate, prioritizing 'content consumption with a flat hierarchy that can fluidly adapt and scale to various screen displays and sizes' (Maramis, 2013).

If technological changes are asserting the primacy of informational content (or the absence thereof), where might this leave recordkeepers' understanding of 'records'? Traditional definitions are founded on records arising from transactions and being retained as information or evidence. In fixing the characteristics of the record, its content, context and structure, important steps are taken to ensure its authenticity, integrity and reliability. It is what it purports to be, is complete and unaltered (or any alterations are properly documented) and can be depended on as a representation (ISO, 2001, 7.2.2–7.2.4). However, the computing metaphors enshrined in Web 2.0 suggest an understanding where the importance of context and structure is diminished and where evidence is a secondary consideration; what Gauld (2013) describes as a 'contingent collection of unstable texts'.

An argument can be made that activities online do leave a trace and that, despite the focus on information, whenever an activity takes place a 'transaction' of sorts occurs, with information or evidence as a by-product. However, this argument stretches a point. 'Transactions' in the sense detailed in ISO 15489 arise from organizational or personal activities conducted in furtherance of particular functions – the classic function, activity, transaction classification at the heart of functional analysis (see, for example, Shepherd and Yeo, 2003, 58–64). Admittedly, a functional approach sits more comfortably in a 'records management' environment or when archiving the papers of an organization, and a combination of professional approaches is required to properly articulate both the organizational and personal in the archive (see, for example, the discussion in Cook, 1997), but the point that familiar definitions of the record are challenged by technological change is one that, in this context, bears scrutiny.

## 3.4 A new definition of records?

As noted in Chapter 1, Yeo (2007 and 2008), in two articles published in the *American Archivist*, recognized that common prototypical definitions of the record, insofar as they represent a mental concept held by most recordkeepers (Yeo, 2008, 122), identify strongly with the definition given in much of the literature and international standards such as ISO 15489:2001 or the *General International Standard Archival Description (ISAD(G))* (International Council on Archives, 2000). He notes that '[i]n Western culture in the twenty-first century, such a prototype might be a written document, created for business purposes with some pretensions to objectivity and maintained in a formal recordkeeping system' (Yeo, 2008, 122). He also notes that this mental prototype can be applied to both physical and electronic information, echoing the analysis of the entrenched nature of the document metaphor above.

Yeo's articles provide a compelling case for this prototype to be revised and for a new definition of records to be developed based on their characterization as 'persistent representation of activities' (Yeo, 2008, 118). Although acknowledging the danger inherent in definition (Yeo, 2007, 315–19) and that there is no one way of looking at records, Yeo's examination of the 'rich, complex and multifaceted' nature of the record (Yeo, 2007, 319) provides a framework through which professional concerns regarding records and the fluid memetic nature of information online can be reconciled. He suggests that records represent activities, but does not define those activities on the basis of organizational structures or functions, thus allowing both personal and organizational records to be encompassed by his definition and the application of the definition to records created and recreated by technology. Similarly, in recognizing the complex and multifaceted nature of records in developing his definition, Yeo provides a means through which the fact that electronic records consist of multiple elements (Smith, 2007, 21) is acknowledged implicitly. Indeed, in many ways he returns the dialogue on the nature of the record to that of an analysis of its characteristics, removing any discussion of format altogether and maintaining the long-held position in recordkeeping that format is something which must be considered practically, but that has little bearing on recordness (notwithstanding any diplomatic implications).

Yeo's definition of records in respect of their persistence also adds a substantive element to his argument, facilitating a distinction between the record and the transitory or ephemeral. If persistence is fundamental, then it seems logical to suggest that, either as a result of a conscious decision or through serendipity, it represents a point of separation between records and information and imparts a status upon the former that is not held by the latter, speaking to the instability noted above in Gauld's (2013) characterization of information online. A focus on persistence acknowledges the centrality and practical importance of the identification of the 'record' and, therefore, the agency of the recordkeeper as the mediator of this relationship.

Such mediation is, of course, problematic. Appraisal and selection is the mechanism by which 'records' can be distinguished from everything else, or 'instantiated' to use Morelli's term (1998). Yet, appraisal is not a simple process, not without significant societal implications, and decisions in this respect are perhaps the most political of all actions taken by the recordkeeper (see, for example, Jimerson, 2009, 11–14, 220–1 and 344 and Harris, 2007, 101–5). However, where persistence is managed or mediated in any recordkeeping sense, the relationship with appraisal decisions is clear. If persistence is accepted as one element required in an assessment of recordness, then an engagement with the political dimension of appraisal and the danger for the recordkeeper of being associated with the Truth is not simply helpful; it is wholly necessary to properly understand and articulate the role and agency of the recordkeeper as *a* recordmaker, not *the* recordmaker. (See Chapter 2 for a discussion of appraisal.)

Another interesting aspect of Yeo's definition is the characterization of information and evidence as affordances that arise from the record, rather than central to the record itself (Yeo, 2008, 118). This, again, is helpful in the context of the challenges to recordkeeping arising from technological change. If information is considered as something arising from records, the record as the container for information, then multiple characterizations or interpretations can be maintained within and around the record without difficulty. The record becomes the locus and the expression of contradiction, depending upon the context in which it is questioned. Accordingly, multiple instances of information and expressions of evidence can arise from the record, all of which represent a truth, rather than the Truth. Yeo's characterization of records as 'boundary objects' (2008, 130–2), borrowing a mechanism from the scientific literature which allows multiple perspectives to exist based upon the same set of facts or results, recognizes their role as 'objects that both inhabit several communities of practice and satisfy the informational requirements of each' (Bowker and Star, 2000, 297). In doing so he acknowledges the circular nature of 'archivization' (Harris, 2007, 41), provides a means by which a definition of records can exist which overcomes the paradox of the observer (Gleick, 2012, 10) and facilitates an introduction of the challenges raised by technology into the discourse on recordkeeping which does not require a rejection of the centrality of the record to professional theory and practice. This analysis acknowledges the record as something apart or, indeed, more significant than Gauld's (2013) 'contingent collection of unstable texts'.

Yeo's definition also represents an opportunity for a considered critique of Bailey's claim (2008, 62), made as part of his articulation of 'Records Management 2.0', that the distinction between records and information is breaking down and that recordkeepers should concern themselves with all information because 'records' are no longer the most important element of the informational resource. Such a critique is not a simple expression of recordkeeping traditionalism and a refusal to evolve professionally. Rather, it is a recognition that the record as a persistent boundary object is more than a carrier for its informational content. The very reason that it can be a locus of contradiction is that it is more than a piece of information; that through an analysis of its characteristics and a recognition that it is the container for multiple evidences and perspectives it has been validated (however problematic that notion) as what it purports to be. From that assertion, the 'unique quality' and 'vital necessity' of records and archives, as identified in the *Universal Declaration on Archives* (International Council on Archives, 2010), can arise.

However, it is important to assert that Archives 2.0 and Records Management 2.0 are not wholesale rejections of professional principle. They are a mindset; an opportunity for the engagement with change, a framework for a consideration of the role of the recordkeeper and an expression of recordkeepers' 'continuously evolving relationship with [their] users' (Theimer, 2011a, 345). They are a structure under which recordkeepers can consider how to balance the requirement 'to provide descriptive information in ways that meet ... users' needs, using systems and tools that users understand' with the responsibility for 'identifying and preserving collections' (Theimer, 2011b, 61). They are a call for innovative and equitable access to records and, as such, perhaps they are most usefully seen as a continuation of the 'rich history of managing access', acknowledged recently in the preface to the International Council on Archives' (2012, 5) *Principles of Access to Archives*, rather than as a step-change in the relationship of the recordmaker with the record.

## 4 Conceit, hyperbole and overstatement?

At this point, it seems prudent to acknowledge some shared conceits and overstatements at the heart of this chapter which have been used to facilitate the foregoing analysis. Firstly, it is important to recognize that the chapter presumes throughout that technological change does represent a challenge to recordkeeping; that an analysis of the relevance of recordkeeping theory in this context begins with an acceptance that technological change represents a significant disruption to the utility of recordkeeping and diminishes the role of recordkeepers. However, the analysis of recordkeeping theory throughout the preceding sections indicates that the recordkeeping profession does have a basis through which it can engage with the challenges created by technological change. Indeed, especially in this context, it should be remembered that recordkeeping theory and practice is a state of continual evolution and has never been static. Cox (2006, Ch. 6) points to the 'mythical shrouding' of technology and the fact that records professionals have been engaging with the implications of technological change since the 1940s. In fact, he suggests, technology does 'not so much change the principles used by records professionals ... as change the expectations they are asked to meet' (Cox, 2006, 154), calling to mind some of the debate around Archives 2.0 noted briefly above. Similarly, Cook, in his seminal article 'What is Past is Prologue' (Cook, 1997) and more recently (Cook, 2013), charts the evolution of recordkeeping theory not just as a response to technological change but as an expression of the discipline and the foundation of its practice.

Technological change is also raising issues concerning the nature of community and communities, but this, in and of itself, is not new to recordkeeping. Flinn (see, for example, Flinn, 2008) notes how groups at the margin of society recognize the need to document their narratives independently of recordkeepers, where the record of those activities falls outside of the archival mainstream and does not fit neatly with collecting policies, highlighting the tensions that this creates for the view of the recordkeeper as the passive arbiter of Truth. He notes (as does Cook, 2013) that is a process that has been accelerated by the development of participatory technology, but that it is not exclusively a response to that development.

In many ways, scholars in other disciplines may be surprised by the current focus on community in recordkeeping, expressions of community being fundamental to their own discourse. The importance of community in identity negotiation is noted above; novelists recognize that '[t]o dream in isolation can be properly splendid to be sure; but to dream in company seems … infinitely preferable' (Barker, 2009, loc. 235), and historians have long acknowledged the development of horizontal consciousnesses of purpose where communities coalesce around a shared agenda, as opposed to vertical consciousnesses of status (Thompson, 1978), however fleeting those horizontal allegiances may be. As Hobsbawm (1997, 113) suggested, 'no understanding of society is possible without an understanding of the major components of all societies no longer based primarily on kinship'. If his argument is extended to mean the multiple and ever-changing societies, communities and kinship bonds within which any individual exists (amplified by technological change), then echoes of Harris' (2007) 'archivization' process can be heard.

Perhaps the clearest articulation of the adaptability of recordkeeping theory is the increasing acceptance of postcustodialism ('the idea that archivists will no longer physically acquire and maintain records, but that they will provide management oversight for records that will remain in the custody of the record creators' (Pearce-Moses, 2005)) and the records continuum model (see, for example, Upward, 1996 and 1997). Despite concerns regarding authenticity, postcustodialsim, as Tough (2004) points out, provides a way for certain types of record, such as large datasets, to be brought into the purview of the recordkeeper. Similarly, it offers a way for recordkeepers to engage with electronic objects during the 'messy transitional phase' that he identifies as (citing Flynn) he points out that the incoherent nature of electronic information and records may not remain the reality (Tough, 2004, 21). However, at almost 10 years of removal from Tough's article, and given the preceding analysis of the memetic relationship with information promoted and accelerated by Web 2.0, it seems reasonable to suggest that postcustodial approaches are being normalized, particularly where information and records are identified as residing in third-party systems.

The records continuum provided a way of conceptualizing the value and context of records in a way which was not time bound. The relevance of such a model, with its inherent flexibility, has clearly increased since the advent of Web 2.0. As Flynn (2001, 83–4) explained, the continuum model articulates 'the synchronic existence of a record or an accumulation of records in more than one "dimension" of context', and moves recordkeeping beyond a consideration of records according to a 'diachronic movement ... through one discrete and compartmentalized life-cycle stage after another'. It provides a 'sense of the provenancial, organization and social context in which records are created and maintained'. In essence, it gives recordkeeping a theoretical model against which the many facets of the record can be considered in the light of the 'irruptive violence of time', but not in thrall to its progression. The importance of the continuum here is that although it provides a conceptual model which is helpful when understanding electronic records and information and can, especially in combination with Yeo's more recent work on the nature of the record, provide an element of the theoretical foundation from which recordkeeping can develop its approach to and engagement with technology and technological change, it is not restricted to electronic information. The continuum provides a lens through which recordkeeping in a broad sense can be articulated and the 'irruptive violence' of change can be reconciled with professional principle and tradition.

The second conceit contained within this chapter is that Web 2.0 is a universally accepted and democratizing phenomenon. Clearly, it is not. As early as 2007 Keen railed against the dumbing-down of intellectual and cultural discourse promulgated by participation online, the implications for the 'rich ecosystem of writers, editors, talent scouts, journalists, publishers, musicians, reporters and actors' (Keen, 2007, 204) and the impending death of quality-assured media and comment inculcated by the widespread use of Web 2.0 platforms by 'amateurs'. Similarly, Susan Cain, in her book *Quiet* (2012), notes the need for reflection and introspection in innovation, away from the noise generated by modern 'extrovert' society, and Antony Funnell (2012) spends his volume dissecting the hype surrounding technological change, in an attempt to leave the reader better informed having 'embrac[ed] their inner sceptic' (Funnell, 2012, 8). This is not to suggest that recordkeepers should ignore the web as a platform. The ways that Web 2.0 platforms are used by politicians in areas such as fundraising and campaigning (see, for example, Dean, 2006 and Harfoush, 2009) provide obvious examples of why recordkeepers need to engage with the technologies in which records and information are made, remade and exchanged. However, acknowledgement of the criticisms of Web 2.0 is important when considering its presentation as an agency of change, particularly given the hyperbolic language used by both Web 2.0's advocates and its detractors.

The challenge to the document metaphor and paper paradigm is also similarly overstated above. For better or worse, they remain functional computing metaphors, despite the challenge of Web 2.0 and the changes it is fostering. What seems to be happening is that two paradigms are existing concurrently, a complete shift not yet having taken place. The memetic exchange of information is apparent in the ways that people communicate and in creative uses of technology, whilst the document metaphor endures in the administrative use of computers. Acknowledging this, Microsoft may include a 'boot into desktop' mode in the next update of Windows 8, following users' feedback indicating that the 'content consumption' is not inherent to their workflow and that they require familiar metaphors to be productive (see, for example, Pachal, 2013).

A further conceit in preceding sections is the focus on theory and the exclusion of practice. Whilst this may be editorially necessary, there is a danger that it gives an impression that nothing is being done at a practical level to recognize and adapt to the challenges raised by technological change. For example, Wright and Crawford (2013) have detailed the attempts to engage with the recordkeeping social media at a practical level at Victoria University; Prom (2009–13) has developed strategies to cope practically with electronic records and information; and Lee's edited volume (2011) contains chapters on the theoretical and practical implications for recordkeepers of personal digital collections. At every level the recordkeeping profession is facing up to the challenge posed by technology, taking steps to combat the mythical shrouding identified by Cox and considering digital objects at all levels of aggregation.

The final conceit contained in the chapter that must be acknowledged is that it is written from a Western, bureaucratic recordkeeping perspective. Whilst it avoids defining records by format, it is true that no explicit acknowledgement or analysis of the recordkeeping practices of indigenous peoples or oral recordkeeping traditions is made. Similarly, the challenge of technology to recordkeeping presumes the economic means which give access to that technology, and technical sophistication on the part of the recordmakers that engage with it. Clearly, there is no one recordkeeper, user or record, and that is recognized. Space precludes further analysis here, but there is much scope to extend the analysis of the impact of technology in these areas, especially given the democratizing, non-linear, non-traditional and memetic nature of the issues under investigation.

## 5 Some thoughts in conclusion

Despite the complexities and uncertainties detailed in this chapter, it does appear that recordkeeping is simply responding to another stage in an evolutionary process to which records professionals, theories and practices will adapt. To conclude, then, perhaps a return to a question posed in the introduction is instructive; do current trends in technology marginalize recordkeeping theory? Is recordkeeping in danger of becoming an irrelevance, dismissed as 'nothing more than the nomination of the visible'?

Foucault uses the example of 'the nomination of the visible' in a discussion of the development of classification in natural history, articulating one of the criticisms of the discipline when viewed at its most simplistic. However, he notes that the evolution of natural history was a result not of people looking harder than they had done previously, but of the distance between language and observation being reduced, 'limiting and filtering the visible' through classification. The resultant application of controlled and structured language 'permit[ed] the visibility of the animal or plant to pass over in its entirety into the discourse that receiv[ed] it. And, ultimately, perhaps it may manage to reconstitute itself in visible form by means of words' (Foucault, 2002, 144–7).

When applied to recordkeeping this analysis is interesting. The same criticism – that of the simple nomination of the visible – can be made of recordkeeping, if it is reduced to the most basic aspects of processing. This reductionism, however, neglects the emergence of narratives arising from a consideration of language and structure both within the record and in the archival apparatus surrounding it, and of the evolution and flexibility in definitions of the record. If it is accepted that information and evidence arise from the record (Yeo, 2007 and 2008), then the role of the recordkeeper remains, at one level, to be the arbiter of that relationship; to exist at the boundary point, not claiming neutrality, recognizing the political nature of their decisions (and the decisions of those who went before them) and allowing all recordmakers to use the record in ways that let them access their information, their evidence, their truth. This is not a rejection of the enabling role of the recordkeeper. Rather, it is a refinement of that role which acknowledges the centrality and importance of the record to the profession, to societies and to communities, and the enduring nature of the record as a conceptual construct, whilst recognizing the multiple claims upon records and the need for equal and innovative access to them. It is a refinement placed into sharp focus by the recordmaker's continually changing relationship with information and records and the acceleration of those changes by technology.

It seems logical, therefore, to suggest that the role of recordkeeping theory in this discourse is to 'limit the distance' between users, communities, the record and the recordkeeper. It recognizes the fractured, politicized and uneven influence of records and recordmakers. It is not necessarily that recordkeepers are looking harder. Rather, they are thinking in a more nuanced way about their role, the nature of the record and the interface with the user in the context provided by increased participation, sense of ownership (on all sides) and technological change. The theoretical underpinnings of recordkeeping acknowledge that an analysis of language or the evaluation of the context in which language was selected and applied reveals multiple meanings and has varied political overtones; 'recordmaking … both invites politics in and generates a politics of its own' (Harris, 2007, 244). Such meanings will be both intended and unintended by the author, originator, user or recordkeeper. Similarly, the act of scrutiny and the drawing of inferences creates new and different meanings in turn, as do attempts to apply structure, to preserve or to capture – to control.

This analysis, then, leads towards an exploration of a relevance for recordkeeping (or recordmaking) not wholly predicated on control and fixity, but one which arises from the application of a variety of archival or recordkeeping theoretical and practical constructs. Such constructs facilitate visibility in respect of the narratives and meanings surrounding a record and allow those narratives to be reconstituted on the basis of the record's content or the identification of elements missing or hidden, the actions taken or not taken, the decisions informed by or taken upon it. Or, and perhaps more simply, this discussion returns recordkeeping or recordmaking to an analysis at the heart of the records continuum; of records existing in multiple contexts and encompassing multiple value propositions concurrently. In its doing so, a suggestion emerges naturally that recordkeeping, when expressed in this manner, retains relevance, providing practical and analytical frameworks (or filters) for society collectively and people individually. It does so both because of and despite the profound and ongoing changes in the cultural relationship with information witnessed during the last decades of the twentieth century and the first decades of the twenty-first. Recordkeeping theory and practice is not static. There is little to suggest that it will, or should, become so.

The final thoughts are left to Terry Cook (1997). His analysis remains the most eloquent expression of the enduring and metamorphosing nature of recordkeeping theory and practice:

> Archival history is … a rich collage of overlapping layers, of contradictory ideas existing simultaneously or even blended together, of thinkers exhibiting differences of emphasis more than of fundamental ideas, of individual thinkers changing their ideas in light of new circumstances, of old ideas appearing in new guises in new places. The pendulum of thought swings back and forth, as one generation solves its predecessor's problems, but thereby creates new problems for the next generation to address, with ideas having their day, being discarded, and then even being revitalised in modified form in later work. And so it should be.

## Acknowledgements

Parts of sections 2 and 3 of this chapter draw on work that originally appeared (in a limited form) in the Electronic Records chapter of P. Whatley, A. R. Bell and C. Brown (2013) *The Recordkeepers' Bookshelf*, self-published e-book with the support of the Programme Commission International Council on Archives, Centre for Archive and Information Studies, University of Dundee. It is used here with permission.

The early outline of some of the ideas in this chapter was first presented in two keynote papers for Records and Information Management Professionals, Australasia (RIMPA) in 2012. I wish to thank RIMPA and to acknowledge the help, encouragement and friendship of our late colleague Dr Marian Hoy, who arranged that opportunity.

I would also like to recognize my colleagues in the Centre for Archive and Information Studies at the University of Dundee and the atmosphere of spirited debate and mutual support that we enjoy.

## Notes

1 This chapter returns to Foucault's argument in greater depth in the conclusion.

2 *Memetics* is 'a catch-all term for the study of human social evolution as opposed to biological evolution (i.e., genetics) … [R]eligion is meme. Art is a meme. [An argument can be made that e]very form of human social expression is memetic [to some extent] … Memes are simply mental expressions that behave like genes … [which is why] we often refer to memes as "going viral" … Most of the time we don't even realise we are spreading them, the same way a beast plays host to an intestinal parasite … Memes can be ideologies, trends, fads, gossip, jokes, music, fashion or adages – any concept that can be shared from one person to another. They're distinct and repeatable, and they live and die by natural selection … If a meme fails to spread, it's dead' (Stryker, 2012, 18–19).

3 Foley (2008, 12) notes the difficulty with defining Web 2.0, pointing out that since O'Reilly's (2005) seminal conference papers and articles from the early 2000s, Web 2.0 has become a somewhat loaded, imprecise and overused term, ascribed multiple meanings and often used to identify technological developments which are seen to be (or are pilloried as not) forward thinking or current. Indeed, only five years after the initial Web 2.0 conference in 2004, O'Reilly and Battelle (2009) recognized the dramatic changes and enormous potential of the web as a platform, identifying the 'collision course' between the web and the physical world. The imprecision in the use of the term 'Web 2.0' leads to the slight fluidity in the way that it is used throughout this chapter. For the purposes of this discussion, Web 2.0 is defined in its broadest sense, so as to facilitate analysis: as the use of the web as a platform (although the inherent lack of specificity in the definition is acknowledged). The transition from Web 1.0 to Web 2.0 is characterized as the web's moving from being primarily a source of consumption for the majority (i.e. a majority of people accessing content posted by an engaged minority) to being part of the cultural and social mainstream; a platform used by the majority (where economic, social, cultural and political conditions allow) for the creation of and interaction with information and as a platform for communication and social engagement, again defined in their broadest terms. These definitions are not restricted to specific tools, applications,

platforms or services, and the focus of the chapter is personal and community relationships with information, not the technical aspects of Web 2.0 or how Web 2.0 might be exploited by recordkeepers.

4 From Wikipedia: 'A *skeuomorph* is a physical ornament or design on an object made to resemble another material or technique. Examples include … a software calendar application which displays the days organized on animated month pages in imitation of a paper desk calendar.'

## References and further reading


Bailey, S. (2008) *Managing the Crowd: rethinking records management for the Web 2.0 world*, Facet Publishing.

Bantin, P. (2008) *Understanding Data and Information Systems for Recordkeeping*, Facet Publishing.

Barker, C. (2009) *Weaveworld*, Amazon Kindle ebook of Voyager paperback edn, Harper Collins Publishers.

BBC News, Technology (2013) *Privacy 'Impossible' with Google Glass Warn Campaigners*, www.bbc.co.uk/news/technology-21937145.

Bowker, G. C. and Star, S. L. (2000) *Sorting Things Out: classification and its consequences*, paperback edn, MIT Press.

Cain, S. (2012) *Quiet: the power of introverts in a world that can't stop talking*, Penguin.

Cook, T. (1997) What is Past is Prologue: a history of archival ideas since 1898, and the future paradigm shift, *Archivaria*, **43**, 17–26.

Cook, T. (2013) Evidence, Memory, Identity and Community: four shifting archival paradigms, *Archival Science*, **13** (2–3), 95–120.

Cox, R. J. (2006) *Ethics, Accountability and Recordkeeping in a Dangerous World*, Facet Publishing.

Dawkins, R. (1976) *The Selfish Gene*, Oxford University Press.

Dean, H. (2006) *You Have the Power: how to take back our country and restore democracy in America*, Simon & Schuster.

Derrida, J. (1998) *Archive Fever: a Freudian impression*, paperback edn, University of Chicago Press Ltd.

Duranti, L. (1995) Reliability and Authenticity: the concepts and their implications, *Archivaria*, **39**, 5–10.

Flinn, A. (2008) Other Ways of Thinking, Other Ways of Being. Documenting the margins and the transitory: what to preserve, how to collect. In Craven, L. (ed.),

*What Are Archives? Cultural and theoretical perspectives: a reader*, Ashgate Publishing Limited.

Flynn, S. J. A. (2001) The Records Continuum Model in Context and its Implications for Archival Practice, *Journal of the Society of Archivists*, **22** (1), 79–93.

Foley, M. J. (2008) *Microsoft 2.0: how Microsoft plans to stay relevant in the post-Gates era*, Wiley Publishing Inc.

Foucault, M. (2002) *The Order of Things*, Routledge.

Funnell, A. (2012) *The Future and #relatednonsense*, Harper Collins Publishers Australia.

Gauld, C. (2013) Democratising and Privileging: an evaluation of the role of gatekeeper in the twenty-first century. Paper presented at Centre for Archive and Information Studies, University of Dundee conference *Democratising or Privileging: the future of access to archives*, unpublished.

Gleick, J. (2012) *The Information*, paperback edn, Fourth Estate.

Harfoush, R. (2009) *Yes We Did: an inside look at how social media built the Obama Brand*, New Riders.

Harris, V. (2005) Ethics and Electronic Recordmaking. In McLeod, J. and Hare, C. (eds), *Managing Electronic Records*, Facet Publishing.

Harris, V. (2007) *Archives and Justice: a South African perspective*, Society of American Archivists.

Hobsbawm, E. H. (1997) *On History*, Abacus.

ICA (2000) *General International Standard Archival Description (ISAD(G))*, 2nd edn, International Council on Archives, www.ica.org/10207/standards/isadggeneralinternationalstandardarchivaldescriptionsecondedition.html.

ICA (2010) *Universal Declaration on Archives*, International Council on Archives.

ICA (2012) *Principles of Access to Archives*, International Council on Archives.

Isaacson, W. (2011) *Steve Jobs*, Little, Brown Book Group.

ISO (2001) 15489:2001 *Information and Documentation: Records Management, Parts 1 and 2*, International Organization for Standardization.

Jenkinson, H. (1965) *A Manual of Archive Administration*, 2nd edn, Lund Humphries.

Jimerson, R. (2009) *Archives Power: memory, accountability and social justice*, Society of American Archivists.

Keen, A. (2007) *The Cult of the Amateur*, Nicholas Brealey Publishing.

Lee, C. A. (ed.) (2011) *I Digital: personal collections in the digital era*, Society of American Archivists.

Levy, S. (2000) *Insanely Great: the life and times of Macintosh, the computer that changed everything*, Penguin.

Levy, S. (2001) *Hackers: heros of the computer revolution*, Penguin.

Maramis, I. (2013) *Windows 8 UI Design and Apple Skeuomorphism*, Nerdery, http://blog.nerdery.com/?s=Windows+8+UI+design+and+Apple+skeuomorphism%2C.

McDonald, J. (2005) The Wild Frontier Ten Years On. In McLeod, J. and Hare, C. (eds), *Managing Electronic Records*, Facet Publishing.

Morelli, J. D. (1998) Defining Electronic Records: problems of terminology. In Higgs, E. (ed.), *History and Electronic Artefacts*, Oxford University Press.

The National Archives (2004) *Appraisal Policy*, www.nationalarchives.gov.uk/documents/information-management/appraisal_policy.pdf.

O'Reilly, T. (2005) *What Is Web 2.0: design patterns and business models for the next generation of software*, O'Reilly Media, http://oreilly.com/web2/archive/what-is-web-20.html.

O'Reilly, T. and Battelle, J. (2009) *Web Squared: Web 2.0 five years on*. White paper for the Web 2.0 Summit, O'Reilly Media and Techweb, www.web2summit.com/web2009/public/schedule/detail/10194.

Pachal, P. (2013) Windows 8.1 May Include a 'Boot to Desktop' Option, *Mashable*, http://mashable.com/2013/04/15/windows-8-boot-to-desktop/.

Pattakos, A. and Duncan, E. (2010) The Meaning of Friendship in a Social Networked World, *Fast Company*, www.fastcompany.com/1694484/meaning-friendship-social-networked-world.

Pearce-Moses, R. (2005) *A Glossary of Archival and Records Terminology*, Society of American Archivists, www2.archivists.org/glossary/.

Prom, C. (2009–13) *Practical E-Records*, http://e-records.chrisprom.com/.

Rao, V. (2010) How Conceptual Metaphors Are Stunting Web Innovation, *Mashable*, http://mashable.com/2010/01/13/conceptual-metaphors/.

Schellenberg, T. R. (2003) *Modern Archives: principles and techniques*, reprinted edn, Society of American Archivists.

Semple, E. (2012) *Organizations Don't Tweet, People Do: a manager's guide to the social web*, John Wiley & Sons Ltd.

Shepherd, E. and Yeo, G. (2003) *Managing Records: a handbook of principles and practice*, Facet Publishing.

Smith, K. (2007) *Planning and Implementing Electronic Records Management: a practical guide*, Facet Publishing.

Stryker, C. (2012) *Epic Win for Anonymous: how 4chan's army conquered the web*, Gerald Duckworth Publishers Ltd.

Swann, W. B. Jr. and Bosson, J. K. (2008) Identity Negotiation: a theory of self and social interaction. In John, O. P., Robins, R. W. and Pervin, L. A. (eds), *Handbook of Personality: theory and research*, Guilford Press.

Theimer, K. (2010) *Web 2.0 Tools and Strategies for Archives and Local History Collections*, Facet Publishing.

Theimer, K. (ed.) (2011a) *A Different Kind of Web: new connections between archives and users*, Society of American Archivists.

Theimer, K. (2011b) What Is the Meaning of Archives 2.0? *American Archivist*, **74**, 58–68.

Thompson, C. (2007) Your Outboard Brain Knows All, *Wired Magazine*, **15** (10), www.wired.com/techbiz/people/magazine/15-10/st_thompson.

Thompson, E. P. (1978) Eighteenth-century English Society: class struggle without class? *Social History*, **3** (2), 135–65.

Tough, A. (2004) The Post-custodial/Pro-custodial Argument from a Records Management Perspective, *Journal of the Society of Archivists*, **25** (1), 19–26.

Upward, F. (1996) Structuring the Records Continuum – Part One: postcustodial principles and properties, *Archives and Manuscripts*, **24** (2), 268–85.

Upward, F. (1997) Structuring the Records Continuum – Part Two: Structuration Theory and Recordkeeping, *Archives and Manuscripts*, **25** (1), 10–35.

Wikipedia, *Desktop Metaphor*, http://en.wikipedia.org/wiki/Desktop_metaphor.

Wikipedia, *Moore's Law*, http://en.wikipedia.org/wiki/Moore's_law.

Wikipedia, *Skeuomorph*, http://en.wikipedia.org/wiki/Skeuomorph.

Wozniak, S. and Smith, G. (2006) *iWoz – Computer Geek to Cult Icon: getting to the core of Apple's inventor*, Headline Review.

Wright, K. and Crawford, K. (2013) Tweets, Check-ins and Status Updates: keeping track of social media at Victoria University, *IQ – The RIM Professionals Australasia Quarterly*, **29** (1), 36–9.

Yeo, G. (2007) Concepts of Record (1): evidence, information, and persistent representations, *American Archivist*, **70** (2), 315–43.

Yeo, G. (2008) Concepts of Record (2): prototypes and boundary objects, *American Archivist*, **71** (1), 118–43.

# Index